THE BODY
Alan Cotton

ALAN COTTON
GIVING LIFE A SHAPE

Jenny Pery

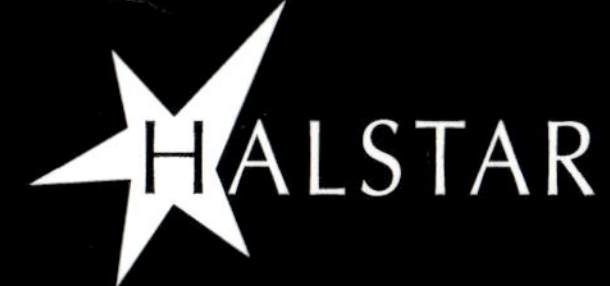

First published in Great Britain in 2010

British Library Cataloguing-in-Publication Data
A CIP record for this title is available from the British Library

ISBN 978 1 906690 24 3

HALSTAR
Halsgrove House,
Ryelands Industrial Estate,
Bagley Road, Wellington, Somerset TA21 9PZ
Tel: 01823 653777   Fax: 01823 216796
email: sales@halsgrove.com

An imprint of Halstar Ltd, part of the Halsgrove group of companies
Information on all Halsgrove titles is available at: www.halsgrove.com

Printed and bound in Italy by Grafiche Flaminia

All paintings photographed by
John Saunders and Steve Russell.

Recent location photography by
Steve Russell unless otherwise stated.

Designed by
The Studio Fine Art Publications

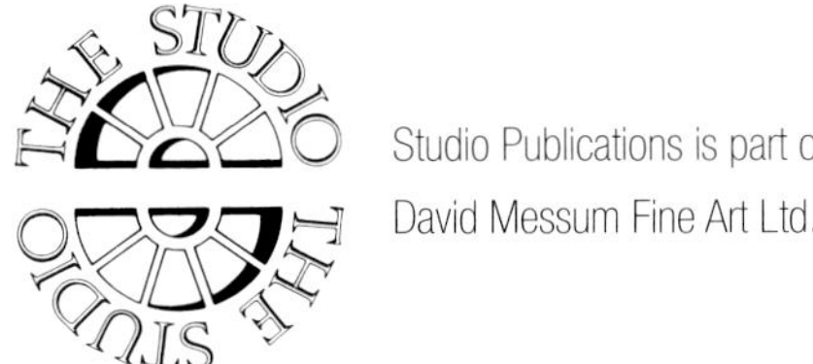

Studio Publications is part of
David Messum Fine Art Ltd.

Dedication

I would like to dedicate this book to all the members of my immediate and wider family, whose constant support and affection has enabled me to sustain my career as a painter.

To many friends. On my journey as a painter I have been fortunate enough to meet some extraordinary people, in this country and from my travels around the world, and their friendships have greatly enriched my life.

To David Messum for his friendship and encouragement during my years with the gallery.

To Jenny Pery, whose insight into the process of painting, and the lives of artists, illuminates all her writing.

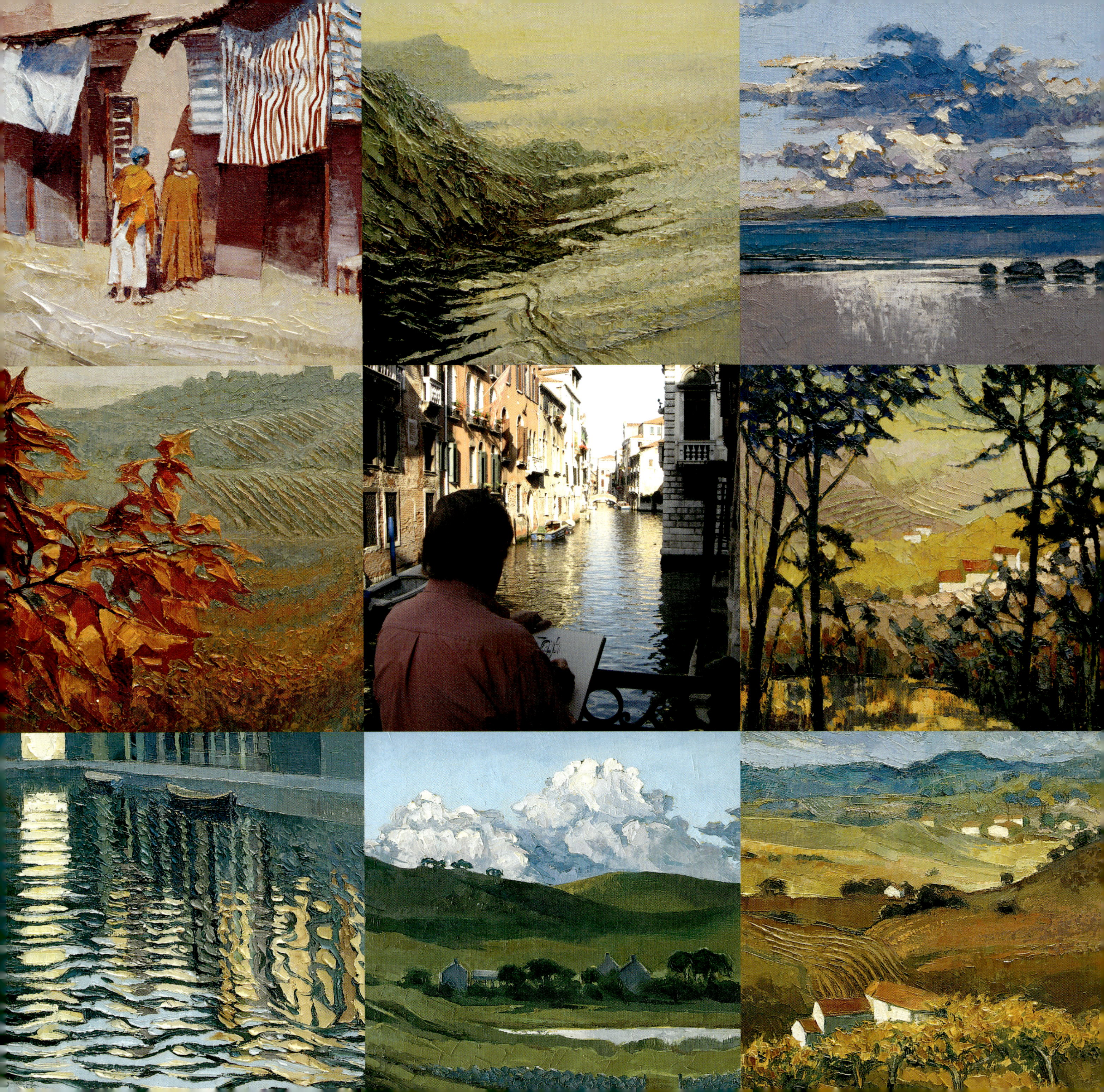

Contents

Unless otherwise indicated, all quotations in the book are from recorded conversations between Alan Cotton and the author.

ALAN MADE SEVERAL TRIPS to Snowdonia in his search for a more rugged landscape as a contrast to the softness of South Devon and his home painting grounds. Inspired by the drama of Wales's mountain scenery and the way the rapidly changing light picked out the contortions of the rocky terrain, he found motifs that were perfectly adapted to his method of painting with knives, each knife mark equivalent to a particular angle or plane in the land. From many exploratory drawings made on the spot he worked on a series of paintings of Snowdonia which show the influence of the British Neo-Romantics, particularly John Piper's mixed media renderings of Wales.

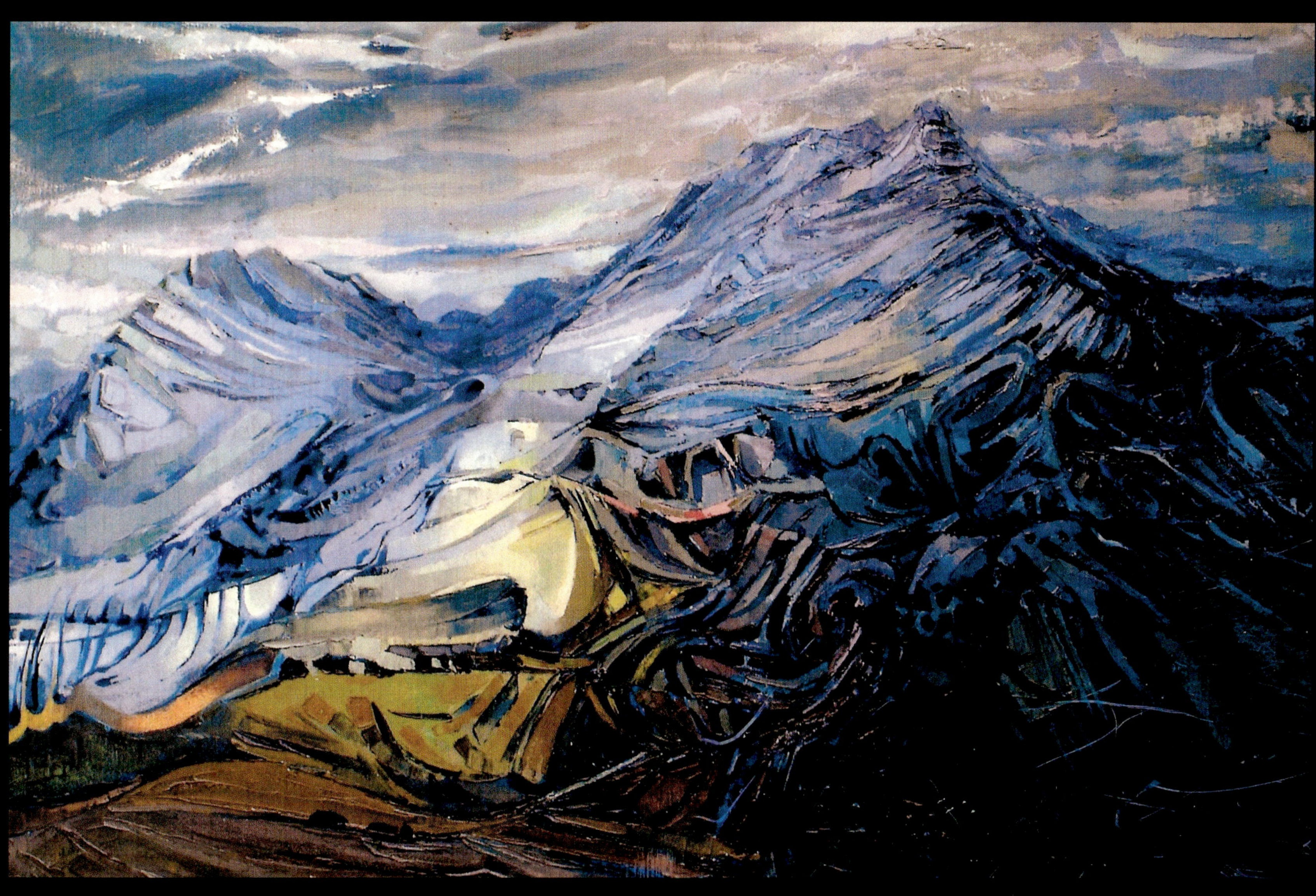

Snowdonia, 1976
oil on canvas 40 x 60 ins
Collection University of Southampton

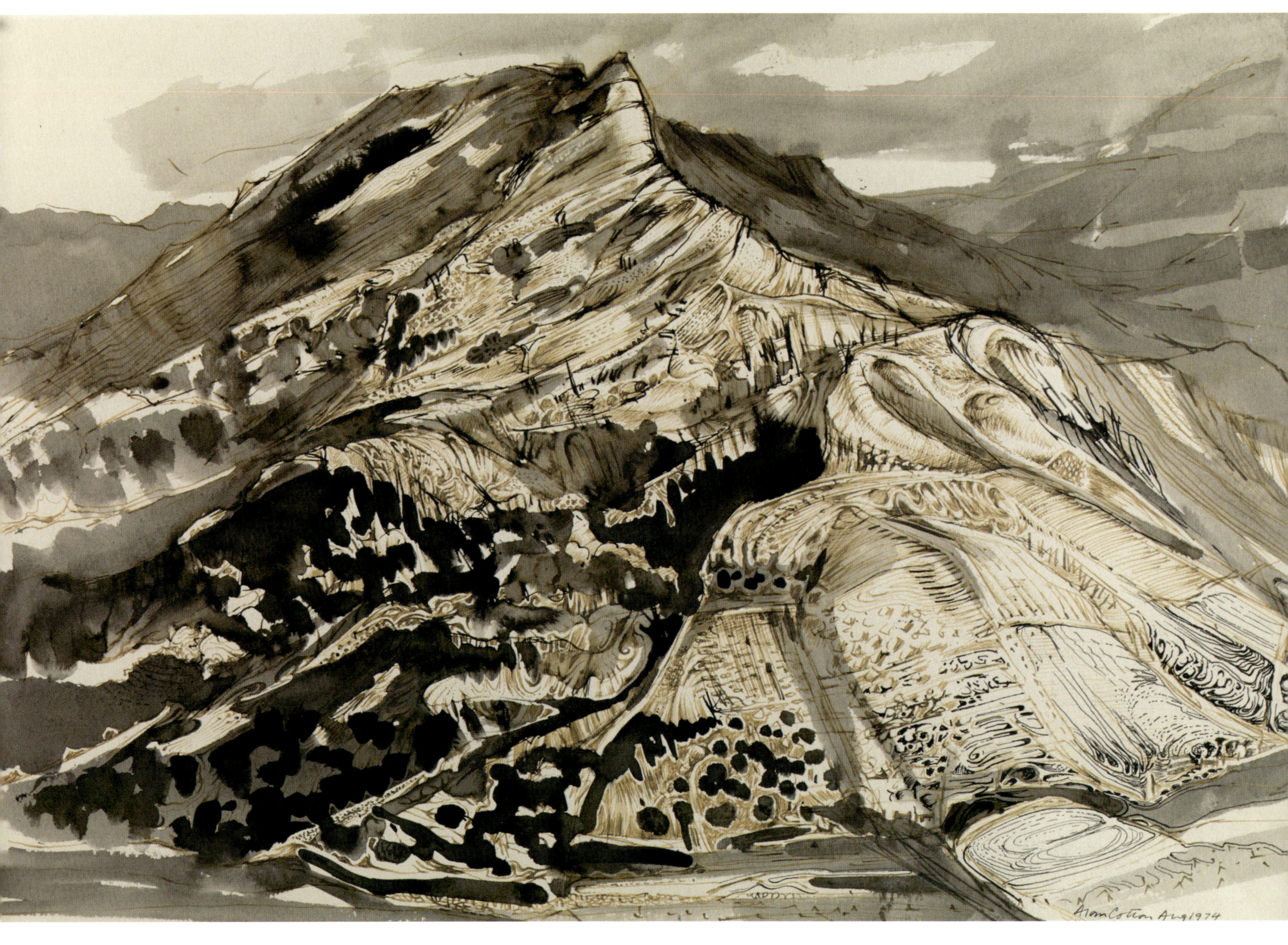

Study for Snowdonia, 1976
ink and wash

Chapter One

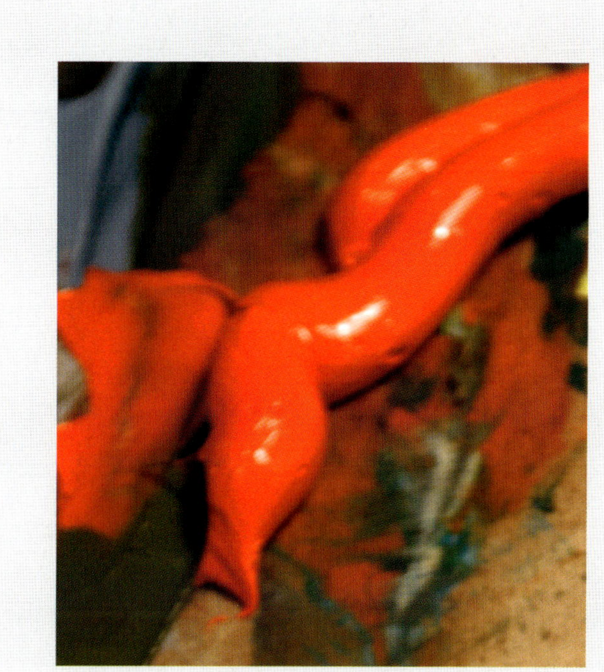

Show Business

Donegal – Spiralling Clouds over the Estuary, 2009
oil on canvas 24 x 24 ins

Alan Cotton's leap of faith, taken nearly thirty years ago, to abandon the financial security of teaching and become a full-time painter, has been rewarded by unqualified success. His annual exhibitions at Messum's London gallery invariably sell out. These exhibitions have become the focal point of Alan's year, his art now forming the axis around which his life is shaped. A prodigious quantity of paintings, the result of long hours spent in the studio, appears before the public in spectacular shows. Alan's dogged work at the coalface begins a process that ends in the razzmatazz of show business.

Every year Alan Cotton produces a substantial number of paintings for exhibition. He is a prolific painter, and well over a thousand oils have emerged from his studio over the years. In his studio at home in Devon he works in oil on canvas, transposing and composing images from drawings that he has made on his travels. Early on in the process much time is spent in gathering new source material to furnish the paintings, and each year is carefully planned. Once the date of an exhibition is fixed, Alan arranges various trips, in Britain and abroad, to collect new material. Having long ago learnt that painting on the spot, with all the paraphernalia of easels and oil paints, was not for him, he now travels light, with sketchbooks and pens, to explore and draw those places that excite him, making rapid notes to catch the particular quality of the place. Back in his studio, a period of intense activity follows as he reinterprets in oils the sheaves of drawings made on the hoof. As the thickly painted canvases begin to crowd the walls of his studio, one image sparks off another until the whole series seems to reach a natural conclusion. Then, having assembled a suitably large body of work, he arranges for the paintings, often still wet, to be photographed. The photography is essential as a record of his work and as illustration for the all-important catalogue that accompanies each exhibition. After being photographed, the paintings go off to be framed in specially bespoke frames. Finally, the carrier comes to transport the work to London for display in the gallery.

For Alan Cotton this cycle of activity has now become the norm. And, just as exhibiting his art gives a distinct shape to his life, Alan Cotton's life is devoted to giving a formal shape to the world he sees around him. Jean Anouilh's observation that 'the object of art is to give life an shape' is doubly apposite in Alan's case. His pictures give painted shape to the places he loves. Using his drawings as starting points, he calls on his memory and imagination to compose images that distil the experience of being in certain places at certain times. Following in the British Romantic landscape tradition, Alan's paintings, carefully constructed edge to edge, generally look at the world from a single viewpoint. Well versed in Western traditions of perspective and unashamedly traditional, he is usually content to

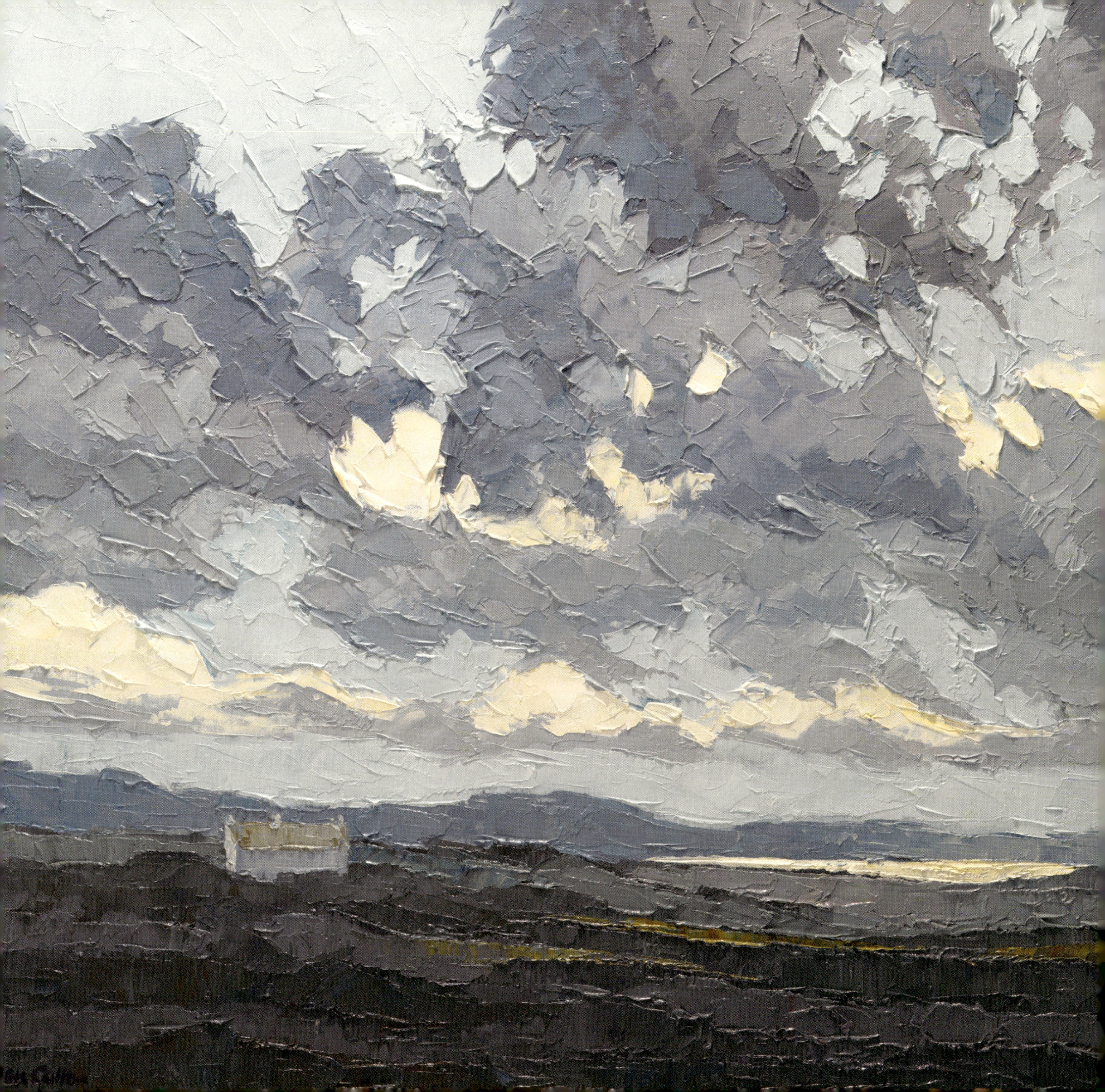

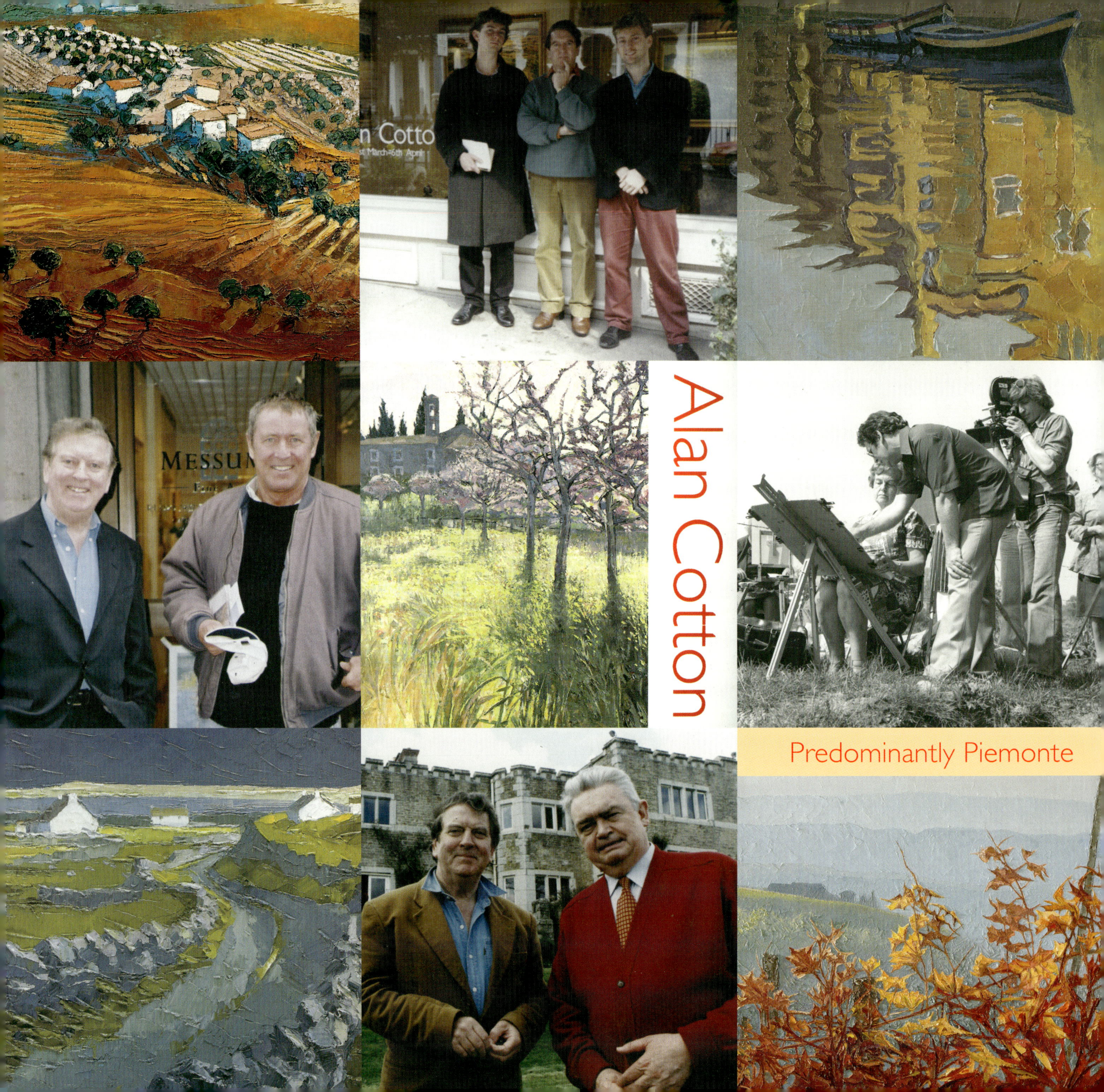
Alan Cotton
Predominantly Piemonte

present a conventional view of the land from foreground to background, although he breaks with tradition when he raises his viewpoint to take an aerial view, so that the land seems to swoop upwards from foreground to a lost horizon. Alan's originality lies in the little-known places that he often chooses to depict, and in the gestural, expressive gusto with which he uses his painting knives to lay the paint on canvas.

Alan Cotton's vision of the world is consistently upbeat. He is a 'worshipper of nature' in the Wordsworthian sense. Whether depicting the sunlit expanses of Provence or the weather-lashed rocks of the Irish coast, his paintings show a clear delight in the variety of forms and patterns to be found in nature. There is no anthropomorphsm here. Alan's hills are hills and his seas are seas, but even at their most sombre they carry a human message of unquenchable optimism. There is hope in the fingers of light that pierce the stormy Irish skies. A world of wonder is revealed in the brilliant autumn colours that burn hrough the mists of Piemonte. A silver lining shines through tempestuous Fijian clouds. Nature is presented in many different moods, but always in celebratory fashion.

It was the sense of freedom and the beauty of the country around the grimy Midlands town of Redditch, where he grew up, that first fired Alan Cotton's imagination. Although born a 'townie', his boyhood escapades into the surrounding countryside opened up a limitless world of colour and life. The contrast between the arid dinginess of the town and the riot of colour in the summer cornfields, where golden heads of wheat waved against an azure sky, was astonishing. Not only was he enchanted by what he saw but he was overwhelmed by the power of nature. By drawing and painting in the countryside he tried to possess it, to make himself a part of it. Now, decades later, in paintings inspired by his travels, he tries to regain that boyhood thrill of excitement. The convolutions of land, worked by man or buffetted by the sea, constantly amaze him, and with juicy paint he tries to recapture the feeling of awe in front of nature. Many subjects capture his imagination, from the rugged cliffs of New Zealand to the sun-soaked plains of Provence, and he puts his enthusiasms into paint. Alan Cotton's paintings tell us that all is well with the world. No wonder they are popular.

The popularity of Alan Cotton's art could not have been achieved without the help of his long-term dealer David Messum. Alan first met David in the early 1980s, when, having given up teaching, he was having a hard time making ends meet. Alan was in Cornwall collaborating with director David Spires on the BBC feature film *An Artist on Every Corner*, describing the life and work of the Newlyn School of Artists. The crew were filming an auction where a major painting by the Newlyn artist Thomas Cooper Gotch was coming up for sale. Local dealers had told Alan that an

Top row:
Messum's catalogue, 1988;
With sons Richard (left) and Robin (right) at the opening of Alan's London exhibition at Messum's George Street gallery, 1991;
Messum's catalogue, 1995
Middle row:
Alan Cotton and John Nettles outisde Messum's Cork Street gallery;
Messum's catalogue, 1990;
Filming "A Step of Two Away the Picture is Complete", directed by Kevin Crooks;
Bottom row:
Messum's catalogue, 1997;
With Hugh Scully during the filming of "Cotton on Canvas";
Messum's catalogue, 1999.

important London dealer was expected to bid for the picture, but there was no sign of this figure when the bidding began. Then a silhouette appeared in the doorway 'like John Wayne in a Western', as Alan recalled, took over the bidding and acquired the picture. That dealer was David Messum. After the sale, while the wrapped Gotch painting leaned against the dirty hubcap of his car, Alan interviewed David Messum about his contribution to the revival of the Newlyn School. Halfway through the interview David stopped and said 'Hang on a minute, I've just placed you. You are Alan Cotton, the painter. What are you doing this lark for?'

At that time David Messum was a prime mover in rescuing from relative obscurity the work of the Newlyn School and the British Impressionists of the late 19th and early 20th century. Alan took his film crew to David's gallery, then in Beaconsfield, to shoot some more Newlyn footage. He also brought along a portfolio of his own work. David's main focus was on British Impressionist paintings, but he had a few contemporary artists in his 'stable'. He liked Alan's work and agreed to take him on his books. It was not long before he was deeply involved with Alan, not only in supporting him financially by paying him a monthly sum, but also steering the development of his art. David's encouragement was immensely important, and Alan has repaid it with his loyalty. As David records, 'Alan has been amazingly loyal. Our relationship is one of complete trust. I think we have taught each other a few things. I feel we have genuinely been able to help, and I wouldn't say that about a number of painters. I have perhaps saved him from himself a bit, prevented him from going down certain paths. I do admire his colour sense and think he is a wonderful colourist. When I first met him he was doing very sombre paintings. Going to Provence really set fire to his palette.'

Alan Cotton was one of the first of the contemporary artists that David Messum took on; only the painter Brian Horton has been with Messum's gallery longer. For the first few years David paid Alan an annual salary, set against future sales. This considerably eased the Cotton family's precarious financial situation. A first solo exhibition of Alan's work was staged at the Beaconsfield Gallery and, later, a seminal show at David's home in Marlow. Alan's first London exhibition, however, took place at Messum's new St George Street Gallery, and was accompanied by the first in a series of beautifully illustrated catalogues packed with illuminating commentary. This first catalogue set a precedent for the future. Because Alan is an able communicator, his commentary in the catalogues offers an admirable way of allowing the public to get to know the man behind the art.

Kevin Crooks wrote the introduction to the catalogue for the exhibition, which was a momentous event for Alan. Kevin Crooks's colleague at BBC South West, Judi Spiers, later recounted Alan's memories of the opening day. 'How

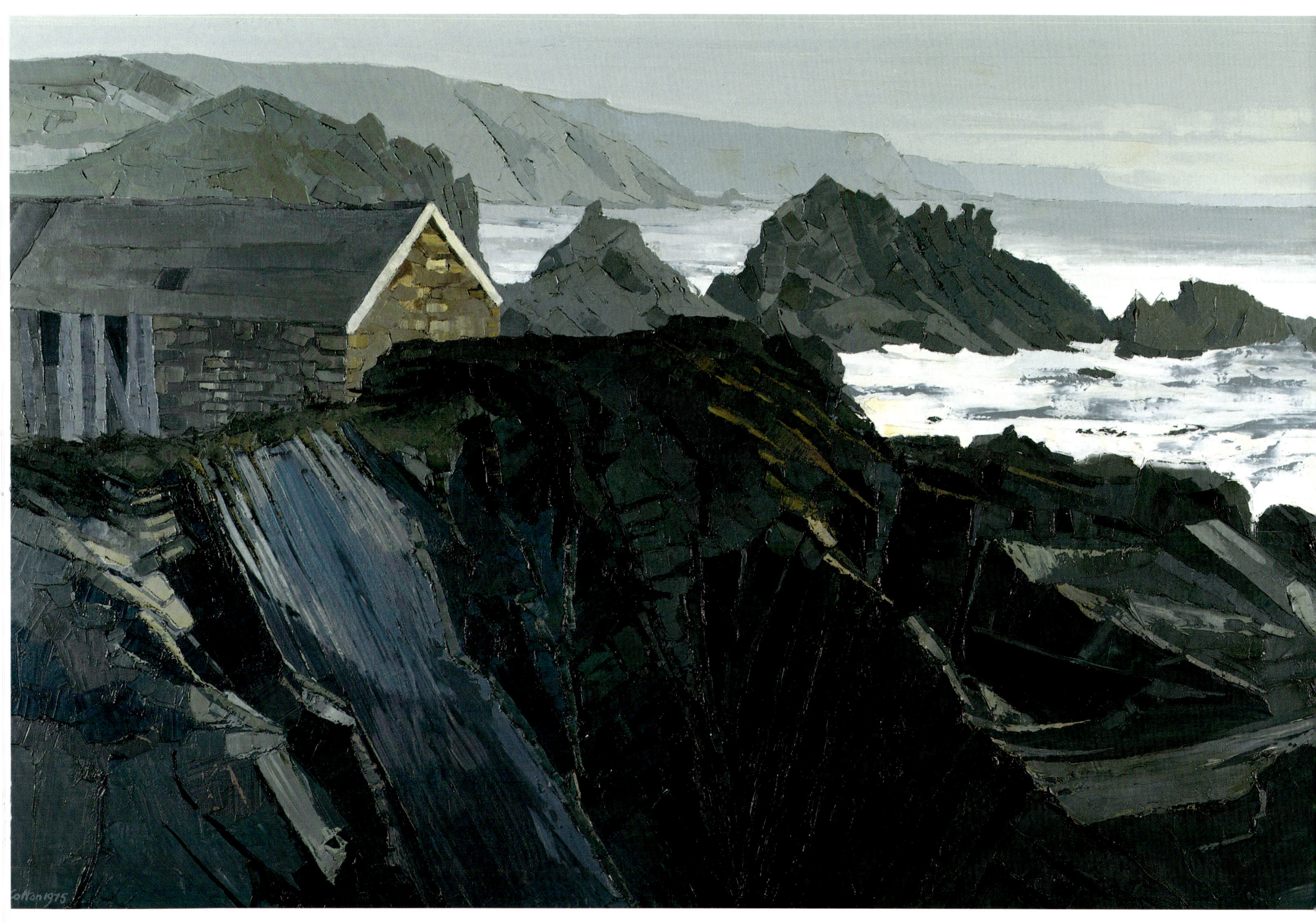

Hartland, 1977
oil on canvas 48 x 60 ins
Collection of City of Plymouth Art Gallery

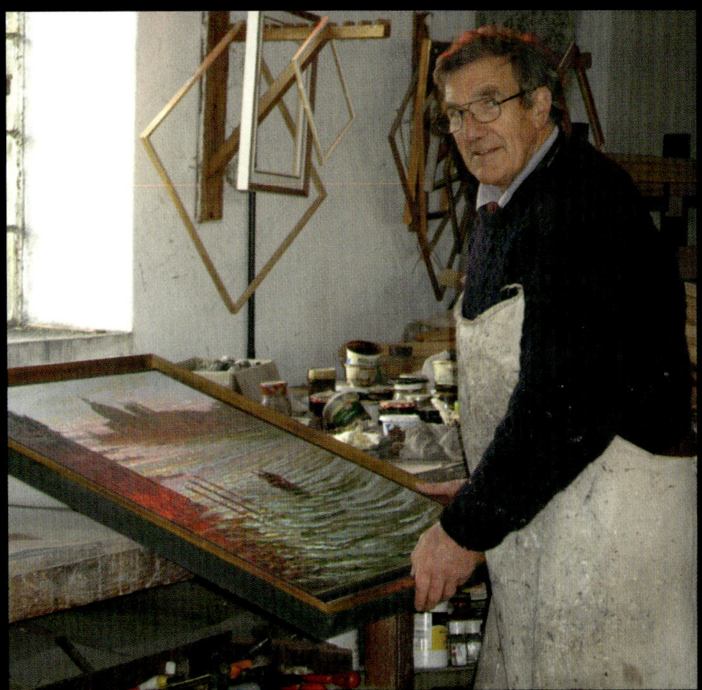

Master frame-maker and gilder Michael Beddoe

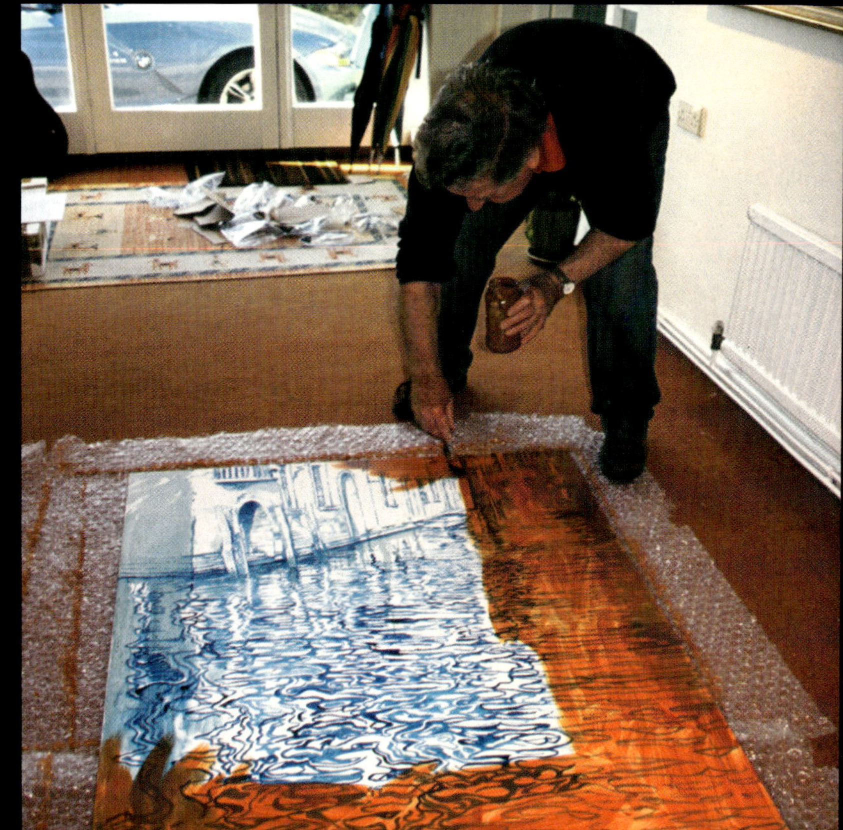

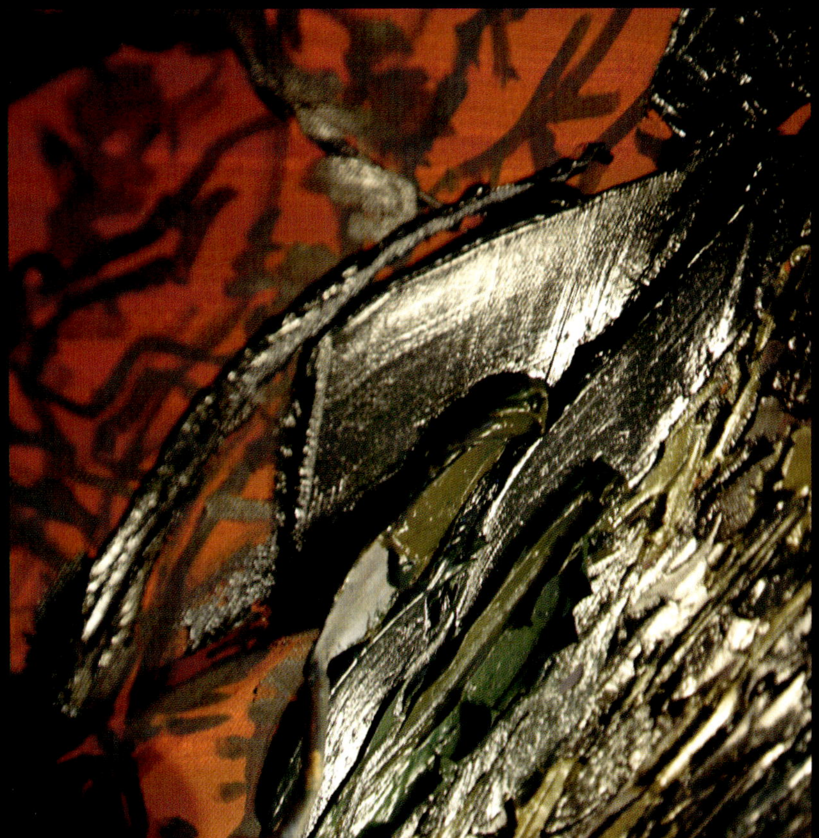

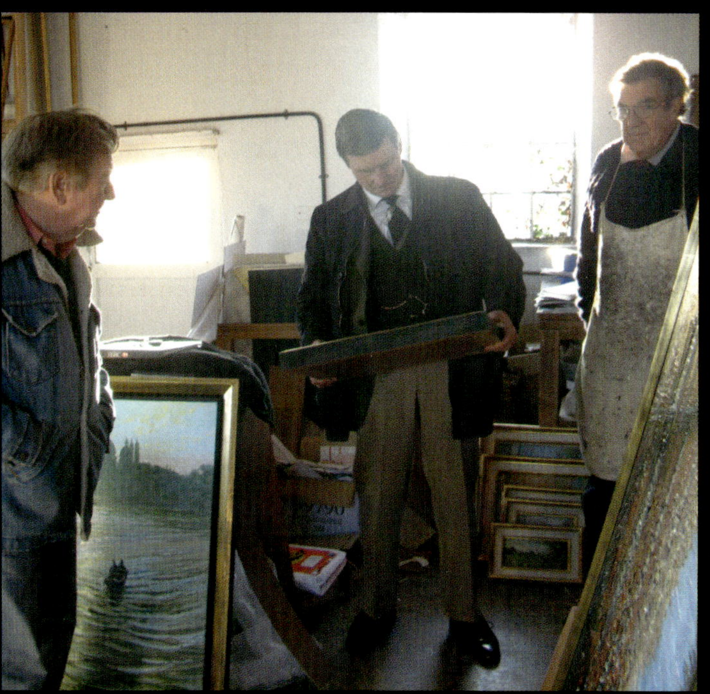

Michael Child, a Director of Messum's, inspecting a newly framed work.

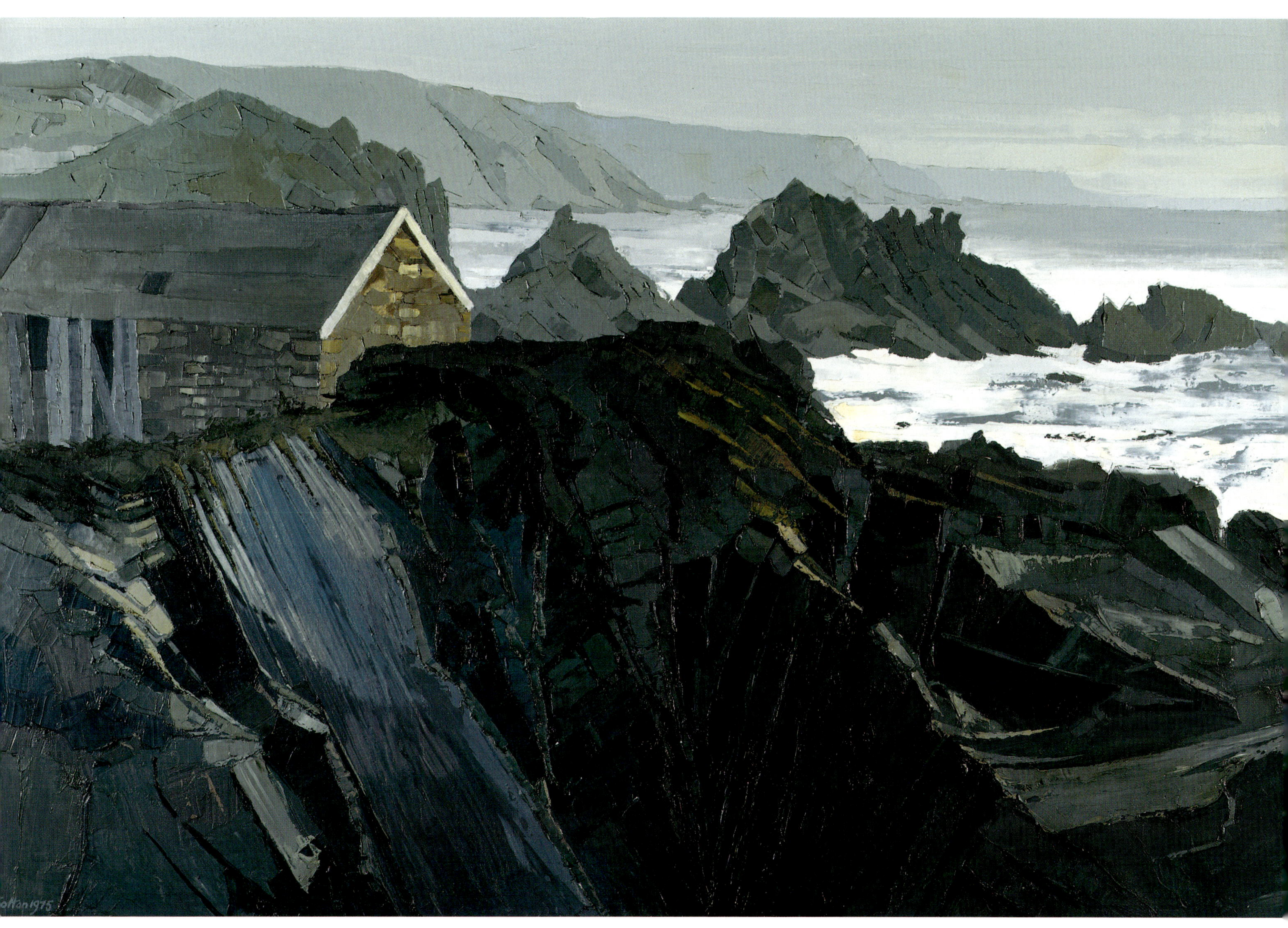

Hartland, 1977
oil on canvas 48 x 60 ins
Collection of City of Plymouth Art Gallery

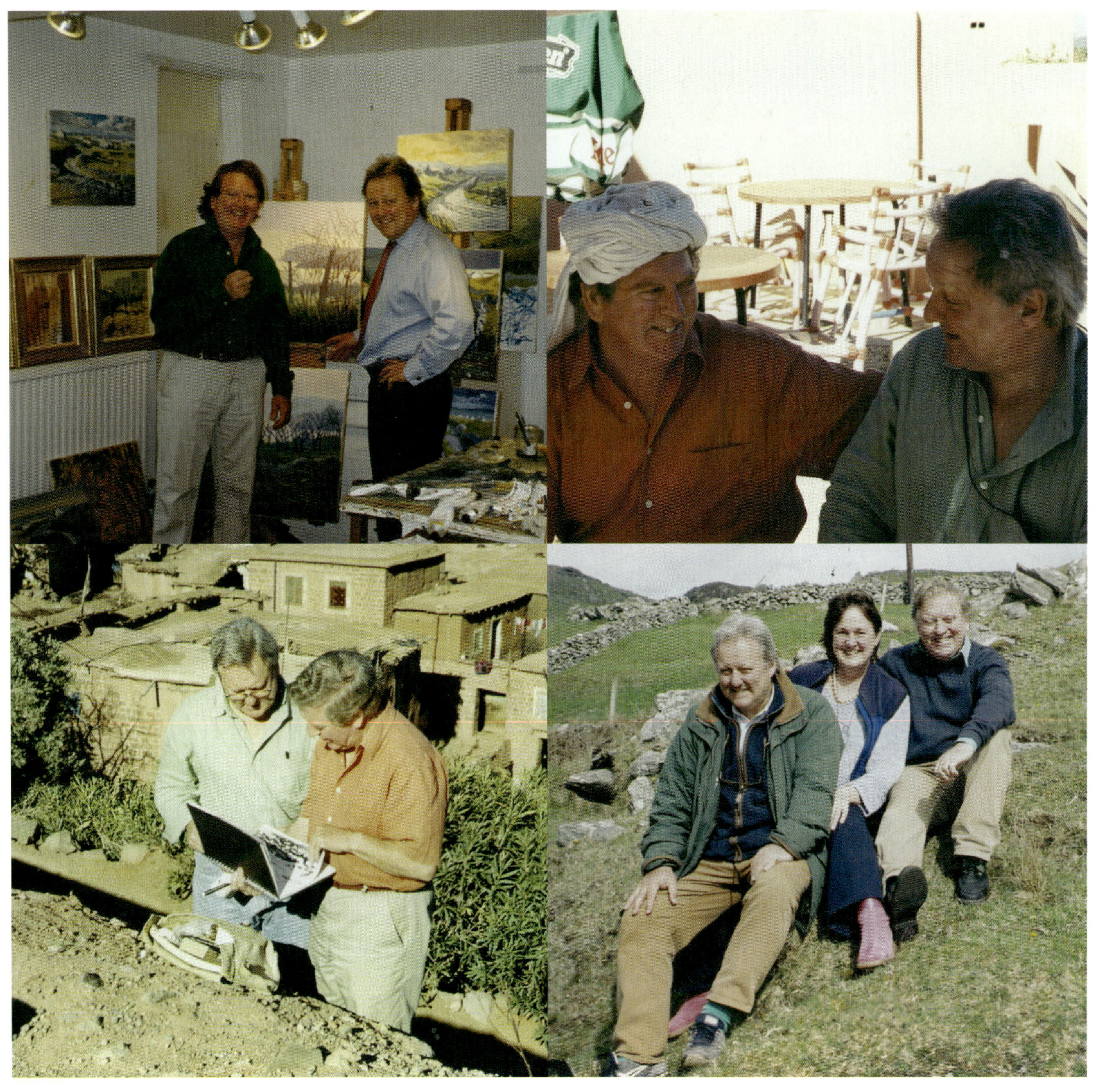

Over the years the partnership between Alan Cotton and David Messum has strengthened into firm firiendship: in the gallery; relaxing in Morocco; working in the High Atlas mountains; with Millie Messum in Donegal.

many times as a young art student had he walked down Cork Street seeing some of the great exhibitions, dreaming of what it would be like to exhibit in the West End? At that time he had found the galleries intimidating and not at all welcoming to young students dripping water over their carpets and polished wooden floors. Now, here he was, working towards his first exhibition in the centre of London. The night before the opening he stayed with David and Millie Messum at their home in Marlow and they drove into London at 5.30 am to avoid the rush hour. They had breakfast at Browns Hotel where, Alan told me, "When I asked for brown sauce to go with my bacon and eggs, it was brought in a silver jug – this is high living, I thought." They crossed the road to Messums' west end gallery and there emblazoned in red across the window were the words ALAN COTTON EXHIBITION. "That was the most exciting feeling" Alan admitted, "and even twenty years later I still feel the same excited anticipation as I arrive to see the show beautifully hung and lit by the gallery team."'

The Alan Cotton exhibition was one of the first to be held in David Messum's new gallery, and David remembers it with mixed feelings. 'We had just put together this very smart gallery on five floors in St George Street and spent about half a million pounds doing it up, and I was itching to show my British Impressionist pictures which were worth huge sums of money, but because I had been without a gallery for a while I felt duty bound to give our contemporary artists, of whom Alan was one, a show in the first quarter of our opening. Alan's was one of our first shows and all his family came to it.' David was perturbed by the influx of family members who were not potential buyers of paintings, but the Private View nevertheless had a great buzz and the show was a success. It set an effective precedent for future shows.

Over the years the partnership between Alan Cotton and David Messum has strengthened into firm friendship. This unusual bond between artist and dealer is in part due to Alan's sunny, easy-going character and in part to David's extraordinary empathy and understanding of art. An occasional painter himself, David has often drawn or painted alongside Alan out in the countryside. With his wife Millie, David has visited Alan in almost all his chosen painting grounds, and experienced for himself the quality of each place whilst gaining real insight into Alan's vision and his working methods. David takes what he regards as his duty of pastoral care seriously. As he says, 'in trying to build a stable of painters I think you do need to make time for them. You can only get the best out of them if you go and see them and see their sources of inspiration. A lot of painters stay in their own landscapes and you need to see their landscape to understand their work. Alan works differently, and I've been away with Alan on location more than with any other artist. I enjoy being at the coalface, as it were, and he does like me to be with him and share the experience. I do feel I have to go and see Alan on a regular basis. He likes to have quiet conversations with me about the work and he does listen to what I say. Some artists don't want to hear what you have to say but when they know that you know something about painting and can speak their language, they will listen. Alan is in that studio under artificial light with the music on, painting, and that's wonderful for a period, but he needs to break from that and concentrate on something new. These journeys he goes on are very important for finding something new.'

With an eye to forthcoming exhibitions, David is naturally keen to see the progress of the work and to select those paintings he would like to show. He is aware that artists are not necessarily the best judges of their own work. 'I always say that the answer to everything is in the stock, so the point of going to see the artist is to discover the stock. If you go down to see Rose Hilton, for instance, you are on your knees looking under the bed at rolled-up work that she thought was no good. Alan, too, might be slaving away on one picture and getting nowhere, and we can pick one out that's fantastic and he'll say "I only did that in five minutes" and we'll say, "well, there you are!" The most important thing is to get hold of the images, for the pre-publicity, and to begin to build the catalogue.'

Messums' first London exhibition of Alan Cotton's paintings featured some of his first paintings of Provence. These early French paintings were based on an area of Provence that he had found particularly for himself. During his student years he had explored the painting grounds of Cézanne and Van Gogh but had found it difficult to see their choice of landscape freshly, through his own eyes. In search of pastures new he was drawn to the vast cultivated stretches of the Luberon plains and the astonishing hilltop town of Gordes, dominated by its Renaissance château. His palette changed dramatically from the subtle tertiary hues and sombre darks of his Devon paintings to brilliant reds, ochres and oranges that positively evoked the sun-baked land. As Alan explained in the exhibition's catalogue, 'the emotional response to the landscape of Provence is simply one of colour. There is no doubt about the sensuality of colour affecting the feeling you have for this region. I think the thing I found most exciting to do was to use a whole new colour vocabulary.' When Kevin Crooks asked him how truthful his painting was, Alan replied 'Some of the landscapes are topographically accurate and try to record my impressions of the light and colour at that moment, but others are… made up from several viewpoints. When you see a landscape which is so wonderful I can only say that you get a terrific gut reaction and can't wait to get drawing and be part of it.'

Solo exhibitions with Messum's in their St George Street gallery followed in 1990, 1991 and 1992. As in the first

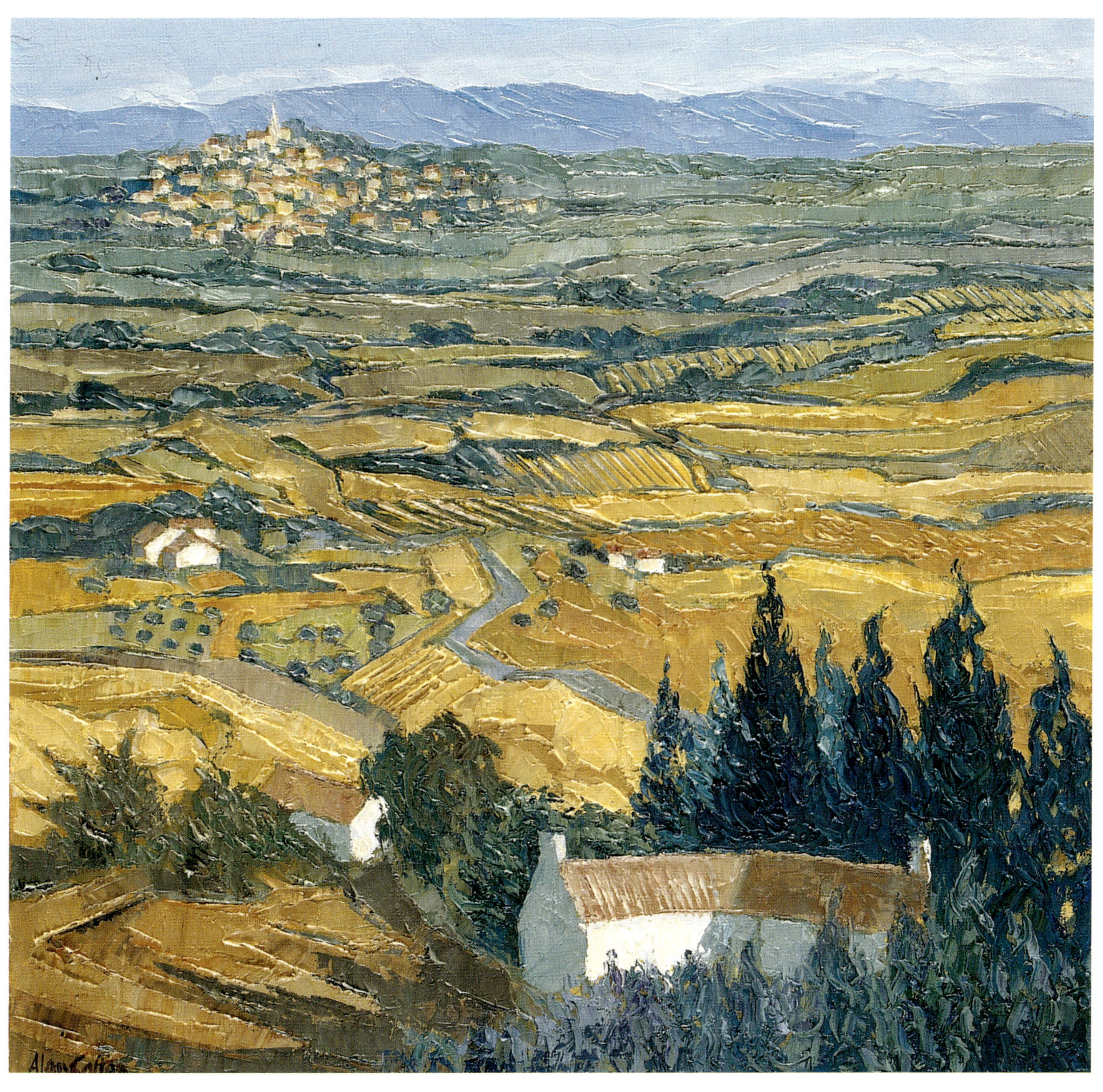

Provence – Bonnieux from the Terrace at Lacoste
oil on canvas 24 x 24 ins

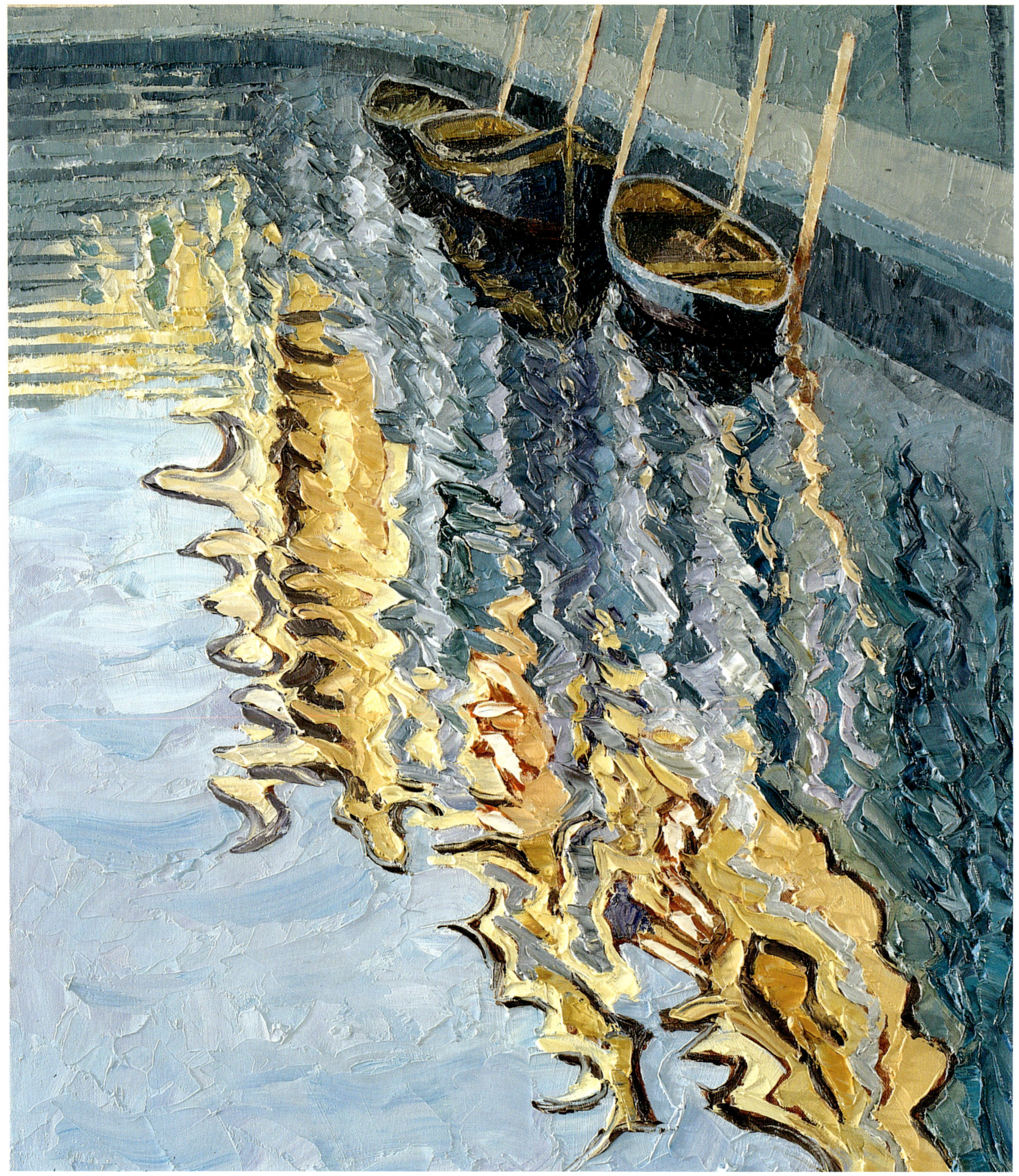

Venice – Façade Abstractions in Blue and Gold
oil on canvas 24 x 20 ins

show, each was accompanied by a well-illustrated catalogue, with images backed up by Alan's own candid comments about his painting. The 1990 show focused on paintings from Tuscany, an area that Alan had explored for the first time in 1989. In the catalogue, for which the television presenter Hugh Scully supplied a foreword, Alan wrote 'When I first arrived here I had a tremendous compulsion to produce images which went beyond the sheer seductive prettiness of the landscape; beyond the great slashes of red poppies, cut into green meadows, and as well, to try and represent other and perhaps more subtle facets of Tuscany… One of the early difficulties I found here at this time of year is that the sun rises high by mid-morning, so that everything is drenched in brilliant sunlight and there is no contrast of light and shade. Soon I began to realise that it was particularly in the early morning and late afternoon, when the sun slants across fields and woodlands, casting long belts of shadow across the landscape and following the contours of the hillsides, that I have found the most satisfying and rewarding times to work. So I have got used to rising early and being out in the fields by seven or so, working feverishly until mid-morning. It sure gives you an appetite for breakfast.'

Venice was the main focus of Alan's 1991 exhibition, which also included pictures of Tuscany, Provence and Cyprus. In his foreword for the catalogue Tom Salmon, then Head of BBC Television South West, remarked 'we have often talked about Venice together, how as a subject for an artist she is often considered a bit of a tart, as so many people have tried her before and everyone feels they know her so well'. For Alan painting in an urban environment, however unusual, was a new departure. Although he had painted the hill towns of Provence many times, he had generally depicted them from afar as part of a landscape, and in Venice his preference for far-reaching views was curtailed by the density of buildings. Alan's answer both to the problem that Tom Salmon posed, and to his own predilection for landscape, was to concentrate on the watery reflections in the canals. 'One of the most appealing features of Venice to me is the abstraction of light and colour created by the reflections of its facades and the movement of its river traffic which cause these reflections – a kind of magic mirror.' Alan's Venetian paintings are among the most abstract of all his work. By looking down into the water he was freed from literal descriptiveness, and by hanging his reflections from a high horizon line, he was able to wallow in the juicy swirls of paint that described the warm-toned watery depths.

David Messum had promoted Alan's work so successfully over four exhibitions and become such a valued friend that Alan was keen to ride to the rescue in 1992, when financial difficulties forced the closure of the gallery in St

George Street. Alan suggested a weekend exhibition at David's home in Marlow, and the Cotton family pledged all their free capital to underwrite the show. David was touched by Alan's loyalty. As he said, 'when we were on the floor, Alan was the only artist who was confident that we would get up'. For this exhibition in the Studio at Lords Wood in Marlow, Alan produced sixty-three paintings, mainly of Provence, but also some new work from Tuscany, Cyprus and Venice. Alan and Pat Cotton stayed with the Messums at Lords Wood to hang the show and help receive the visitors. A proper catalogue was produced and invitations were sent out, but the wait before the show opened on Saturday morning was tense. Nobody knew how many people would turn up, and the first hour of waiting with nobody appearing was agonising. But gradually people began to arrive and the paintings started to sell. By Sunday evening every single painting had been sold, and the Messums, the gallery staff and the Cottons celebrated with stiff drinks all round. David presented Alan with the long list of paintings, each marked with a red dot, that he has on his studio wall to this day.

The success of this exhibition not only helped to put David Messum back in business but proved that Alan's landscapes were finding a most responsive audience. The catalogue for the exhibition, with a foreword by the journalist and photographer Peter Brimacombe, featured a conversation between Alan Cotton and Kevin Crooks, who remarked that 'in television we talk about still pictures and silent pictures, but paintings are rarely silent. Your response to them fills the mind in a way with sound. I think you can actually hear the countryside around you in these paintings.' In his commentary Alan discussed his own emotional response to landscape as well as the painter's responsibility to try and fix a representative image both of the scene and of the emotion it evoked. 'The whole process of selection begins and you set off on this very complicated process of trying to select those ingredients that represent the mood and the feeling and your emotional response to it. So you're trying within the rectangle of the canvas to design a series of images and shapes that represent that idea.... I can be in the same place on many different days and the image might do absolutely nothing for me and then for some reason, and it's usually to do with the light... I can see something so magical that I have this tremendous compulsion to make paintings about it.'

Restored to London with a new gallery in Cork Street, David Messum has kept Alan Cotton at the centre of his stable of artists, giving him a major exhibition every year. Unusually amongst dealers, he likes to put forward a budget for each exhibition and discuss it with his artists beforehand. As he points out, 'not only are you an emotional pillow for your artists, but you do provide the money. The sort of question we ask is how the artist is going to exist. We have

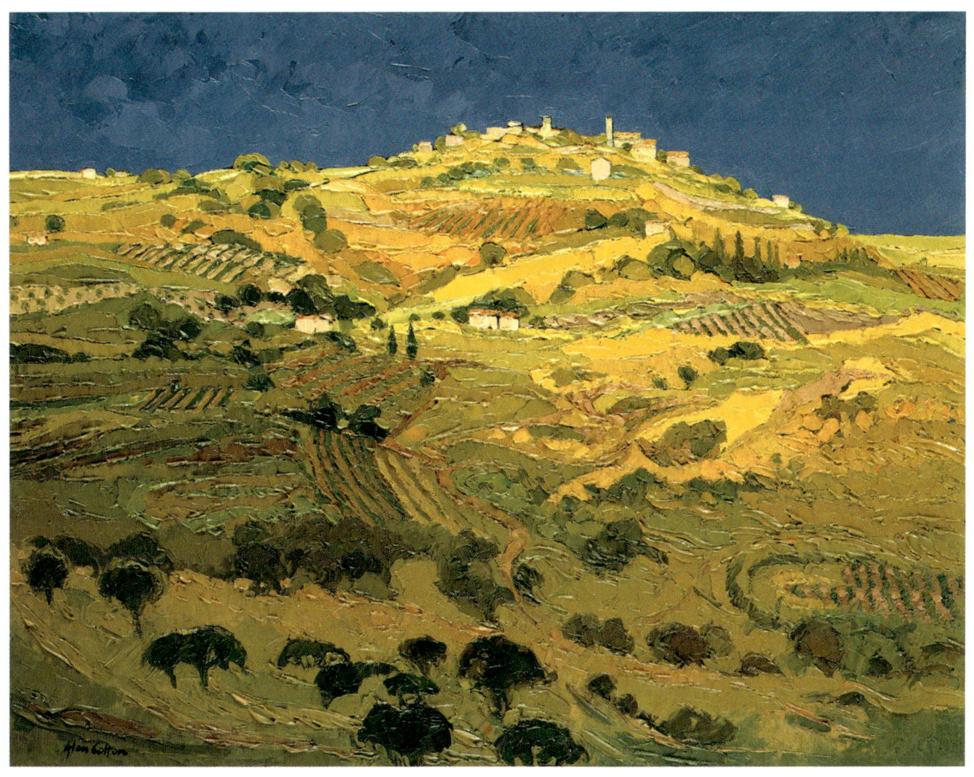

Sunlit Landscape Against Stormy Skies
oil on canvas 24 x 30 ins

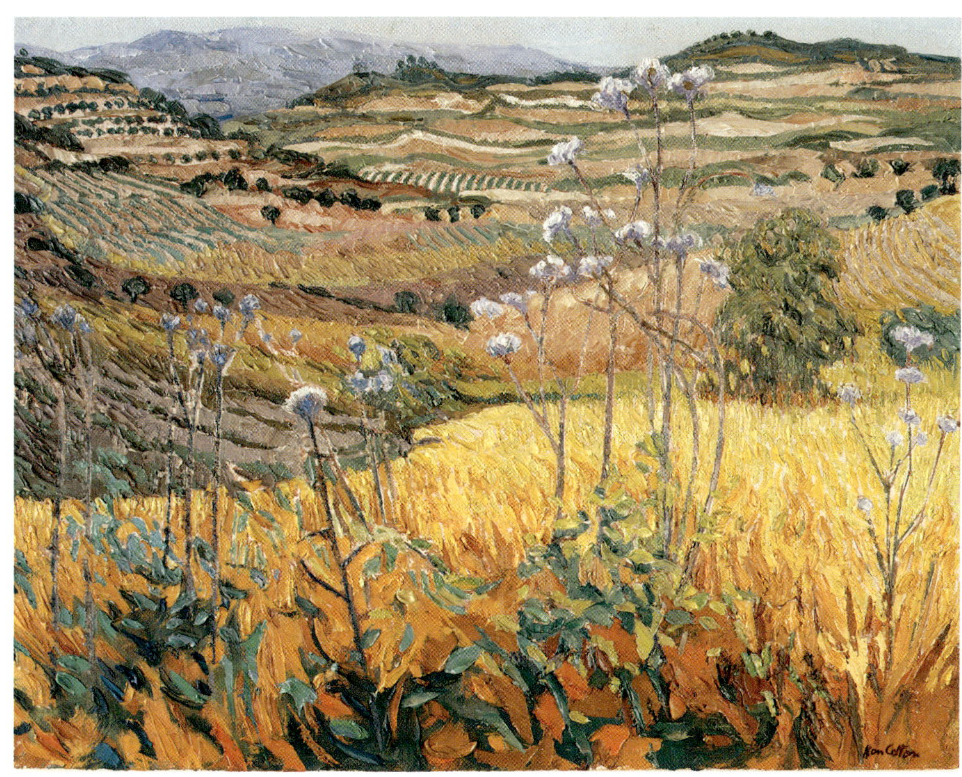

Landscape near Paphos with Wheatfields and Foreground Plants
oil on canvas 24 x 30 ins

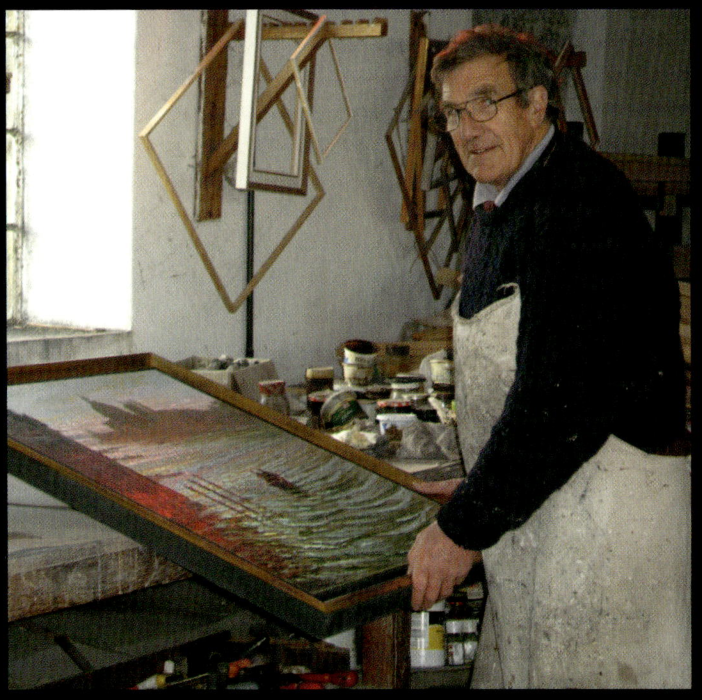
Master frame-maker and gilder Michael Beddoe

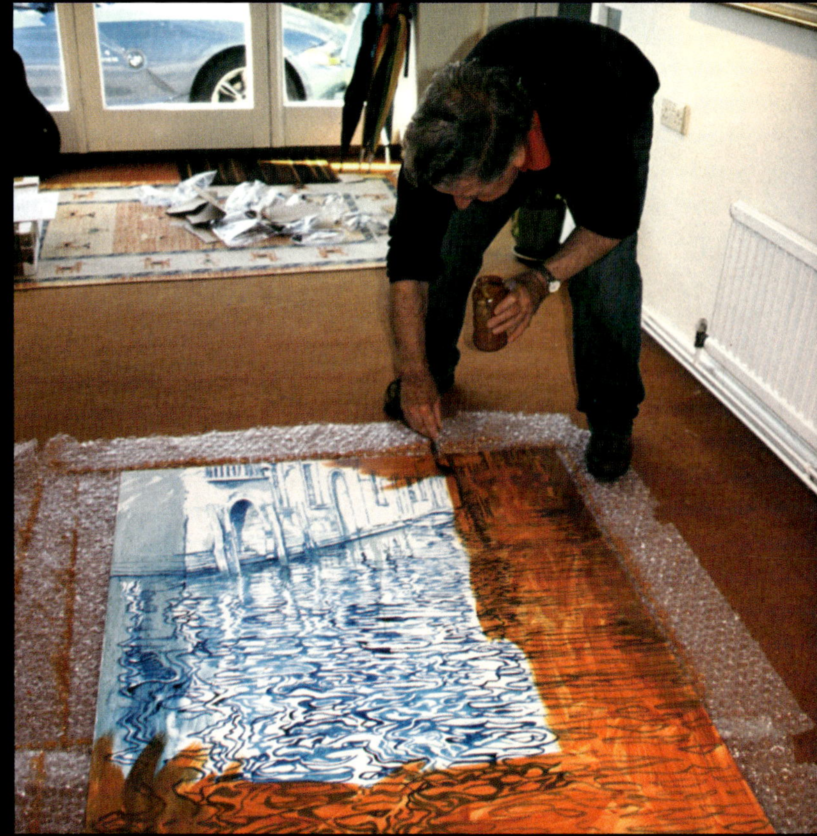

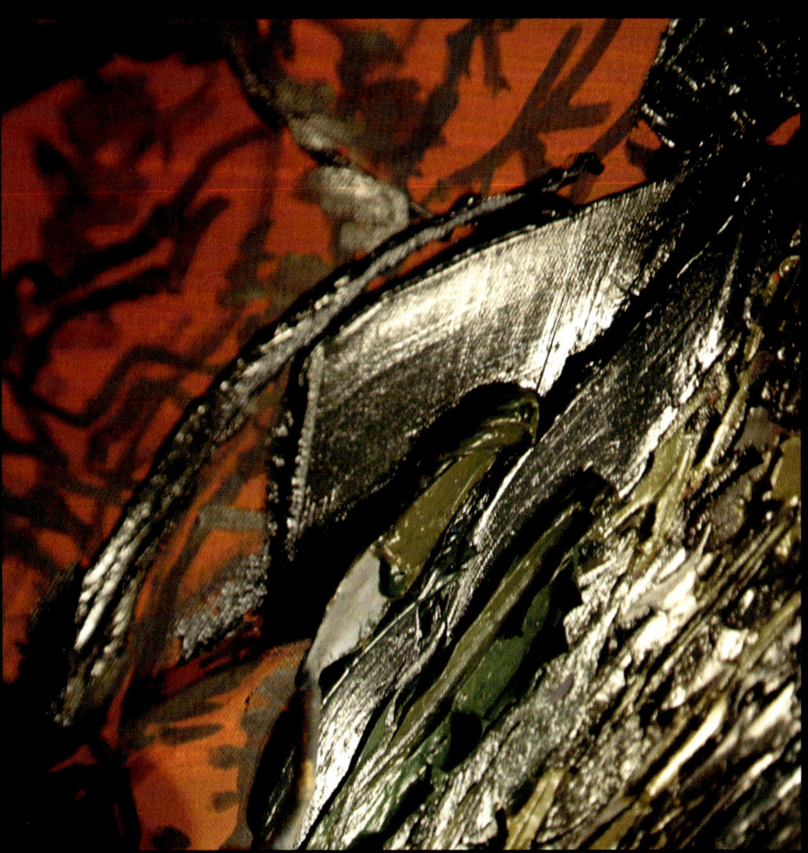

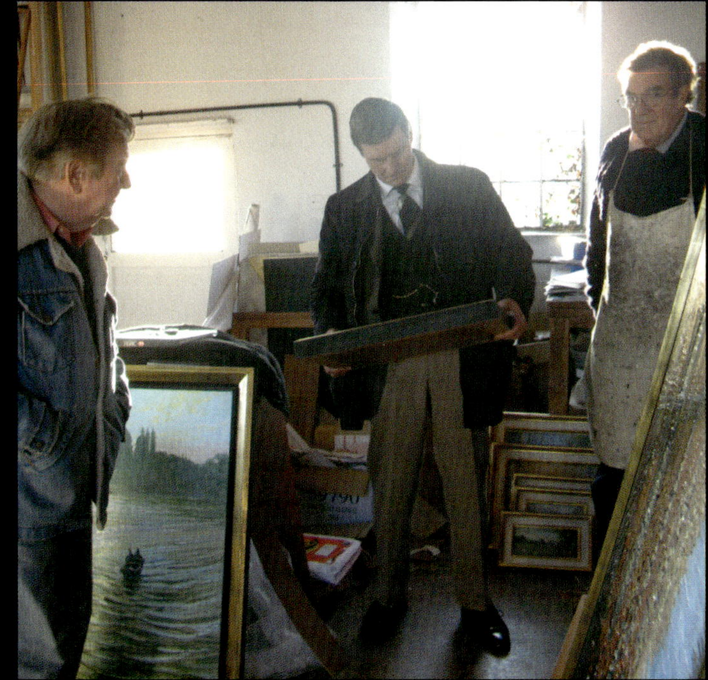
Michael Child, a Director of Messum's, inspecting a newly framed work.

a financial discussion early in the planning. I say to each that I need to have at least a quarter of a million pounds value on the wall in order to make things happen for you. If we sell half the work and half the money goes to the artist, that can quickly be reduced to a sum that we might spend entirely on the one show. I write a programme and give the artists an idea of what they might expect. I think it is quite helpful as artists are terrible worriers and frequently very unrealistic about money.'

These business meetings are particularly helpful both to Alan and to Pat Cotton, who deals with the family finances. Alan confirms that his relationship with David Messum is built on total trust. As he says, 'over the years David comes frequently with his director Carol Tee to discuss and plan each show, but I never have a contract. At one point in the gallery's development they brought in solicitors, but the documents were so long that I thought, this is not what I'm about. I told David that I couldn't sign and he was a bit aghast, but I don't need that. I know how David and all the gallery people work and I trust them. Now he jokes that Alan never signs a contract. We agree in a letter what we will spend upfront and it's always pretty exact. We have no arguments.'

A set chain of events for each exhibition now gives distinct shape both to Alan's life and to the life of the gallery. The gallery team refer to him as 'Big Al' because of his ability to facilitate and draw in new clients. A superbly designed and illustrated catalogue is sent out a few weeks before each Private View. Paintings shown in the catalogue are now sold before the exhibition opens. Although in the past nothing was sold before the Private View of an exhibition, the advent of the Internet with its worldwide reach has changed everything, and selling from the catalogue has become the norm. Each of the Messum's catalogues is a mini-book, on which the gallery team work very hard. David Messum himself does most of the layout at weekends, when he can get a bit of peace and quiet to spread out the images. 'Everything goes on the floor and everywhere. You have to see it all together and see just what you have got.' By this time the photographer has already done his work. For many years John Saunders, formerly of the University of Exeter, has photographed Alan's paintings, skilfully bringing out the impasto on the canvas by backlighting the work. The photography must be completed before framing, because the frames impede the acute angle required to illuminate the painted surface. Because pictures illustrated in the catalogue are more likely to sell, Alan works feverishly to catch up with the demands of the photography. He is invariably delighted with the catalogues. 'David does the best catalogues in London and has a terrific facility for variety, giving a different approach for each artist. When the catalogues finally arrive I salivate – it's such an important moment in my life to get a fresh-minted catalogue. Pat and I sit down and look at it and are full of pride. David has always done that for me – a real attempt to surprise and please me… He usually gives me the September slot, undoubtedly the best slot of the year, the start of the autumn season. I am aware that it is a responsibility. If you are given the best slot you have to use it.'

After the photography the pictures go to the framer. For many years all Alan's work has been framed by the master frame-maker and gilder Michael Beddoe. Alan tells the story of how they first met. In the Chelsea Arts Club some of the art displayed was framed in exceptional frames. Alan had not seen frames like these before and he lusted after them. Discovering that they were made by Soar & Son in London, he and Pat took a taxi to their shop. There were splendid frames were on the walls, hanging by their corners. When Alan asked if he could buy several, he was met with disdain. 'You can't buy them, sir, they are made for artists' individual paintings. Alan remarked 'It's a pity that nobody in the West Country can make frames as wonderful as these, with gesso and coloured clays underneath the gilding.' He was asked where he lived, and, answering that he lived in Devon, was told 'Well, our man lives in Somerset and if you give him a ring he may care to accommodate you.' Alan rang Michael Beddoe, who sounded wary, obviously wanting to make sure that Alan's work was worthy of his efforts. But when Alan took some of his work to the workshop in Martock, he received a very warm response. Michael Beddoe has framed his work ever since. As Alan admits, 'it's a huge job for him to frame at least sixty paintings with those wonderful frames. I'm afraid I do put him under pressure at times.' Beddoe's beautifully constructed frames, each tailored to show off the particular image it contains, have played an important part in the presentation of Alan Cotton's work.

Making a start on working for a new exhibition perhaps a year away is daunting. Alan compares it to climbing Everest. Back in his studio after the latest bout of travelling, he pores over his drawings and begins to formulate ideas for paintings. The studio becomes Everest Base Camp, and a great deal of preparation is necessary. The canvases are stretched, sized and painted with two coats of acrylic gesso before being washed over with a mid-tone, often red, ground. Over this ground Alan begins each painting with a brushed-in compositional sketch. Onto this sketched armature he lays the paint with painting knives. He has a plentiful supply of knives of different sizes so that he can obtain a wide variety of marks. As he begins to build up completed pictures, he likes to keep the canvases around him. 'I try to have the paintings around in the studio so when I'm creating the work for an exhibition I'm always aware of the paintings and it dawns on me that some could do with more work. With others I know I have gone as far as I can.' As he emphasises, 'being surrounded by the paintings and going with the flow, that's terribly important. It's like

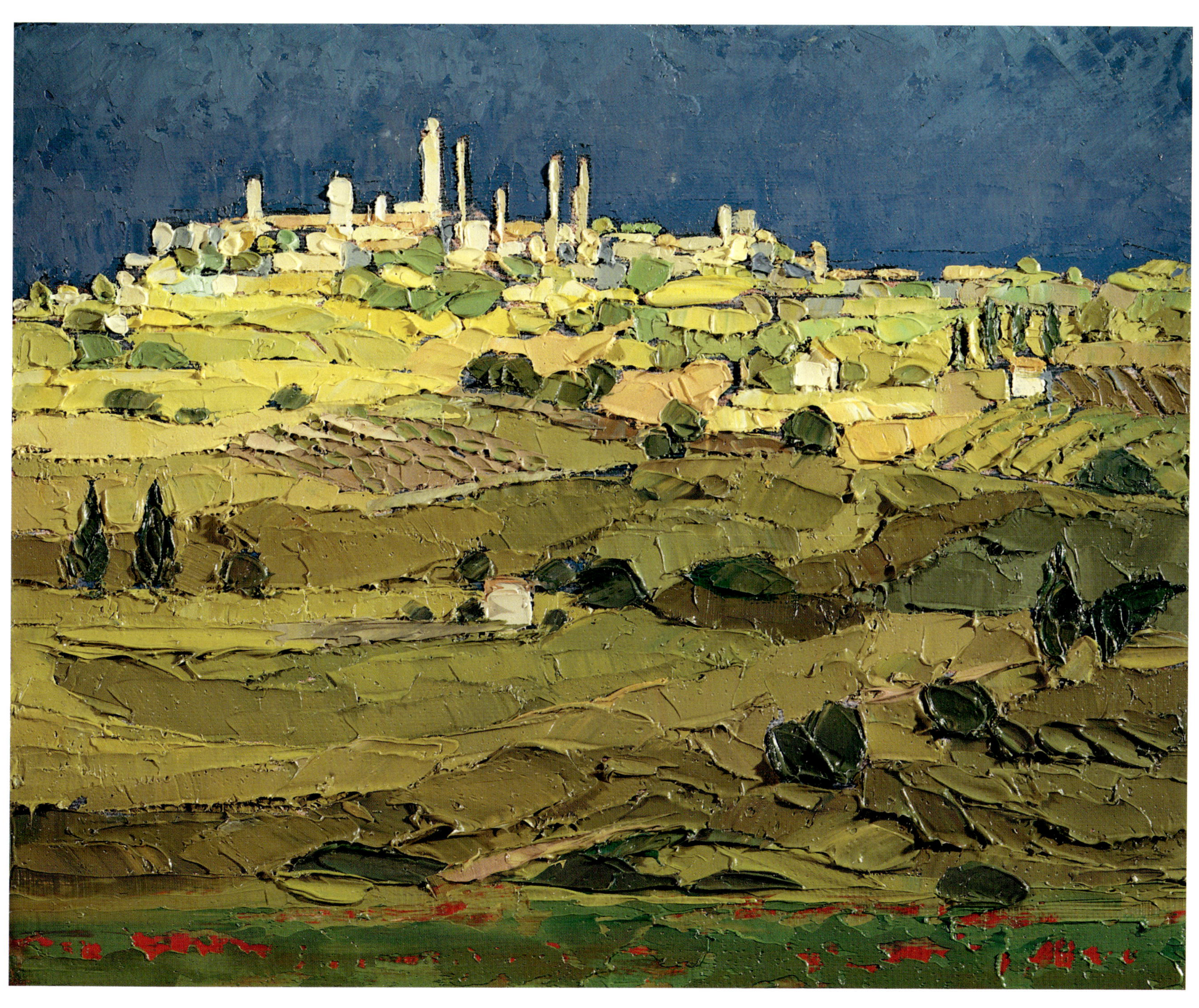

Tuscany – Sunlight after the Storm
oil on canvas 10 x 12 ins

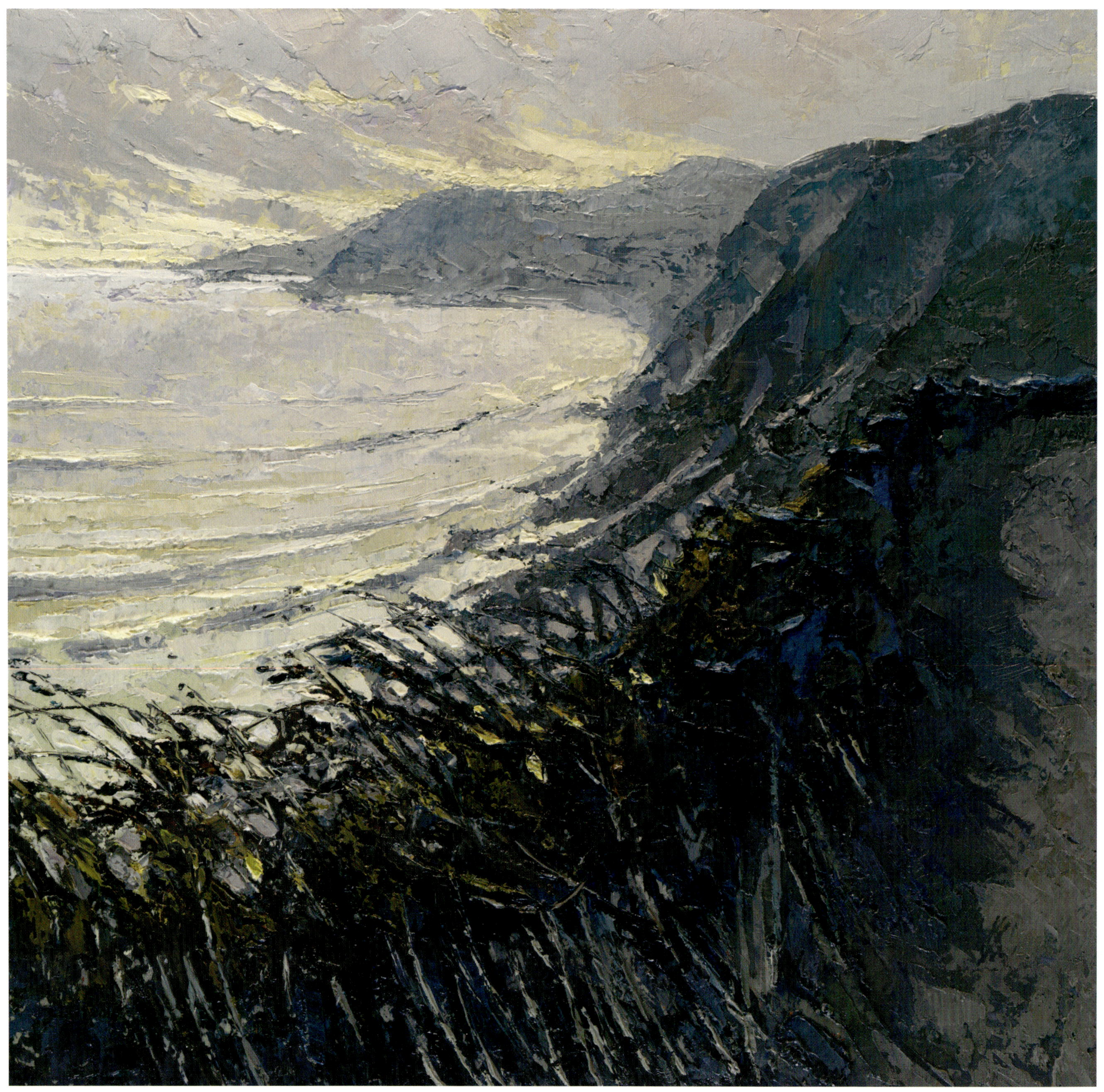

Donegal – Thorny Hedgerows along the Coastal Path, 2009
oil on canvas 24 x 24 ins

being surrounded by your children… One painting influences another. Then the day comes when the carriers come from London and take the paintings off the walls and pack them up. They are packed into the van and off they go. That is quite a downer – it's like the children leaving home and going to university.' He is comforted, however, by knowing that the paintings will appear at their very best in the gallery. 'Messums hang the exhibitions so well. My first exhibition was in a Gas showroom at goodness knows what age and anything I sold was to relatives. You learn – you have to inform yourself. For many years I hung my own exhibitions. But now one of the joys of being with a really good gallery is that they hang the work for you, better than I could, and light it better than I could, and understand the whole business of staging a show.'

The culmination of the year's planning and hard work is the Private View. Nowadays Private Views have become not so much Openings or First Day of Sales but more of an 'Artist's Party', giving artists the chance to see their work afresh and to celebrate with friends. Because Alan lives far from London, for him Messum's stage all-day Private Views with plentiful wine and canapés, giving far-flung family and friends a chance to admire the new work. As Alan reiterates, 'they do the whole thing very well. When I see the work hung in the gallery I am always surprised and on the whole proud of what I have done. You do see your paintings in a totally different way. You detach yourself. It's almost as if they belong to someone else already, and you can be objective about what you've done. Selling the work is mostly a good experience. While you are doing the work you care passionately about it and then you realise it will go and that's fine because (a) you need the money and (b) lots of charming people buy and enjoy it.'

Knowing that many paintings are sold from the catalogue before the Private View greatly increases Alan's anticipatory buzz. As he says, 'I am gregarious and I love it. I never have any fear. There you are, centre stage, and a lot of family and friends come, and I really love it. This is not a hostile audience. Essentially people come because they like you and like your work and want to be part of it. It's always a friendly thing. I am pleased to see my collectors, and I get a lot of feedback, hundreds of letters, from buyers who love the paintings. A lot of people come from the South West and I always host a big dinner afterwards for family and friends and the gallery team. I want everyone to share the experience with me and have a good time.'

ONE OF AN IMPORTANT SERIES of late summer harvest scenes based around the Otter Valley, near Alan's home in Devon. Since childhood Alan had loved the romance of walking through harvest fields, looking through tall plant stalks at the sky and the distant landscape. This painting, on a white ground, was composed from his drawings in the fields, with some of the foreground plants standing in pots on his studio windowsill. To vary his mark-making, Alan 'printed' the strong verticals of the plant stems on the canvas with the edge of a painting knife, and dragged paint across an underpainted surface to suggest the warm haze of a summer evening sky. The influence of Alan Reynolds, whose paintings of the four seasons Alan admired as a student, is clear in this lyrical image.

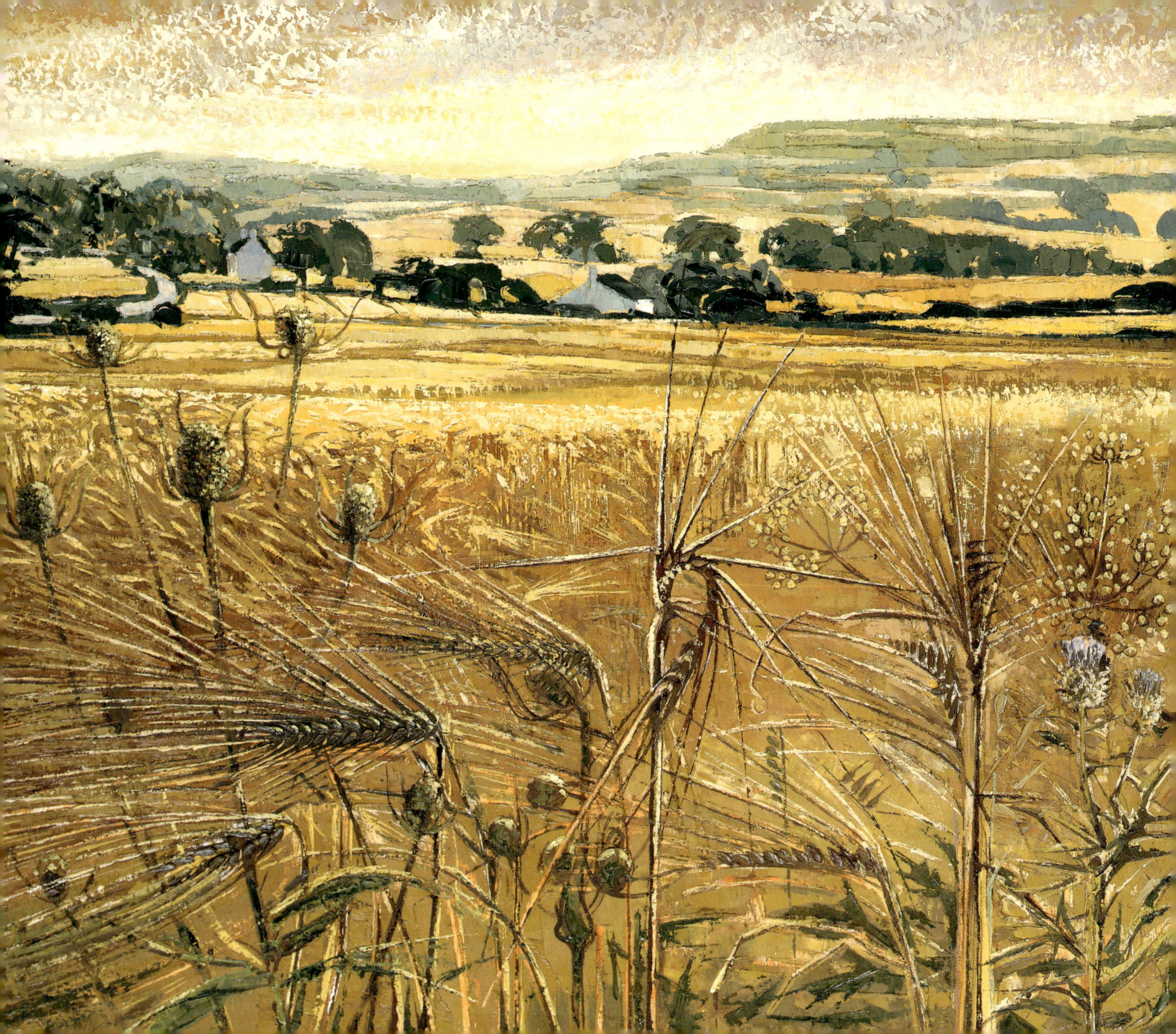

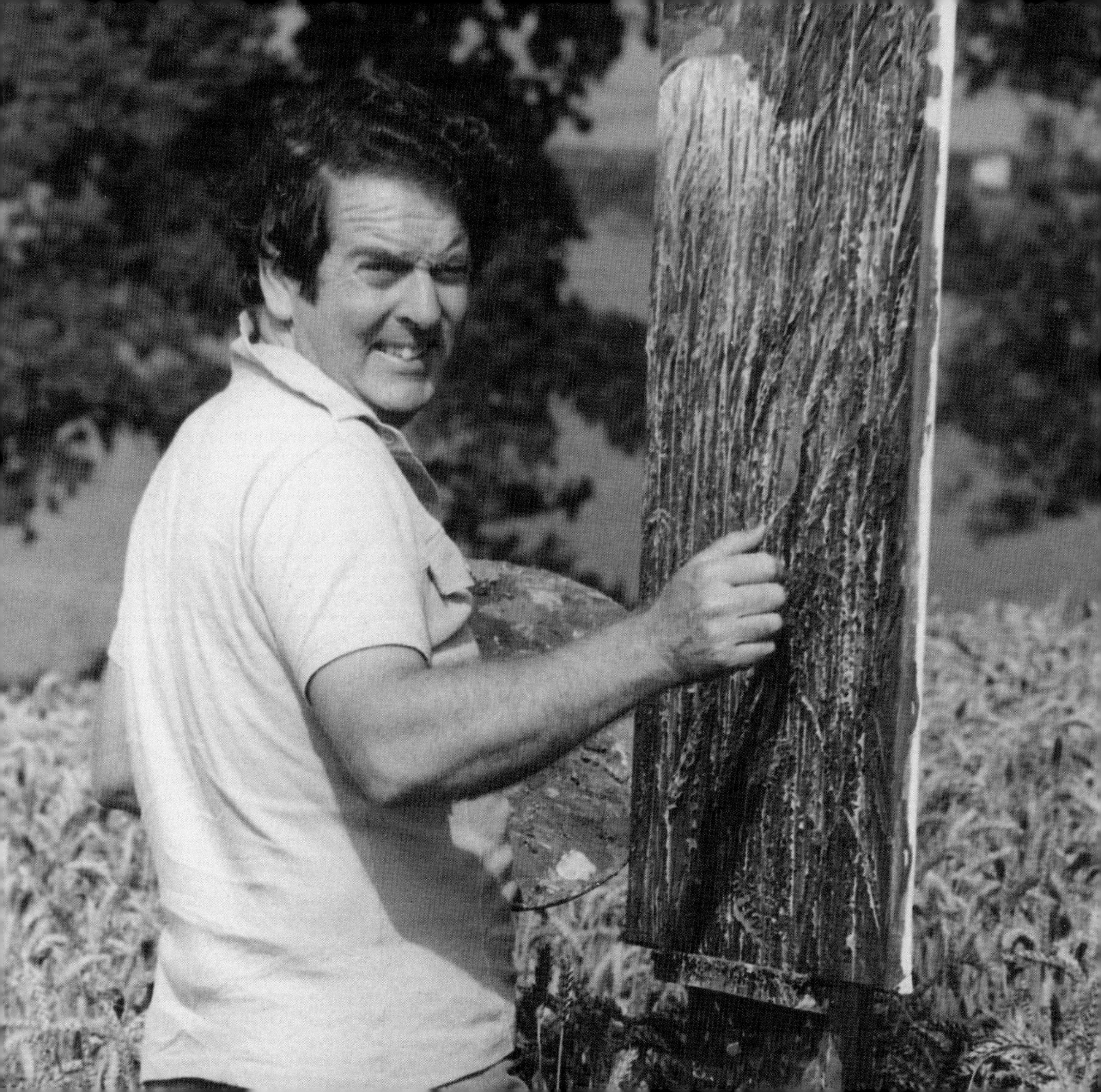

Chapter Two

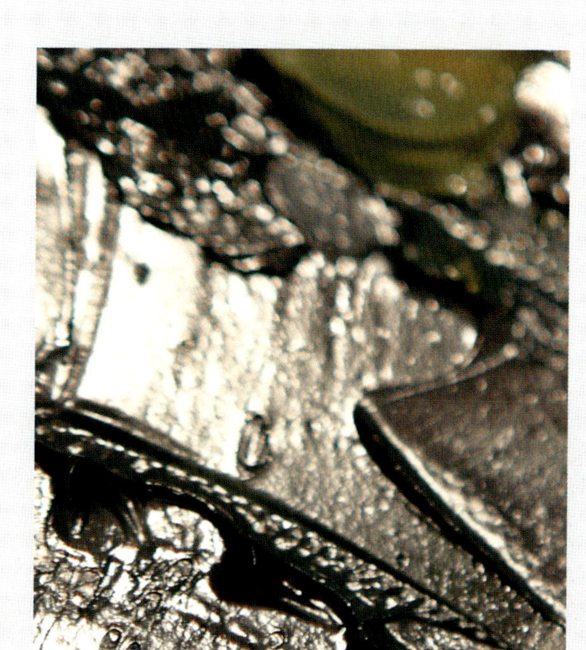

Reaching Out

Morocco – Jemaa el Fna at Midday, Marrakech
oil on canvas 20 x 20 ins

Through Messum's gallery Alan Cotton's expressive and celebratory landscapes have a wide reach, attracting collectors and commissions from around the world. Through his art he has made many friends, some of whom are ardent collectors. It seems fitting that many of his collectors are actors, as his wife Pat taught drama and his son Richard is an actor. John Nettles of *Midsomer Murders* fame has acquired several Cotton paintings. The actress Sheila Hancock bought from the gallery a painting of Bonnieux, the village close to the house that she and her husband, John Thaw, owned. She also liked a Provencal landscape that had already been sold, so she commissioned a similar, larger picture to give to her daughter. Alan's painting of a Provencal orchard with spumes of blossom touched by the evening sun so delighted Sheila Hancock that she kept it for herself. The actor Art Malik was also bowled over by Alan's work. He first saw it in the weekend exhibition in Marlow in 1992, and as he recorded, 'the previous summer I had spent three weeks in Provence filming, and to be greeted by the paintings of the Ochre Quarry brought it all back. The colours and the landscape, the light, so unique, were all oozing from every canvas.' Subsequently Art Malik found himself looking at landscape through Alan's eyes. As he attests in his foreword to the catalogue of the 2002 exhibition, he had a passionate desire to see what Alan might make of Morocco. 'I have visited Ouarzarzate many times, making films, but it was whilst travelling by road to Marrakech across the Atlas mountains that Gina, my wife, and I discussed how wonderful it would be for Alan to interpret onto canvas the enigmatic arid landscape. There was little vegetation, and as we turned bend after bend we were occasionally surprised by villages, almost invisible as they blended into the hillside, built of the same rock and substance as the mountains themselves. Having just come from London at that time where we had seen Alan's exhibition of Venice, this spectacular vista made me think of the first show of his I had seen at David Messum's house years before, in which the ochre quarries of Provence had featured. As we were driven round the hairpin bends in the High Atlas, I remarked to Gina who was lying down throwing up in the back of the car, "Alan and Pat must come to Morocco. He has to paint this."... I spoke to Richard, Alan's son, who felt that Alan had surpassed himself with these paintings and when I saw the new work in his studio in Devon, I agreed. They are full of Alan's characteristic vibrancy of colour and drama using light and form, which instantly transported me back to the unforgettable atmosphere and impression of that ruggedly beautiful country. I believe this collection undoubtedly confirms Alan as one of Britain's greatest living landscape artists.'

Martin Bralsford, another collector who has subsequently become a good friend, now owns over thirty Alan

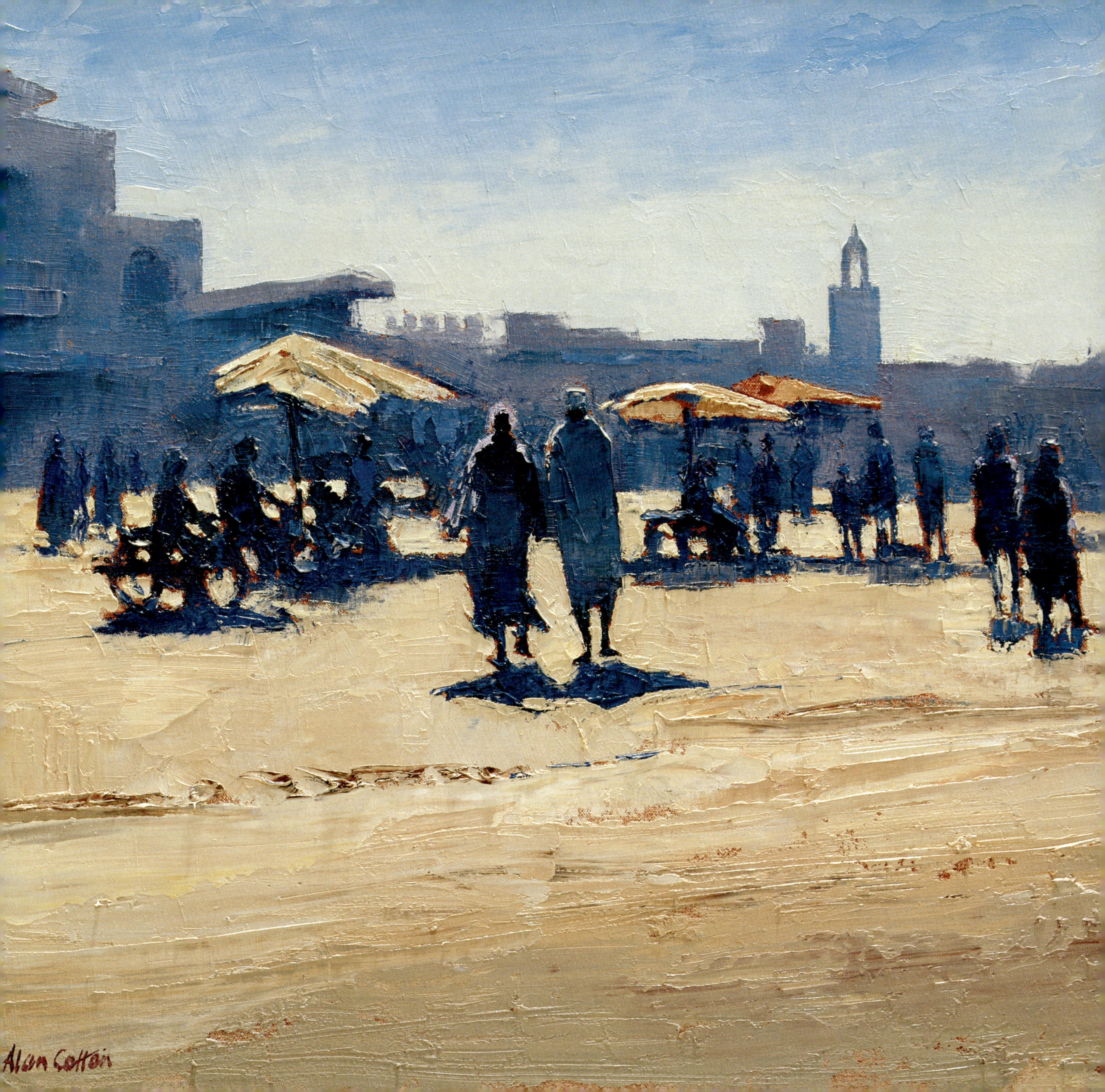
Alan Cotton

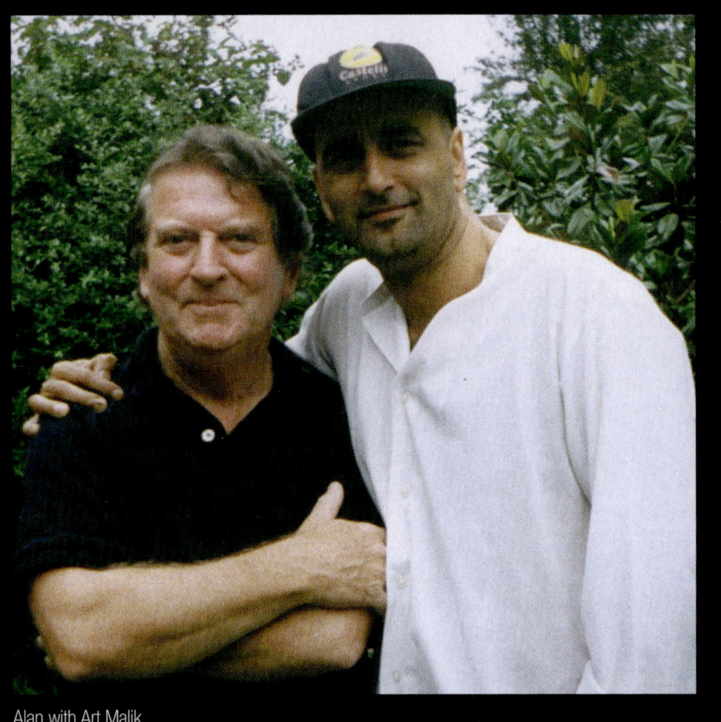

Alan with Art Malik.

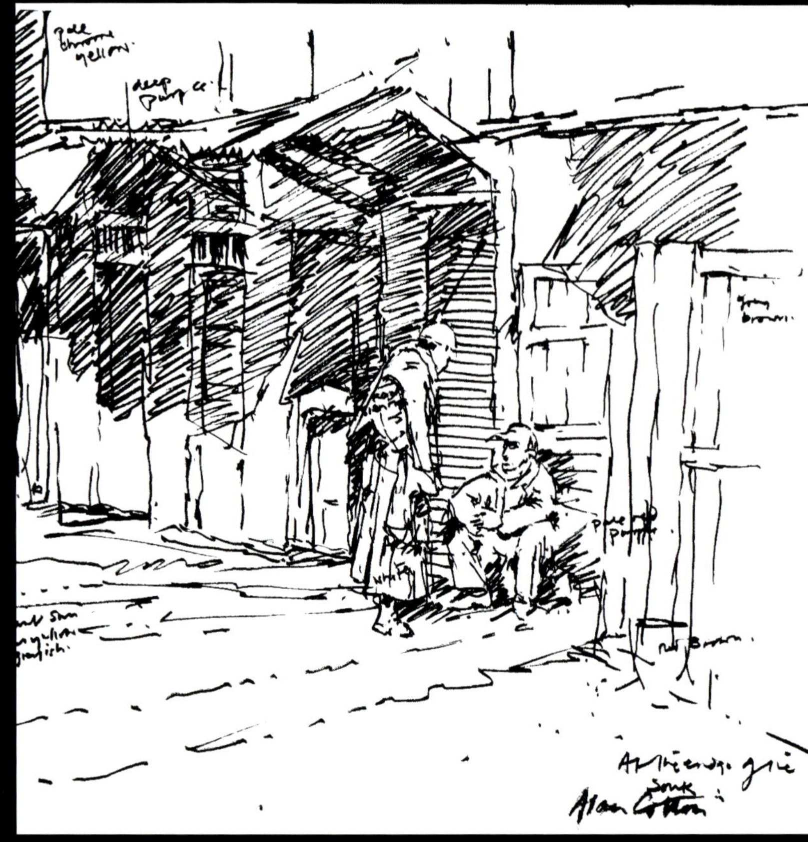

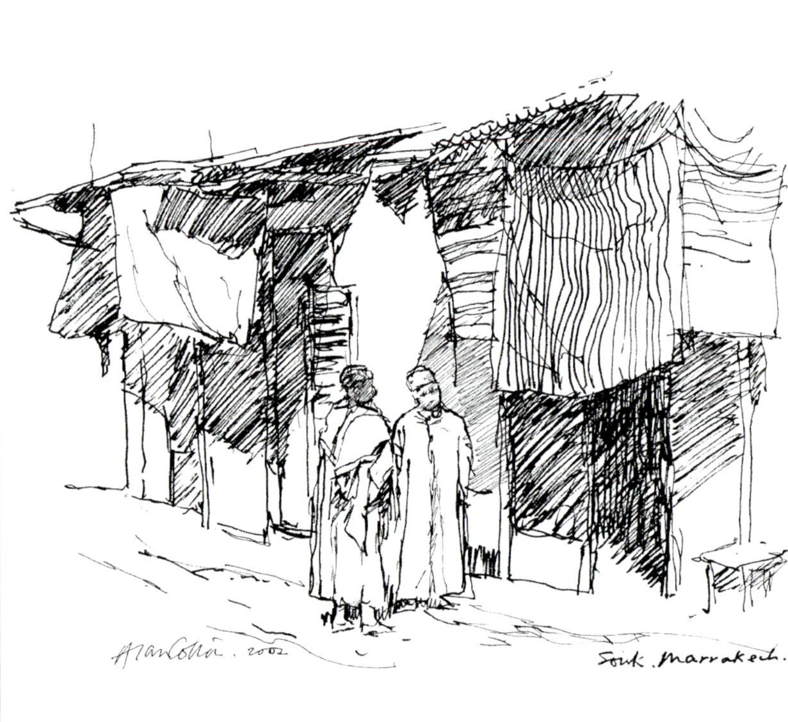

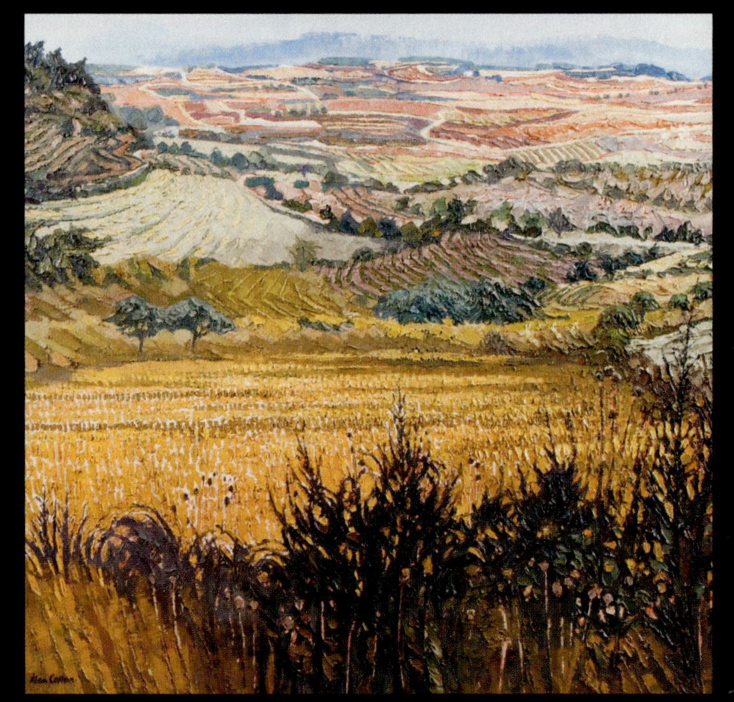

Cyprus – Barley Fields and Vineyards near the Troodos oil on canvas 36 x 36 ins
Collection Martin Bralsford

Cotton paintings. Having recently moved to Jersey, Martin Bralsford first saw Alan's work in an exhibition at John Falle's new gallery, Falle Fine Art, in St Helier, Jersey, in1994. He remembers the occasion vividly. 'I walked into the gallery and facing me on the wall was the big Alan Cotton painting of Cyprus. I said I have got to have that painting. When I turned round the other way there was another painting of a similar scene – slightly smaller – and I said I have got to have that too. I bought those two paintings just like that. They are still the most significant paintings I own. The subject matter, the colours, the effects of paint with knife – the stalks of the plants just scored through the different layers of impasto – the effect was brilliant. When I eventually got to know Alan I asked him if he knew what would happen when he did those things. I was intrigued by him. He was very modest and unassuming and yet had this incredibly vigorous style of painting. I am absolutely fascinated by these paintings, which seem to change colour in different lights. They were what really got me into art collecting.'

Martin Bralsford has followed Alan's career closely and, finding common ground in places where they had lived, asked him to paint some pictures of the Worcestershire countryside. 'I found out that Alan had been at Bournville Art School, and I was working for a while at Bournville. I was living at Barnt Green, south west of Birmingham, and while I was there I got to know the Worcestershire countryside. I loved the Malvern Hills and the fabulous countryside, which I thought of as the quintessential England. I commissioned Alan to paint six or so scenes that he himself picked from the days when he used to cycle round that countryside with his tutor Norman Neasom. He had to fit this around his other work so it was a long time between the idea and the execution. One of the pictures, of Tardebigge Locks, close to where I lived in Barnt Green, was different from the others in light and texture, a yellow/lime green painting, smoothly finished and slightly spooky. There was apparently a painful story behind that painting. It was the place where he was caught in flagrante with his first girlfriend and suffered dreadful abuse from her father. Alan very kindly had all the pen and ink drawings for the paintings framed, and now they are all in my office.'

Alan's successful exhibition at Falle Fine Art in Jersey led to a second show in 1999. For this show he and Pat Cotton stayed with Martin Bralsford in Jersey to collect material for paintings local to the exhibition. This second exhibition contained many paintings of Jersey, the centrepiece being *The St Hélier Day Procession*, a large composition featuring the procession, led by the Dean of Jersey in religious robes, to Elizabeth castle and the big rock where St Hélier had his cell. Alan was particularly fascinated by famous La Corbière lighthouse and the rocky headland that it protects. According to John Falle, he exclaimed that he could have painted the whole exhibition around La Corbière alone.

While together in Jersey Martin Bralsford and Alan discovered a mutual love of opera, and Martin was quick to acquire Alan's CD, *Cotton on Music*, created by Bill Holland, then head of Universal Classics and Jazz, to accompany his 2001 exhibition *A Sense of Place*. In the leaflet wrapping the CD Alan describes what music has meant to him. 'From the time I was a child, when my mother made brushes from her own hair, I painted and aspired to be a painter. From a working class background, where the only music came from the radio, I was truly moved by opera, excited by jazz and sang along to much popular music of the day, which hearing now can provoke a potent nostalgia of time and place. My first 'studio' in my early teens was a box room, where I laid out my paints, stretched canvas over old picture frames, acquired a second-hand record player and bought my first music – the first an old 78 by Beniamina Gigli singing *che gelida manina* from *La Bohème*. With much excitement I also bought Tchaikovsky's *Piano Concerto in B Flat Minor*, which I played endlessly. Listening to music as I drew and painted created in my small world an atmosphere which took me far outside the confines of an urban existence to far away vistas and more exotic places. To this day, things haven't changed very much. My studio in a country village is many times larger, I have better recording equipment, but music is still a central part of my working day.'

Music has created a strong bond between Alan and Bill Holland, now the UK's A&R Consultant at Warner Music, who is another of his collectors. He has taken Alan to the opera and extended his musical knowledge by encouraging him to listen to a wider range of music. Opera is now Alan's greatest source of musical inspiration.

Besides the pressure of working for exhibitions, Alan has frequently found himself squeezing in commissioned work. Two important commissions came his way through his paintings of Venice. Messums' gallery was approached by the company commissioning decorative interior design work for the liner *The Queen Mary II*. Alan Cotton was requested to paint three pictures to adorn one of the main staircases on the ship. Because of the potential fire risk, these pictures had to be painted in acrylic on aluminium. Learning how to use these unfamiliar materials proved quite a challenge, and it took Alan three months of preparation before he could start work on the final images. Now an integral part of *The Queen Mary II*, they carry Alan Cotton's images around the globe.

It was these paintings of Venice that were seen and admired by Howard Frank, Vice President of the international shipping corporation Carnival, and his wife Mary Engel Frank, while they were cruising on the Queen Mary. Mary Engel Frank, an art historian, looked Alan up on the Internet and emailed him about a possible commission. She had an idea that she might like a Venetian theme for her dining room in Florida. The Franks invited Alan and Pat to meet

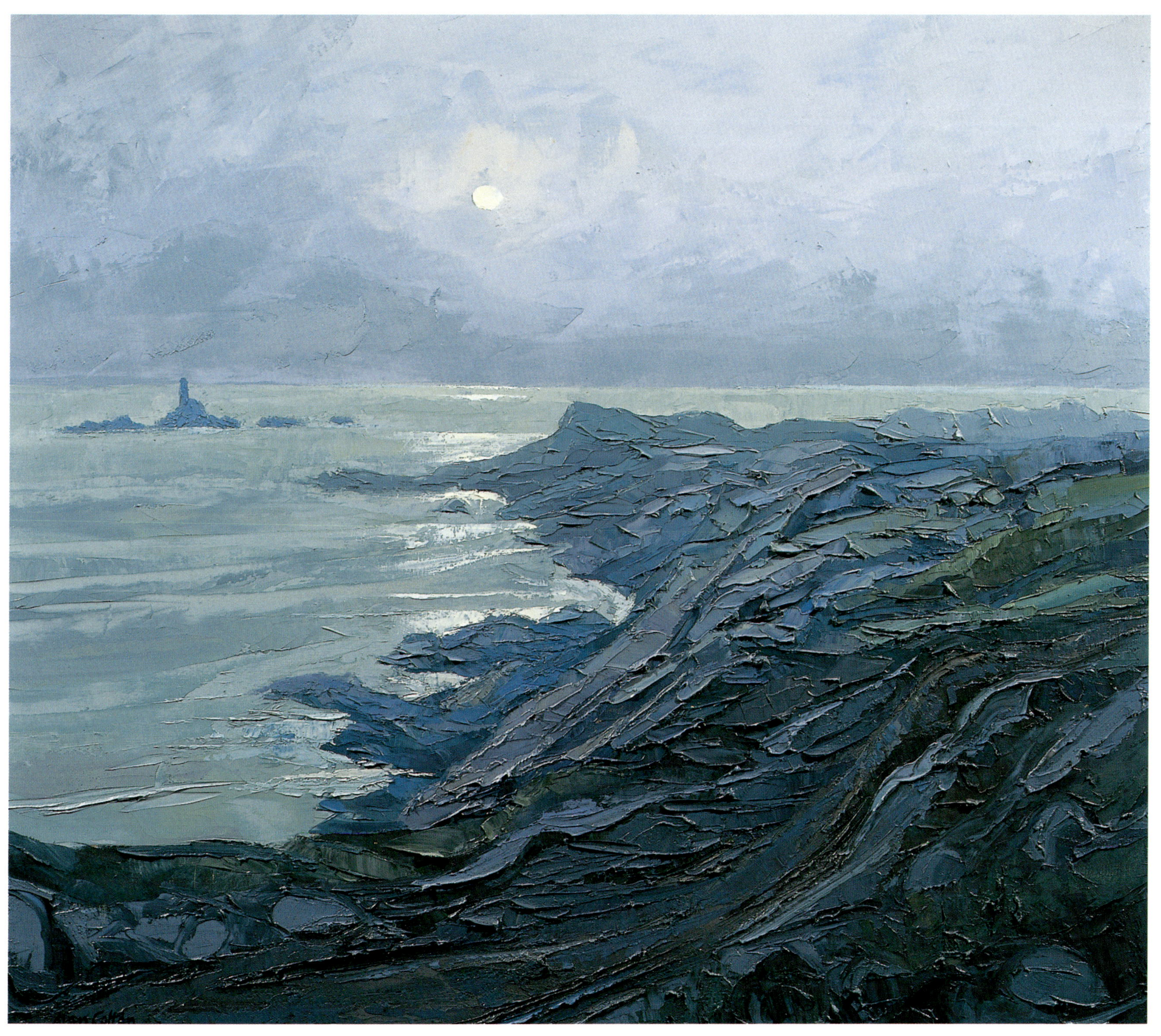

Jersey – La Corbière Lighthouse Towards Evening, 1999
oil on canvas 36 x 40 ins

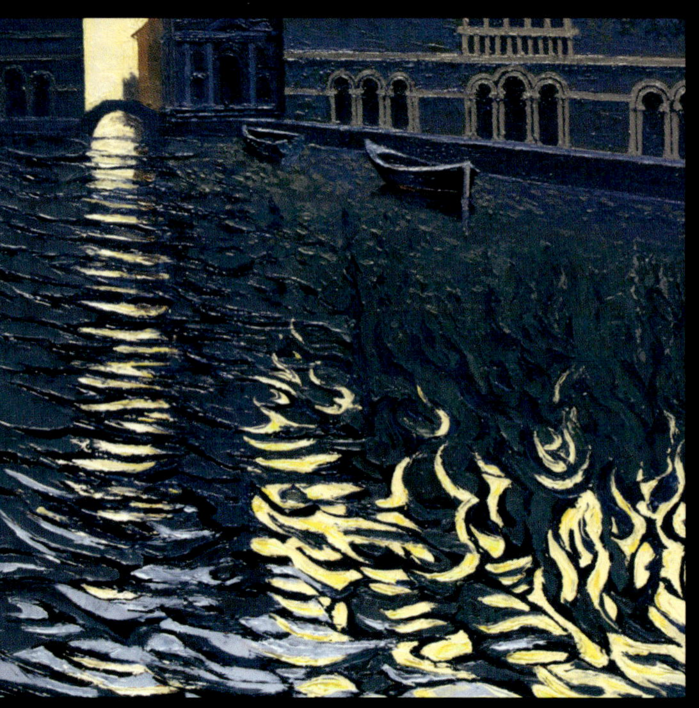

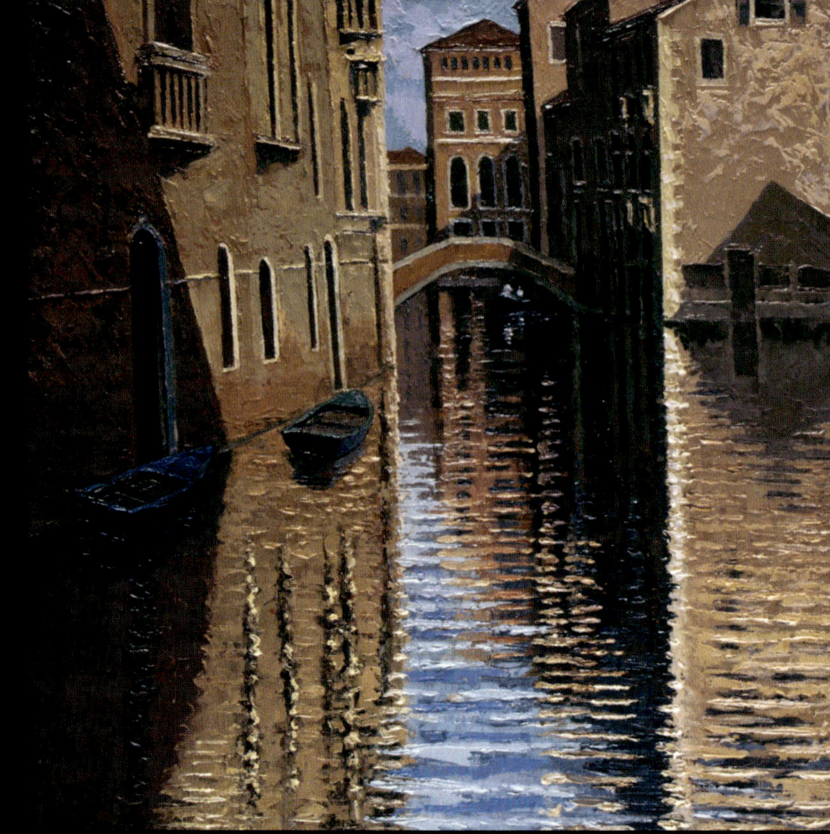

Details from the Franks' Venetian paintings

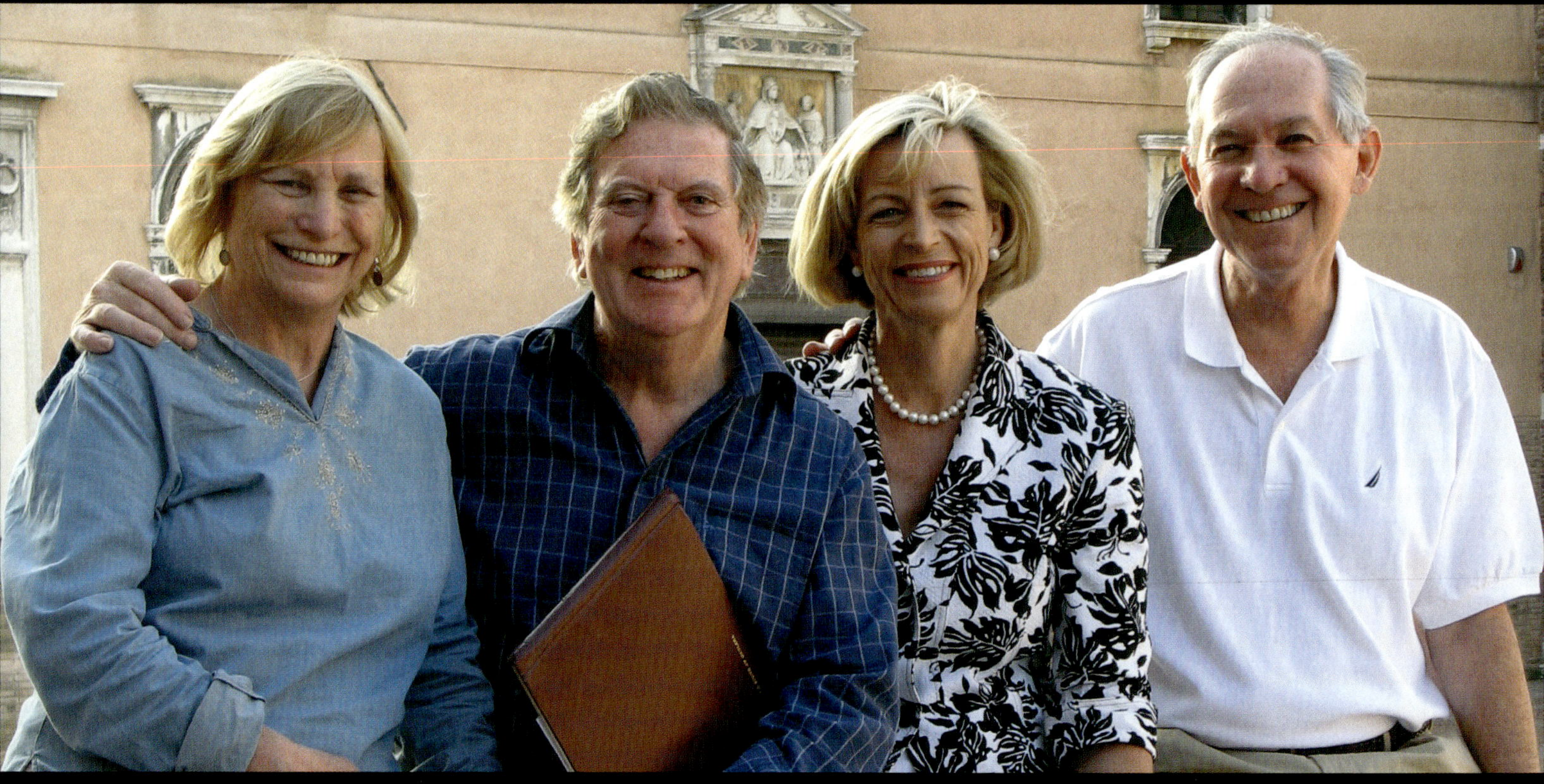

Alan and Pat with Howard and Mary Engel Frank in Venice

them in Venice while they were staying in their apartment there. Feeling that Messum's gallery should mastermind the terms of the commission, Alan persuaded David Messum's son Johnathan (now a director of Messum's) and his wife Catherine to join them in Venice. All six got on famously. Alan and the Franks spent a week walking around Venice together, Alan getting up very early every morning to draw and explore different ideas for paintings. Eventually a plan was hatched for Alan to paint five Venetian pictures for the Franks's dining room in their Miami house. In several subsequent meetings in London they worked out the dimensions of the paintings they wanted. Alan began to formulate ideas for the paintings, while Johnathan Messum and the gallery team worked out details of transport and price. Alan painted all five canvases on a reddish ground, with each one representing a different time of day. Each had a different perspective, with the morning and evening light creating differently coloured reflections. He concentrated on the reflections in the water, enjoying playing about with different viewpoints. As he wandered around Venice, the reflections in the water seemed to suggest a magical underworld, and these became his personal theme. As he recalls, 'it was a wonderful experience going out into Venice at dawn before anyone else was around and walking through all the squares with nobody there. It was like being on a series of empty theatre sets. I felt I must put in a gondola to represent Venice, but I simplified it. There's a lot of invention in them, and the simpler they are the better. '

Venice got into Alan Cotton's blood, as it has done with so many artists. In an effort to find a fresh way of depicting it, Alan chose to study the mirrored image rather than the famous sights themselves, in a reversal of normal landscape composition. In many of his Venetian paintings the watery reflections, hanging from a high horizon line, take up the whole canvas. The reflections of building or boat in water disturbed by passing gondolas or vaporetti fascinated him. In his catalogue commentary for his 2004 exhibition *As I See It* he describes his exploration of Venice, adding: 'One place in Venice I feel I have made my own is the Fish Market, because what I enjoy are reflections. The wet surface reflects the light and in the old fish market, which has been going for hundreds of years, they continually spray the fish to keep it cool and the water is all over the floor. Then everything is in silhouette in this interior and the reflections stream down horizontally and are absolutely wonderful.' For Alan the commission for the Franks was a delight. Throughout the whole process he photographed his paintings, and finally presented the Franks with all his working drawings. Alan's Venetian paintings, now in situ in Miami, are much prized and have joined the Franks' distinguished collection of American art.

One of Alan Cotton's earliest commissions, which seemed at first to present insuperable problems, was commissioned by the Commando Training Centre Royal Marines Lympstone to commemorate their Golden Jubilee in 1990. A committee of marines met Alan to discuss commissioning a painting of East Devon from the air as it appeared after World War II. When Alan said that would need a great deal of investigation to find out what the landscape was like from the air, the committee members replied 'that's easy, we can fly you up there in the Seaking helicopter'. As Alan remembered 'I sat with my legs out of the bomb bay, with a harness on, with my drawing book on my knee – there were fumes coming out of the back and lots of vibration. I did have a camera up there but I thought I can't do this – it's too difficult. I prevaricated for a long time but ordered the canvas of the required size, and then we had an invitation to the opening. The Lord Lieutenant was going to be there and the marine band. That started me. I rang the Commandant and said "I'm in a terrible pickle because you've invited people to see something I haven't even started. I just can't get the material I want." He said "I'll call you back."' He arranged for Alan to go to the Devon and Cornwall Police Headquarters at Middlemoor, and within minutes of arriving he was flying over the estuary in a police surveillance helicopter which he described as being just like his own sports car. 'I said I wanted the evening light with the shadows showing the configuration of the landscape and they said "let's get on with it". They took me up about ten times, and I even prolonged it because I so enjoyed it – it was wonderful flying over the estuary. I made a drawing and then, when I needed to find out what the land had previously looked like, the Press invited farmers, local historians and anyone with old photographs or reminiscences to contact Alan Cotton with their memories. We had a succession of farming people coming to the studio.' Alan wanted to make sure that the shapes of the fields and hedgerows were accurate, and local farmers would walk in to inspect the eight-foot canvas with the drawing and say "in my day, it weren't like that". When the marine officers were training on Woodbury Common they would divert into Alan's studio to see the progress of the painting, looking at it while still jogging on the spot. As Alan remembered, 'the whole project became great fun. At the unveiling by the Lord Lieutenant the cord was pulled and the curtain got stuck on the painting. They had to get a ladder out to free it. But it was a great occasion and a great commission to do.'

Another early commission came through Alan's television connections. The board of West Country Televison wanted a large painting to hang in their main entrance. Alan decided to link the main transmission regions of Devon and Cornwall by painting the river Tamar with Brunel's bridge. The painting was unveiled by Peter Brooke, the then Arts Minister. Other commissions included a painting of Cyprus for the head of the Jaguar Racing team, a work so

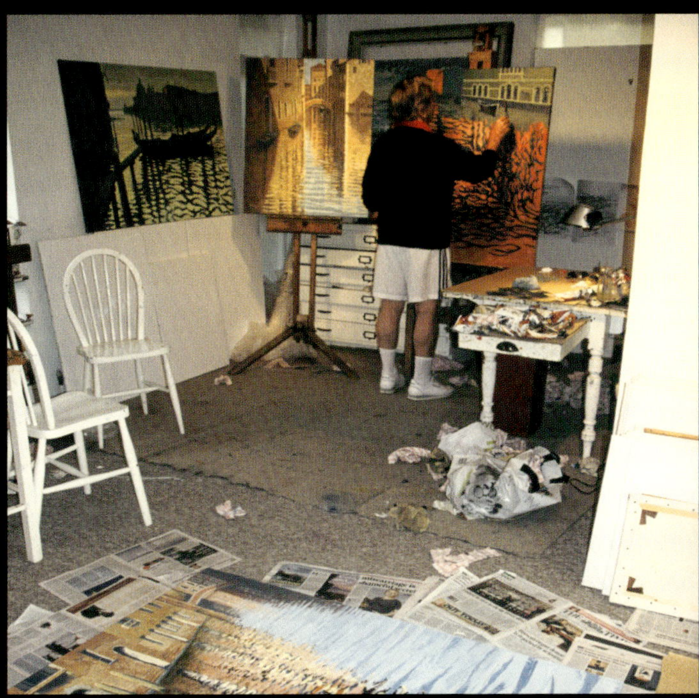

Above: Alan working on one of the Venetian commission paintings

Right and below: details of the Venetian commission paintings

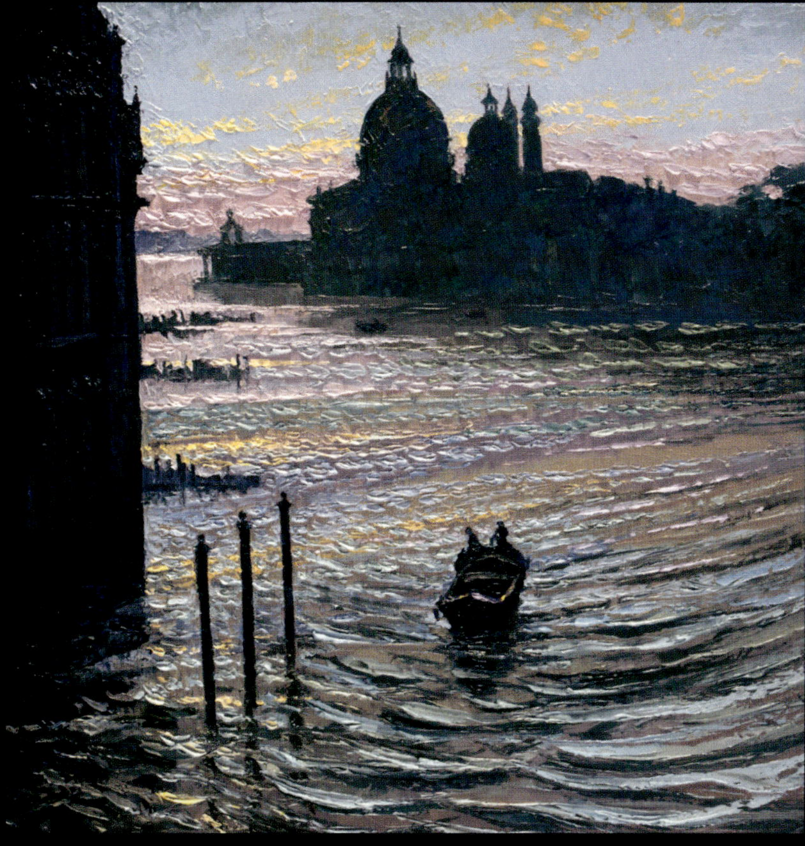

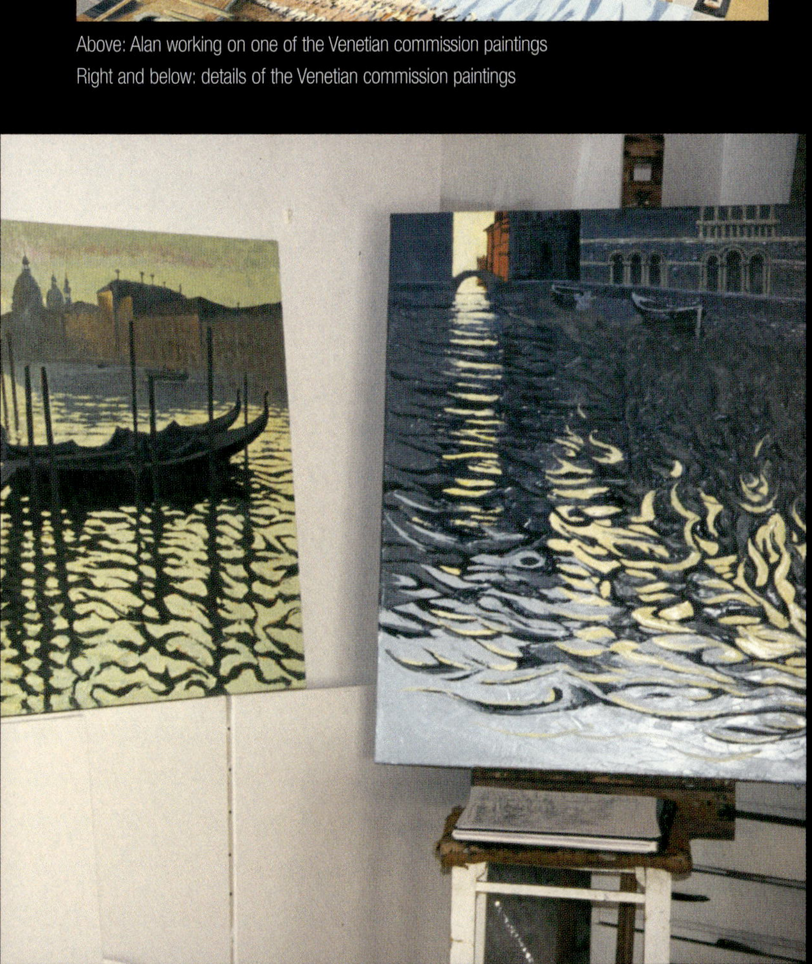

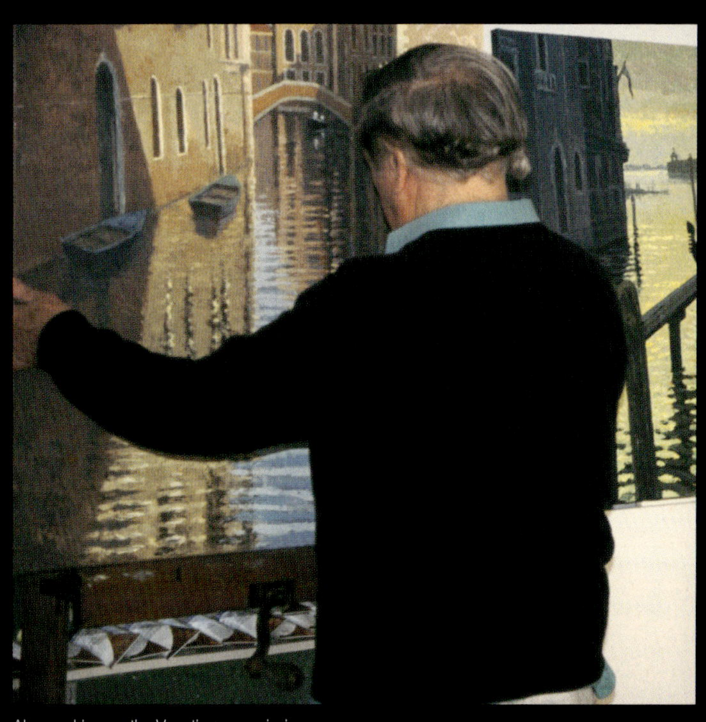

Alan working on the Venetian commission

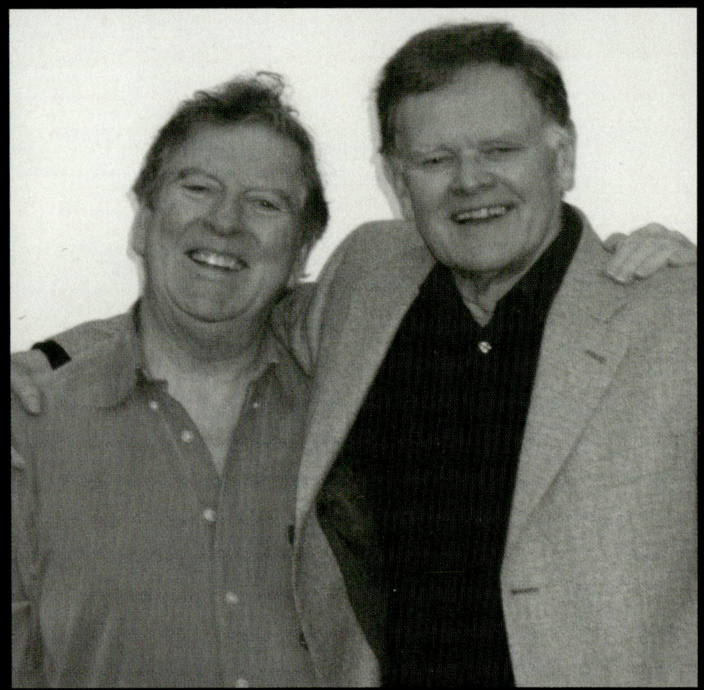

Above: Alan with film director Kevin Crooks

Right: Alan with the Cyprus painting commissioned by Dr Michael Peagram

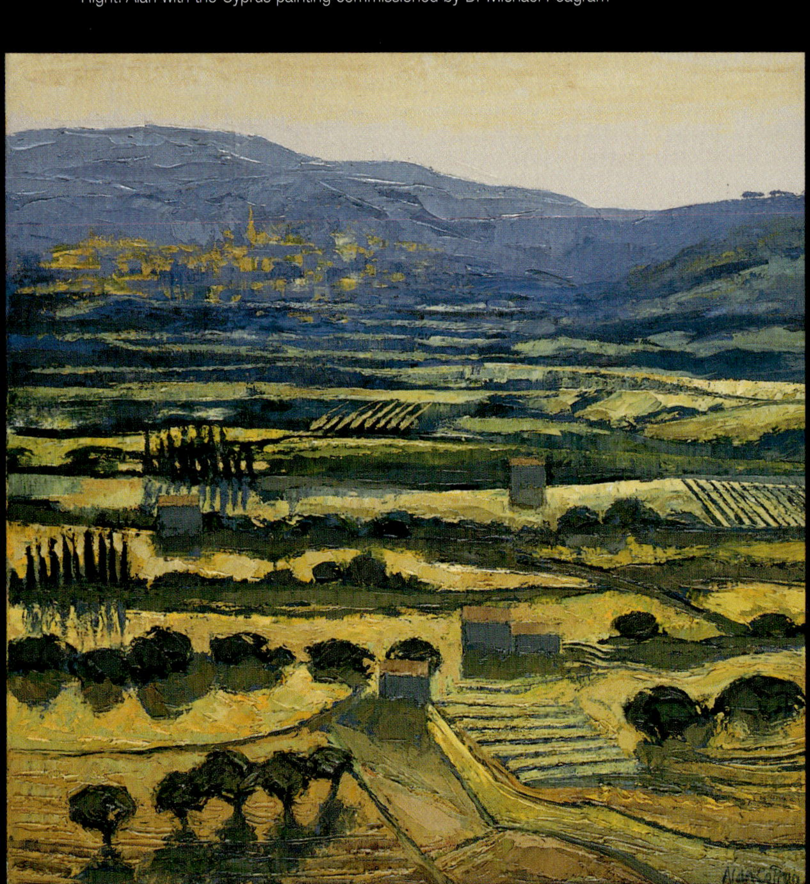

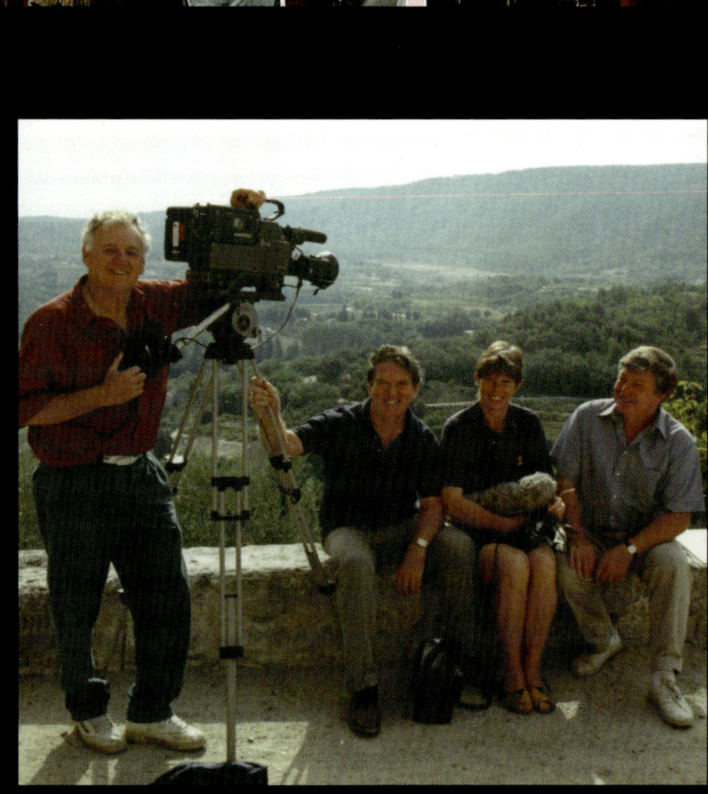

Left: *Provence – Bonnieux in Evening Light,* oil on canvas, 24 x 24 ins

Above: Filming in Provence for the ITV film "Cotton on Canvas" . From left to right: Colin Rowe (cameraman), Alan, Zyna Gaskell-Brown (sound recordist), Philip Speight (director)

large that he needed tall padded ladders to hang the finished picture.

Even larger was the Cyprus painting commissioned through the gallery for his Palladian mansion in Oxfordshire by Dr Michael Peagram, who already owned a number of Cotton paintings. Alan went with David Messum and his director, Michael Child, to hang the completed painting, which was heavy with impasto, only to find that no preparation had been done. The three of them had a difficult job moving the furniture, including a very heavy dresser, and hanging the painting on their own.

Unusual commissions for paintings, lecturing and filming have brought Alan Cotton a wide circle of friends. Perhaps his closest friend of the 1990s was the television presenter Kevin Crooks, whose premature death Alan still mourns. Crooks' s colleague Judi Spiers recalled that the two of them were like brothers, sharing the same sense of humour, always laughing together. When Crooks first saw Alan's work, Alan was still teaching at Rolle College in Exmouth while somehow finding time to paint. After a memo from his boss, Tom Salmon, saying that he had seen a rather interesting painter and that the BBC should make a film, Kevin Crooks recorded their first meeting. 'It seemed to me that the work was intense. Broad sweeps of colour were criss-crossed with subtle marks where flat paint gave way to sculptural forms. The canvases held those extra dimensions that proved the artist was here. The mastery of composition seemed almost secondary to the record of how the artist felt'. Then, as the project got under way, 'we gave ourselves a massive task. Filming days were littered across the calendar. Together we worked on a plan which would need a minimum of five or six locations – just enough to cover Alan's diverse approach to life. The way we laid the schedule far exceeded the available budget.... As our friendship developed, I found myself indulging in the somewhat pointless occupation of embroidering the plan. I was so taken up with these thoughts that I clear forgot to report my progress. The craggy Cornish face of Tom Salmon regarded me over his half moon spectacles... Where the dickens is my blasted film?... We need to film a sequence in Brittany and I don't think the budget will stretch...

Three weeks later, Alan and I, accompanied by Howie Summers, a young and enthusiastic cameraman who later won world acclaim for his shots of the Torcross Disaster, found ourselves in Concarneau. We set about filming six of Alan's students on a field trip...

...To shoot the body of the material we set up in the comfort of Alan's Brockhill Studio. For those times, it was a brave venture. We planned to expose a pre-watershed audience to nudity... as a dozen amateur students experienced their first encounter with the Life Class. Alan's model was bothered about the range of her exposure. We leaned on the budget for an extra ten pounds and her concern was reduced to the worry of her mother seeing her on the programme. The students took to the experience with little trouble. It was a different case with the television crew. As Alan moved from student to student, offering analysis and encouragement, we filmed the young girl from every conceivable angle. This concentration had the amusing effect of reducing my colleagues to talking in whispers and never directly meeting each other's eyes. I glanced at Jim Knight – he was pouring sweat.

The repetition of shots required to build an effective sequence always tests the patience and the session rolled on for hour after hour. By teatime, the lights had raised the studio temperature to nearly ninety degrees and the model had suffered enough. As she rose to stretch her limbs, perspiration glued her bottom firmly to the stool. For a second it clung in this ungainly position. Then, reluctantly parting company, it crashed to the floor like the final chord in Bolero. It broke the spell.

. . . When it came to the time for me to write the narrative, I puzzled over an adequate description of the artist's work. What I decided is not really an appraisal of its competence, romanticism or inspiration – all of that goes without saying. I was fascinated by its effect. "Up close the image is abstract where shards of colour meet or overlap. A little distance back and a different feeling comes into view with hints of the true relationship of shape and texture. A step or two away the picture is complete. . . .'

The resulting film, entitled *A Step or Two Away the Picture is Complete*, gives a vivid insight into Alan Cotton's working practice.

Alan is by nature an 'enabler', always ready to try his hand at promoting the cause of art by teaching, lecturing, filming. He also responds well to painting on commission, approaching each commission in a spirit of adventure, especially if it takes him into new territory. Although he does draw and paint people, particularly his own family, and has painted a commissioned portrait of the Vice Chancellor of Exeter University, the late Harry Kay, he is at heart a landscape painter. The University of Exeter commissioned five paintings of Hartland as part of their Silver Jubilee celebrations. Alan finds commissions for landscape paintings exciting, particularly if the research required involves flying or driving to new places. Nothing seems to daunt him, and his 'can-do' approach enables him to succeed with the unlikeliest subjects. And these commissions play an important part in spreading the word about his art.

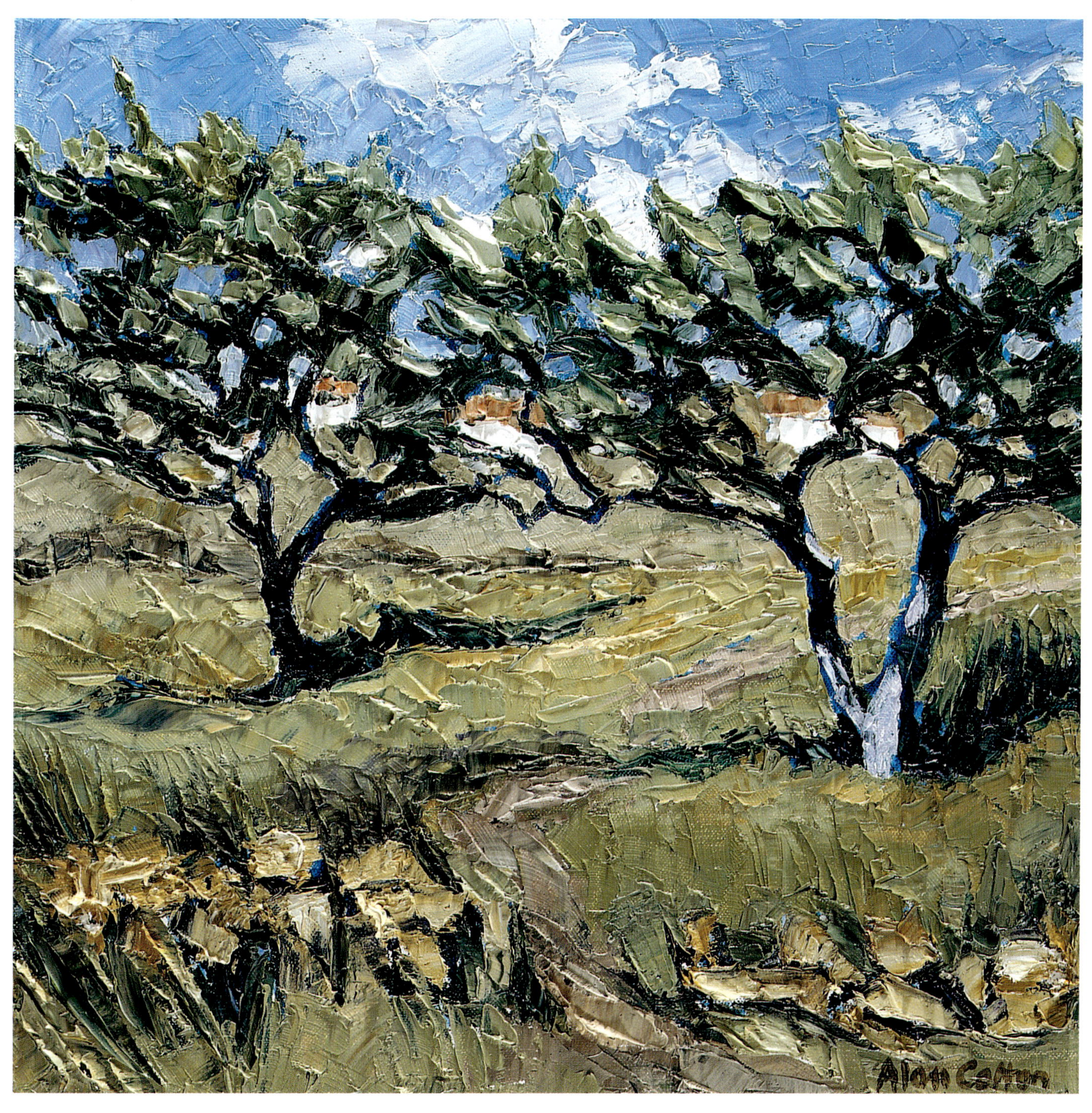

Provence – Cottages through the Olives at Ménerbes
oil on canvas 14 x 14 ins

ON HIS SECOND TRIP to Cyprus Alan was fired up by the wonderful range of hot colours he saw at the foothills of the Troodos mountains, as well as the lovely serpentine contours of the farmed hill terraces and the staccato shapes of the huge umbelliferous plants growing in the valleys. This painting is one of a series of Cyprus landscapes showing Alan's skill in orchestrating colour and depicting deep pictorial space.

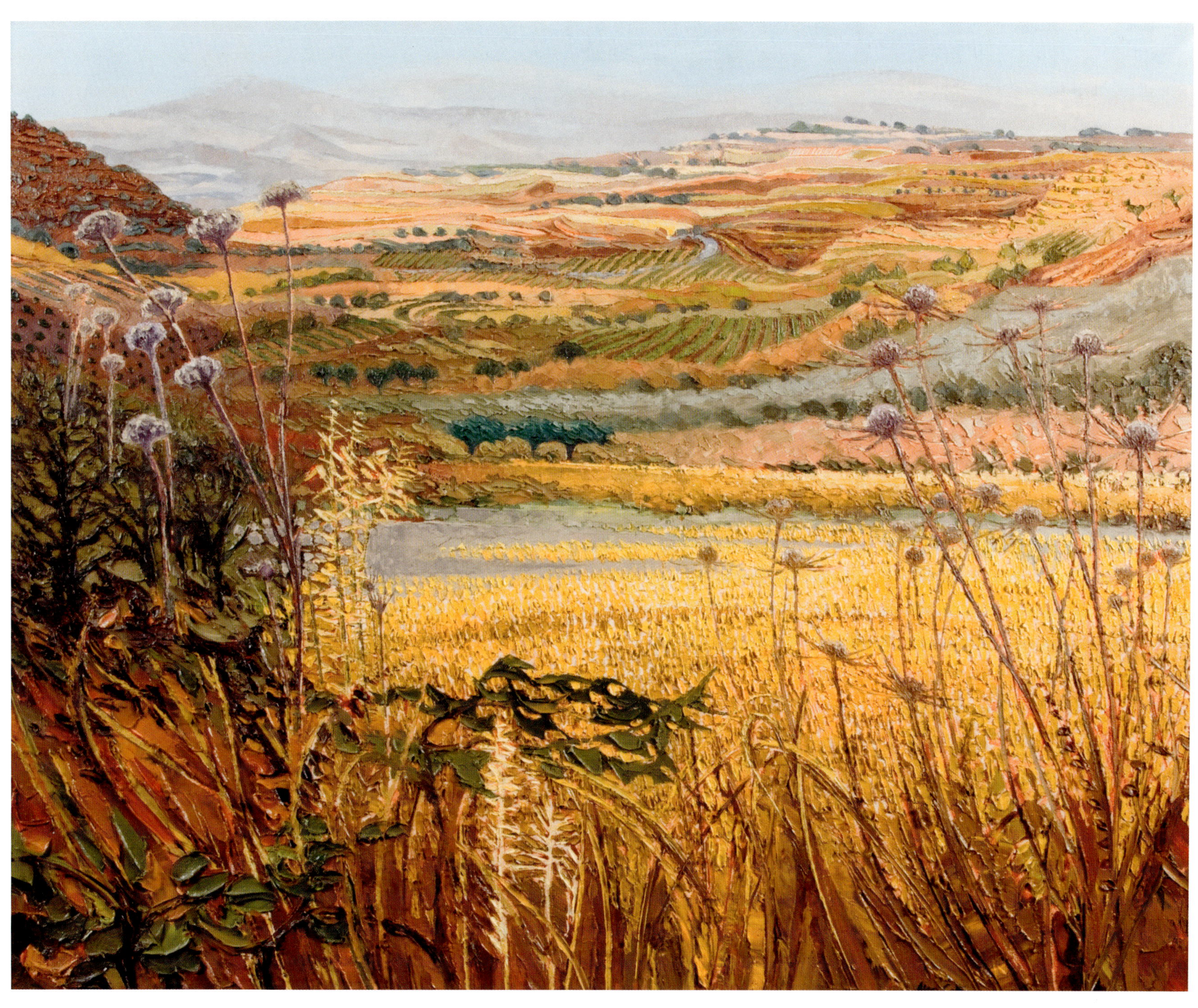

Cyprus – Landscape near Paphos, 1994
oil on canvas 40 x 48 ins
Collection Martin Bralsford

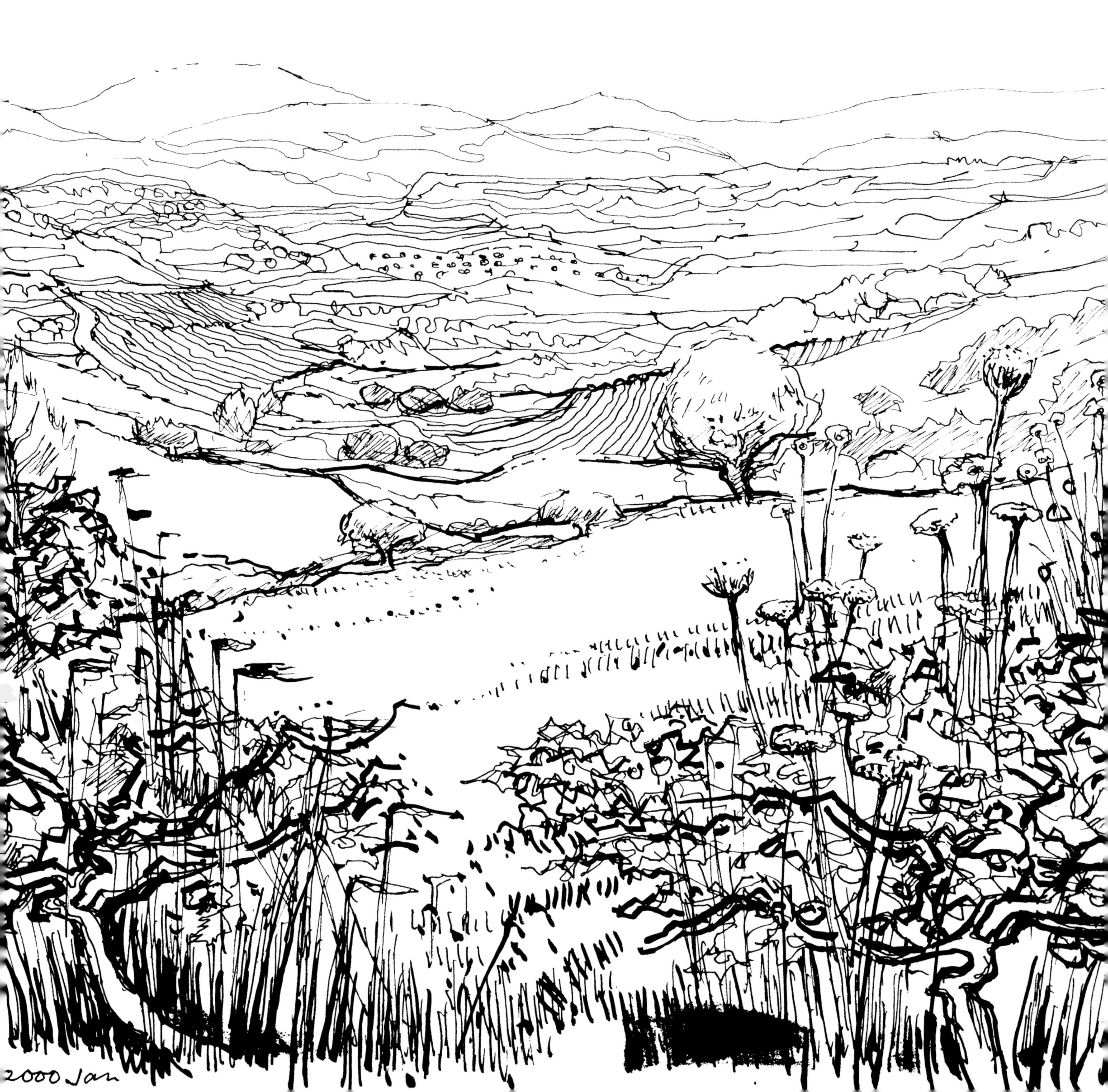
2000 Jan

Chapter Three

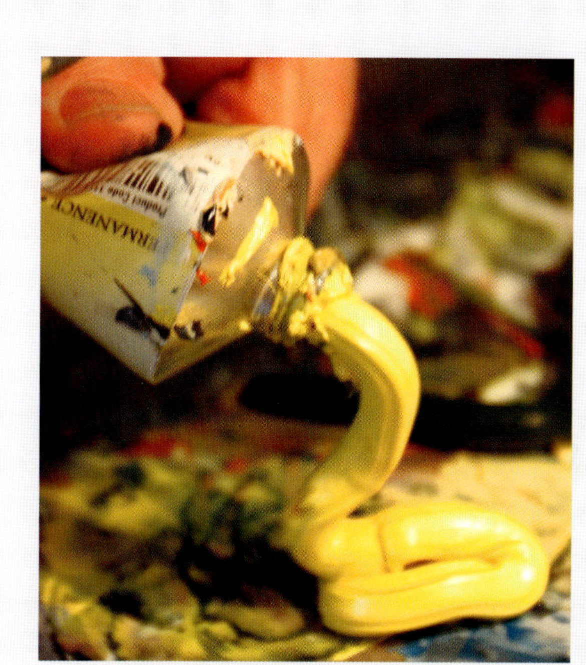

The Home Front

Alan and Pat in the garden at Brockhill Studio, June 2010.

Home in Devon is the axis around which Alan Cotton's life revolves. Since building his own house and studio in the village of Colaton Raleigh all his activities have centred around this vital base. In this house his children grew up, and the studio, built to his own design, became the launch pad for a life of full-time painting. Very much a family man, Alan enjoys having his children and grandchildren around the place while he works. Equally important is being part of the wider community, and the whole Cotton family has always played an active part in their father's life and in local affairs. Alan's pre-Christmas exhibitions in his house, open to friends and neighbours, have ensured his approachability. These exhibitions, begun long before he met David Messum, have become a regular feature of each year and provide an opportunity for locals to catch up on his progress as well as to buy his work. Now that his pictures command high prices the exhibitions have become not so much a selling opportunity as a Christmas party for friends and neighbours.

When Alan gave up teaching to paint full time it had to be a decision for the whole family. One momentous day in 1982 he returned from work at lunchtime and insisted on taking Pat out to lunch. There was, he said, something that he must discuss with her. Pat feared the worst, thinking he was about to disclose some secret affair, but instead Alan announced that he was totally fed up with teaching and simply wanted to spend every day of his life painting. Knowing that Pat was also finding full-time teaching a strain, Alan suggested that she too give up work so that they could start a new life as painter and business partner. They agreed to make the big break. Although Pat continued to teach part-time and her salary was useful, the first few years were extremely difficult. There were family meetings at which likely earnings from future exhibitions were pre-allocated, each child putting in claims for a new coat or a new pair of shoes. Alan and Pat formed a legal partnership, and Pat took over the finances and most of the paperwork, but all four children were expected to lend a hand in the new business, helping with stretching and preparing the canvases and painting the frames. Alan continued to run the painting courses that he had started previously in the village hall. All the family helped with these, serving lunches and teas to the students. They also helped with exhibitions. When he was still teaching Alan had been assiduous in promoting his work wherever possible. He arranged, jointly with a sculptor, the late Professor Moelwyn Merchant, a large travelling exhibition that took his paintings to the Nuffield Gallery, Southampton, Dorchester County Museum, the Butler Gallery in Dillington, the Royal Albert Memorial Museum in Exeter, and the City of Plymouth Art Gallery. Alan also arranged two solo exhibitions in Canada, in 1982 and 1986. These shows were instigated by the Canadian gallery owner Jim Watson, who had met

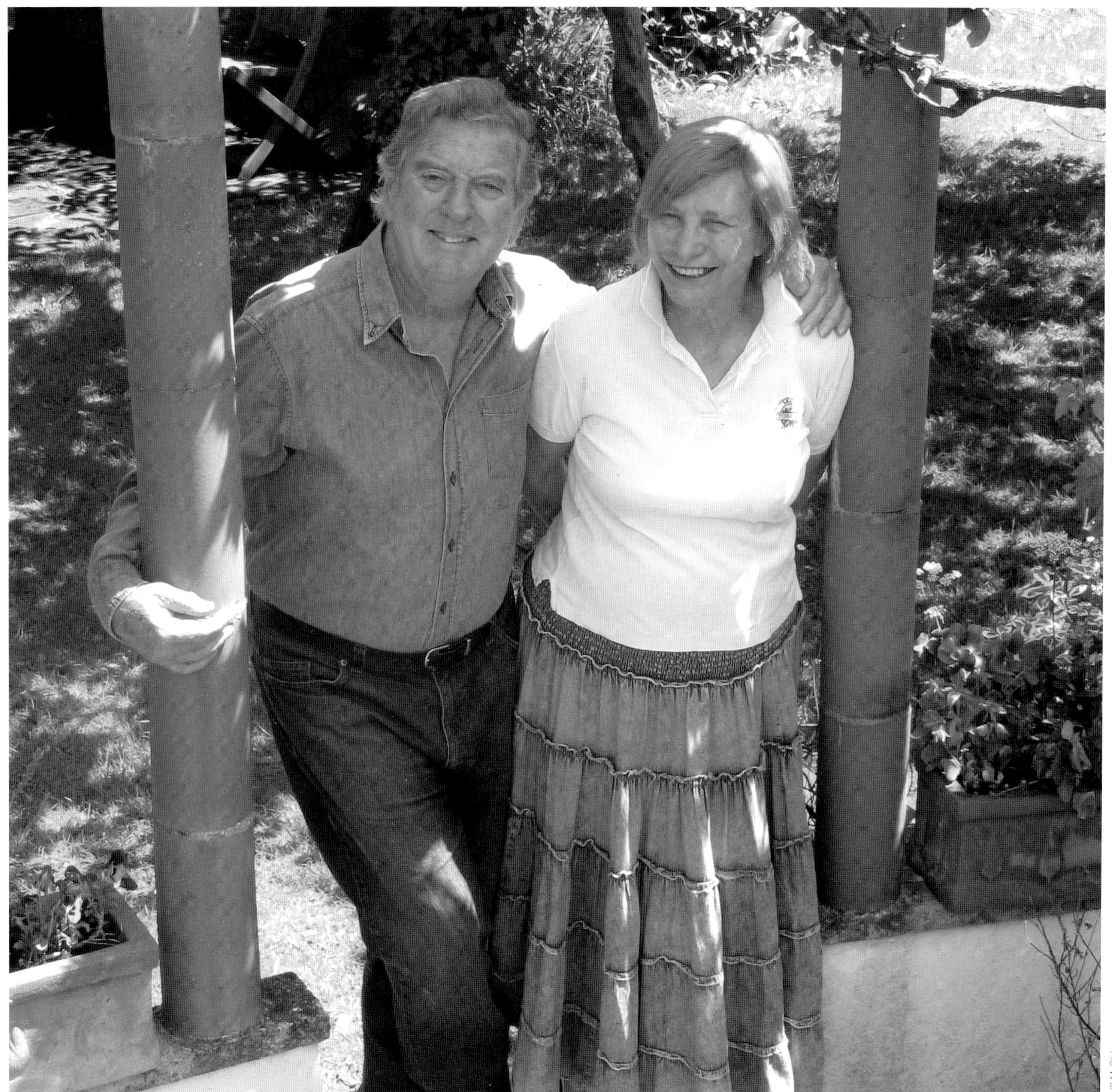
LIS McGILL

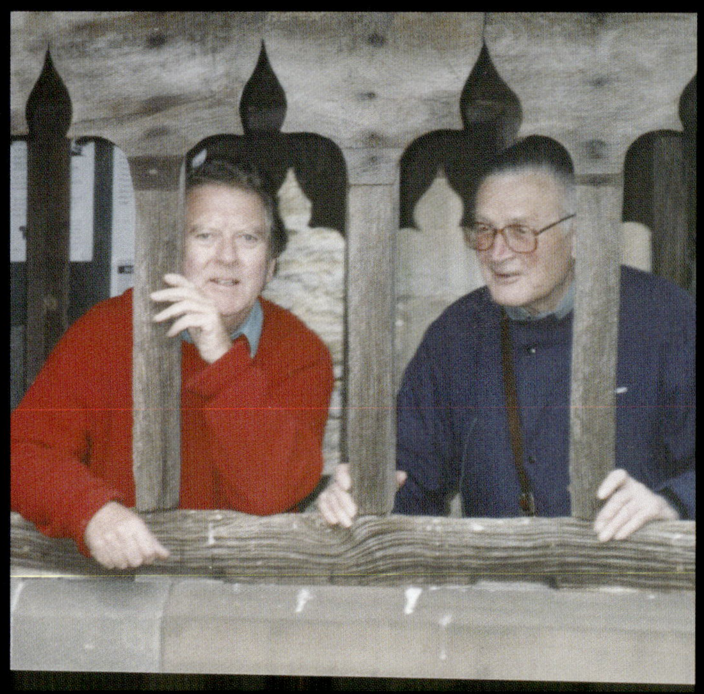

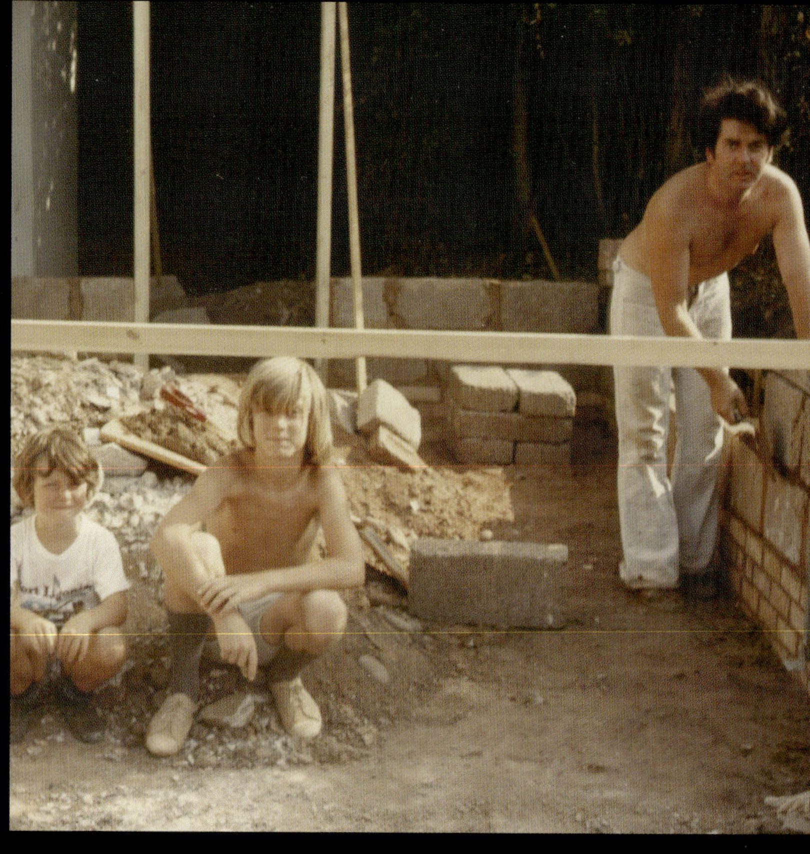

Above: With Norman Neasom
Right: Alan had help building the family garage

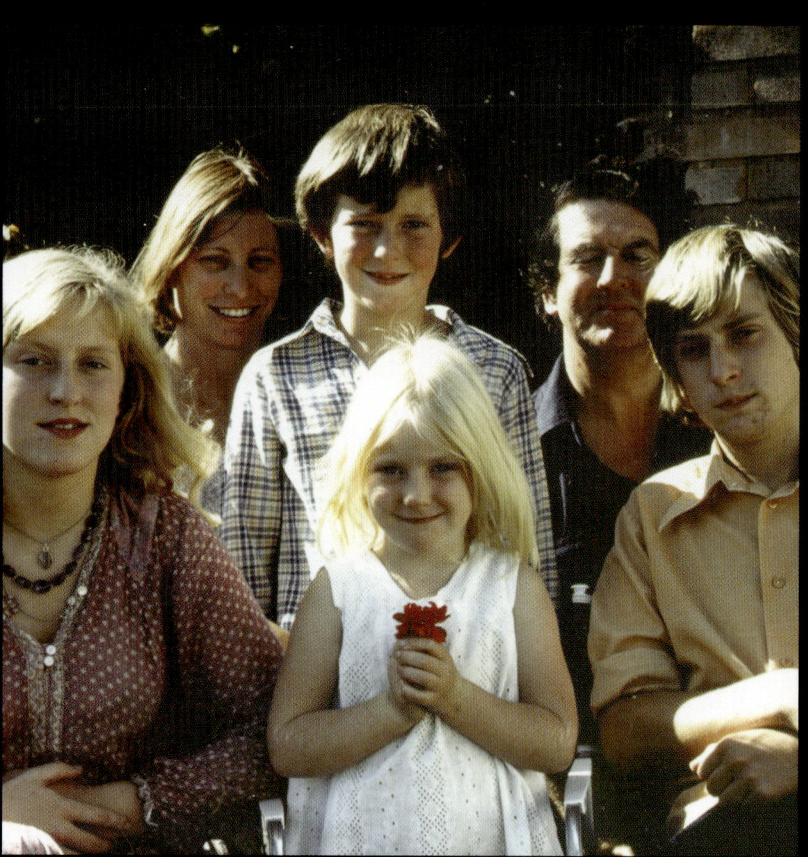

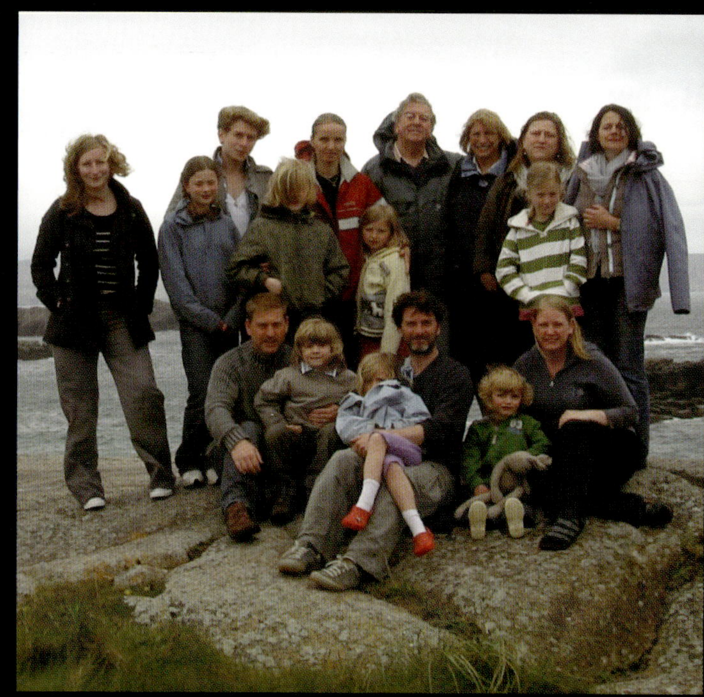

Left: The Cotton family in 1981
Above: The extended family in 2008

Alan in Bristol when Alan gave a lecture to the Fine Art Trade Guild. All two shows, held in Jim Watson's new gallery on Vancouver Island, featured paintings of Devon – the Otter Valley and Hartland – and the paintings sold very well. Alan made several broadcasts in Canada. At home he continued to lecture on art, to work on art educational films with the BBC, amongst them *Out of the Box, The Moving Line, For the Sake of a Lick of Paint, Journeys into Light*, and *An Artist on Every Corner*. Pat and the four children, Juliette, Robin, Richard and Rachel, all still at school, were swept up in this new life.

Alan worked every hour of the day and, despite the financial uncertainty, revelled in the mixture of domestic and artistic life. He was determined to make it succeed. He was used to hard work, and had inherited his mother's formidable energy. His mother's example of stoical determination was often in his mind. She worked all hours to keep her four children afloat. She left her small terraced house in Redditch at 6.30 in the morning to clean offices and was back at home at 8.30 to get her four children to school. From midday until 3pm she worked as a school dinner supervisor, and then cleaned more offices in the evening. From an early age Alan did his bit, working on a milk float, doing a newspaper round, and running all sorts of errands – anything to earn a bob or two. When he was sixteen he worked evenings and Saturday mornings in a butcher's shop. He was often late for school or in trouble with his lessons, because there was never time, or room enough, at home to do his homework. Redditch, where he grew up, was a rough place, with gang warfare amongst the boys. Although Alan was caned for drawing in class and almost expelled, he managed to survive at Grammar School because he was good at art and made himself useful designing all the school posters. He was also somewhat safeguarded from authority by a new young art teacher, Ted Holmes, who encouraged his interest in painting. It was Alan's first crucial encounter with a working artist, and he spent several summer weeks painting in Holmes's studio in the Lake District. At home his mother also encouraged him by providing paints. These he took, in any spare time that he had, into the surrounding countryside to draw and paint.

As he recalls, Alan drew and painted from the age of three or four, when his mother made him paintbrushes from her own hair. 'I remember drawing as a small child in the fields and I painted from very early on, with poster paints. We subscribed to a club on a weekly basis, and one of the things they had in their catalogue was this huge box of watercolours. For a small child to see so many colours was a great excitement. I used to go up town into Redditch and buy little tubes of paint. They had a magic, a mystery about them. I used to display them on my little table. Because our house was chaotic, with too many people living in a small space, I only had one table in the bedroom

Devon – Symphony in Purple and Gold
oil on canvas 24 x 24 ins

and I displayed my paints on that and was very proud of them. Even today I display paints because they turn me on just to look at them. Like lots of kids I painted my heroes, film stars and cricketers. I did a painting of my brother Bernard, swathed in bandages, when he was at home with a bad leg. But because there was no space, nowhere to study, I escaped from the house when I could and I lived my life outside.'

After taking O-level exams Alan went straight to Redditch Art School. During his year there he continued to escape into the countryside to draw and paint rather than work in the art school. This passion for working outside was fostered by one of his tutors, Norman Neasom, who took a special interest in him. Together they cycled around the countryside, studying everything from stained glass to misericords. They would stop at various hostelries where Alan drank cider and had his first taste of shellfish. Working alongside Norman Neasom, who could draw 'like an angel', Alan began to draw very naturally, and saw how he could use his drawing as an analytical process to inform future paintings. As he explains, 'the whole point about drawing is that as you begin to draw you become aware of so many underlying things… you begin to analyse and form a point of view about those aspects you want to make more important when you come to paint.… Going out with Norman Neasom was an amazing thing because he drew so fluently. I learnt so much so quickly with him. We cycled around together and he would stop at some landscape or church, and the speed and facility of his drawing was something very special. Drawing does make your work more articulate, more sensitive to shape and form. Norman Neasom took me under his wing and taught me a lot about life, about architecture and country houses, about women, barmaids, all sorts of things. He had enormous sympathy for what I was trying to do.'

From Redditch Art School Alan moved to Ruskin Hall, Bourneville School of Art, and spent an enjoyable year there building up his portfolio for entry into Birmingham College of Art. But when he arrived there after two satisfying years developing his skills, Birmingham College of Art came as a shock. At its head was the austere figure of the painter Gilbert Mason. Alan, still only seventeen, living at home and commuting daily by bus from Redditch, found him terrifying. He vividly remembers the day when he had an eight by four foot piece of hardboard on his easel and was diligently painting a plump and sumptuous nude. 'I was painting away and was suddenly aware of a presence behind me with a smell of Gauloises. Gilbert Mason always smoked these French cigarettes. I didn't look round but sensed his presence with fear and trepidation. He stood for what seemed an eternity and then he brushed me aside with his elbow, moved to my palette, picked up a rag and started to wipe out my painting. He stood back a few times, drew

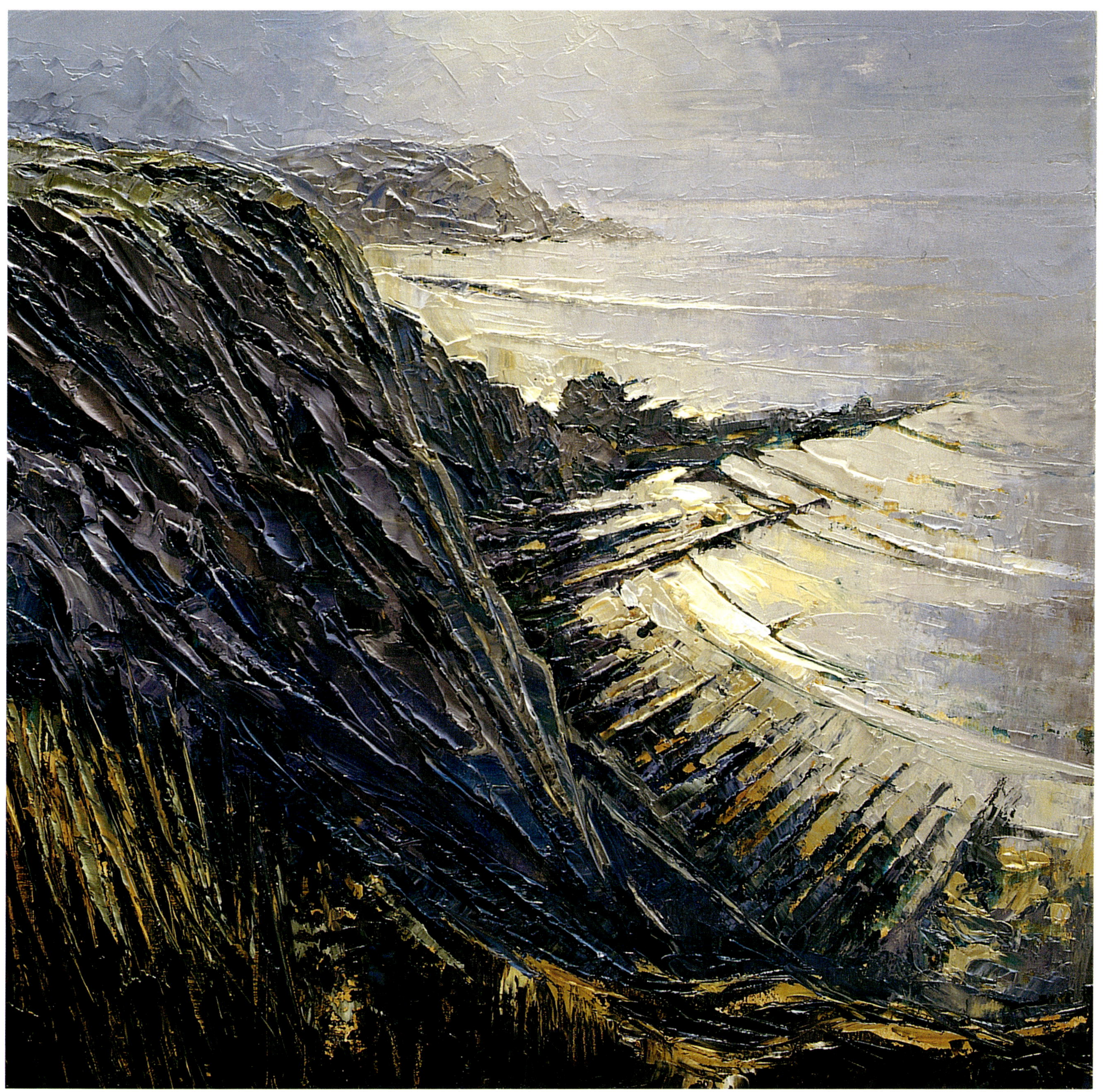

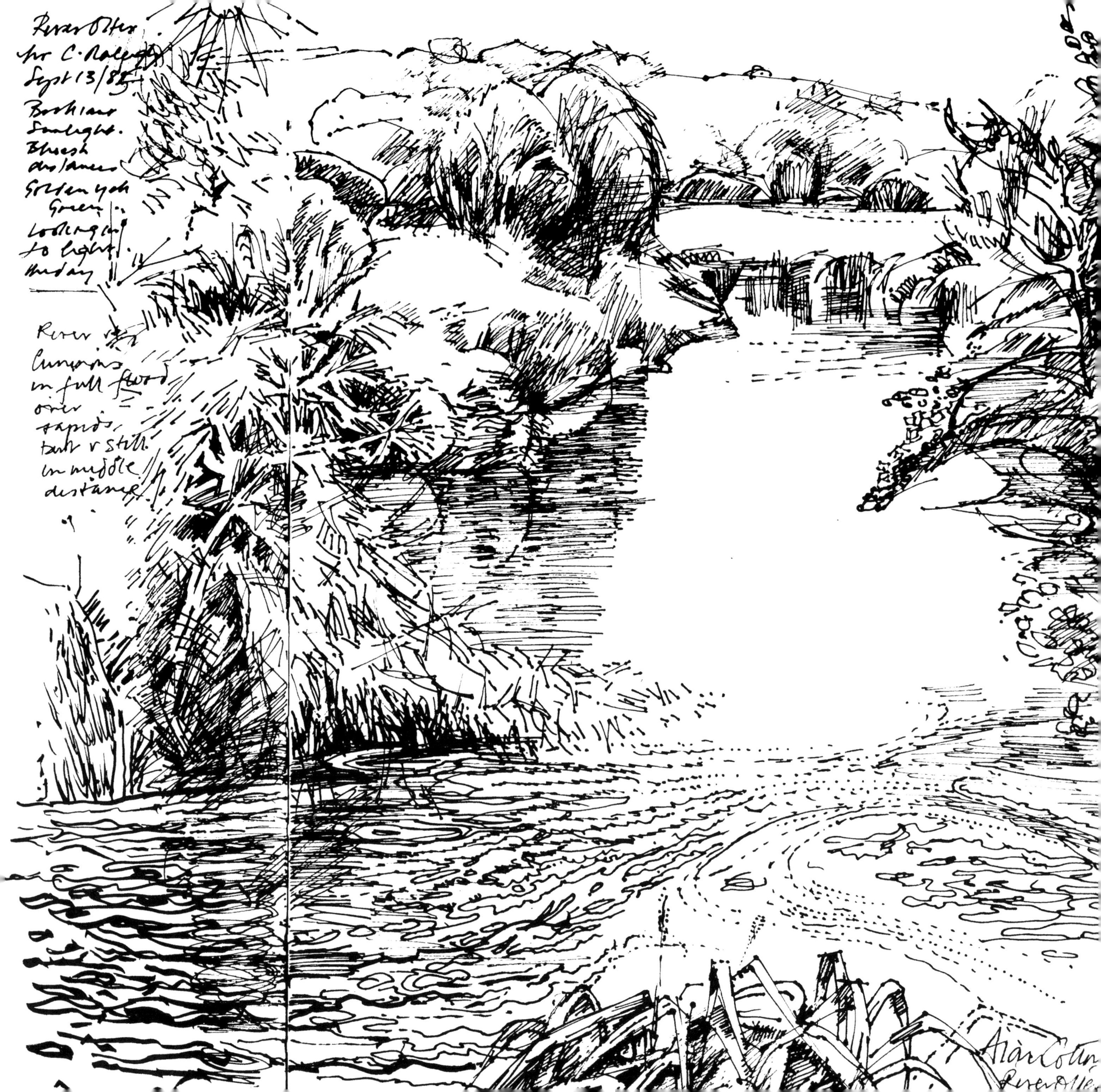
River Otter
Sept 13/85
in full flood
over
rapids.
but v still
in middle
distance
Alan Cotton

on his cigarette, looked at his handiwork and made lots of changes. He didn't say a word to me but stood back and admired his work and finally waved his cigarette and said "That's bloody better, boy" and went off. I was left thinking "what does he mean, what does he think he has achieved, and which direction should I go in?" At the college there was also a man called Hewitt who painted fine paintings of little children. Hewitt used to spend most of his time in the pub. These guys didn't want to teach, they just wanted to paint. They had their own studios at the college and they would disappear for very long periods. The worst time was when they emerged from the pub and would come round, fairly incoherent. I found it a dismal procedure.'

Most of the tutors at Birmingham College of Art at that time seemed very inarticulate. Wanting to get on with their own work, they were not interested in using language to explore their feelings or those of their students. Good teachers need dialogue to demystify things, and there was no dialogue. Nor was there much attempt to study art history. When Alan made a comment in one of Gilbert Mason's talks, Mason sarcastically retorted, "Well, you do the talk then. You know a bloody sight more about it than I do." As Alan has often maintained, he learnt more about painting after he left Birmingham College of Art. He was not one of the favoured students, as his contemporary Michael Upton was, and so did not get the benefit of a travel scholarship. This really rankled. 'We all came back in the second year after a summer vacation and there was a lot of painting around by those who had had travel scholarships. Whereas I worked on a building site the whole summer these guys returned with huge bundles of paintings all tied up with string. I was incredibly envious that they had been given money to travel abroad and paint. That summer I had dug trenches for eight or nine weeks and at the end of it I wasn't paid. That was a bad blow.'

Alan found the general level of teaching at Birmingham College of Art dismally poor. He knew from earlier experience that teaching could be better than that, and decided to become an art teacher himself. Teaching offered a steady job with a steady income. After the art college, his postgraduate teacher training year at Birmingham University was a revelation. It opened his eyes to a wider world beyond the confines of art school and it taught him how to think. Suddenly anything seemed possible, and his buccaneering approach to life led him to take on any part-time teaching or lecturing available, partly for the fun of it, and partly for the ever-present necessity to earn a few shillings. And it was during this momentous year that he met another young trainee teacher, Patricia Stanley (Pat), whom he married in 1961.

By the time Alan and Pat married they had both completed their teacher training and had found themselves

Devon - Hartland Coastline
oil on canvas 91 x 91 cms 36 x 36 ins

teaching jobs. They saved Pat's salary to raise a mortgage for their first home, a pair of conjoined cottages in St Briavels in the Forest of Dean. They worked on the cottages themselves to make them habitable and create a studio at one end, where Alan began to paint furiously in his free time. It was in this studio that he received a surprise visit from the influential writer and art critic John Berger, whose book *Permanent Red* Alan had only recently read and admired. Berger took his time to look at all Alan's work and remarked on two paintings that Alan had made using a painting knife. He said' You have a real feeling for paint. And I really think the knife is the way for you to go.' Alan has used painting knives since that day.

John Berger's writing was an important influence on Alan as a student. Equally important in forming his mature work was the example of certain British painters. As he says, 'in my student days the painter I admired most was Alan Reynolds. His show on *The Four Seasons* at the Redfern Gallery is still deeply etched in my mind. In the gallery's central room he had four big paintings of each of the seasons, with big seed heads in the foreground. I think he is less well known now because he changed to abstract work, although that was lovely, taking the forms of the landscape. Those exhibitions that inspire you when you are young are terribly important. I saw Kyffin Williams's exhibition at the Leicester Galleries after he had been to Patagonia on a Churchill Fellowship. Because he worked to a strict deadline the smell of oil paint pervaded the whole gallery. I also saw a little Sickert painting of a street in Dieppe, so understated, such a joy that it almost makes me salivate when I think of it. You do absorb all these influences and hope that they come out in your own work.'

Amongst European painters, it was perhaps Vincent Van Gogh who had the greatest impact on Alan as a student, and continues to do so today. Alan reads and re-reads the letters of this surprisingly erudite artist. Not only was Van Gogh's idiosyncratic mark-making an important influence, but his whole attitude to painting had a special resonance. In one of his letters to his brother Theo, Vincent wrote 'the duty of the painter is to study nature in depth and to use all his intelligence, to put his feelings into his work so that it becomes comprehensible to others'. Van Gogh's remark that 'Nature is most certainly intangible, yet one must seize it, and with a firm hand' is very much Alan's own belief.

With six years of art training under his belt, Alan was keen to put all his theory into practice. By the time Alan and Pat were set up in their home in St Briavels it was perfectly clear to Pat that her husband was committed to a life as a painter and not really as a teacher. He saw teaching as incidental, a means of making a living. After a few years he found teaching school-age children so tiring and time-consuming that he decided to try teaching at a higher level.

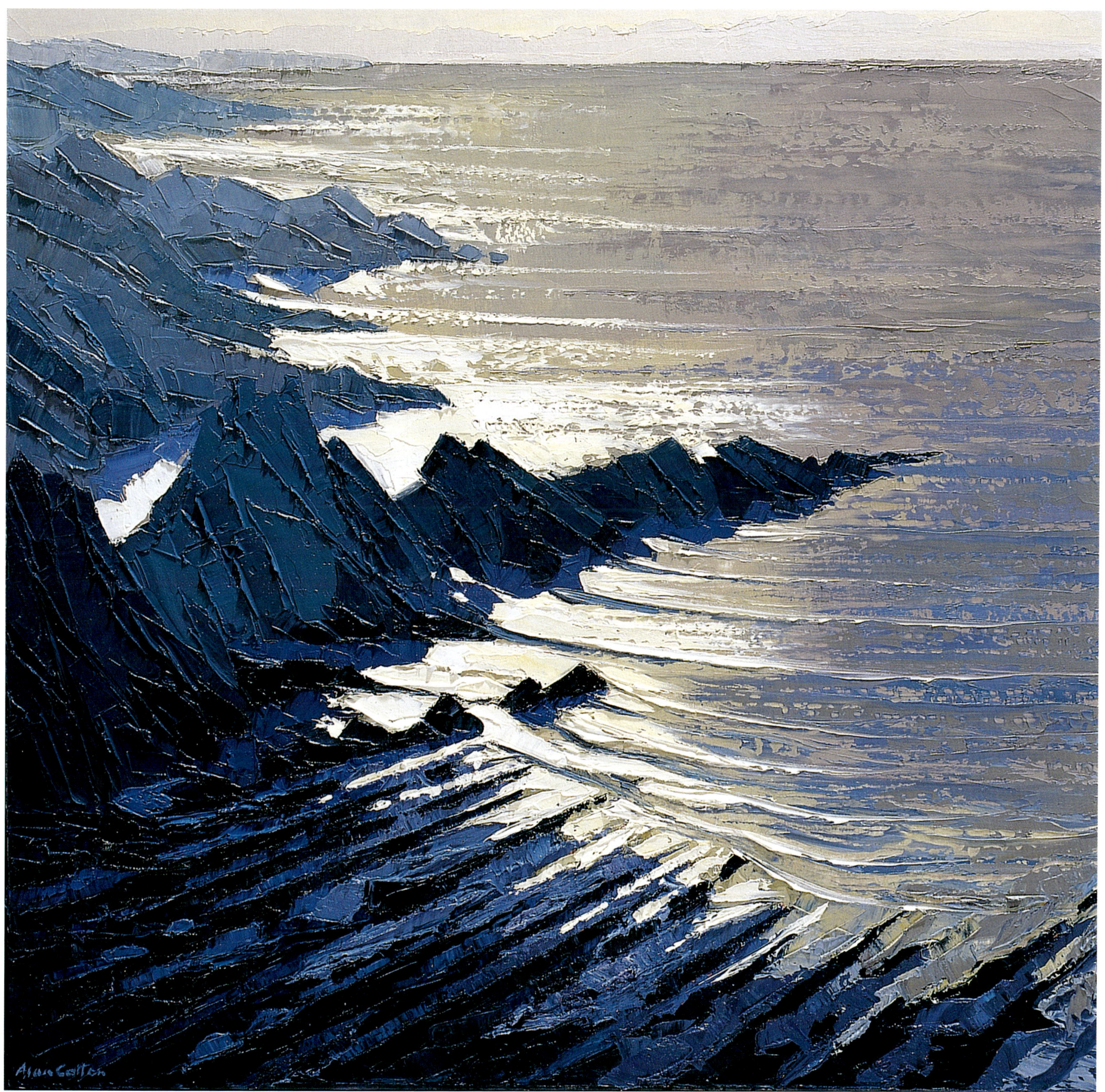

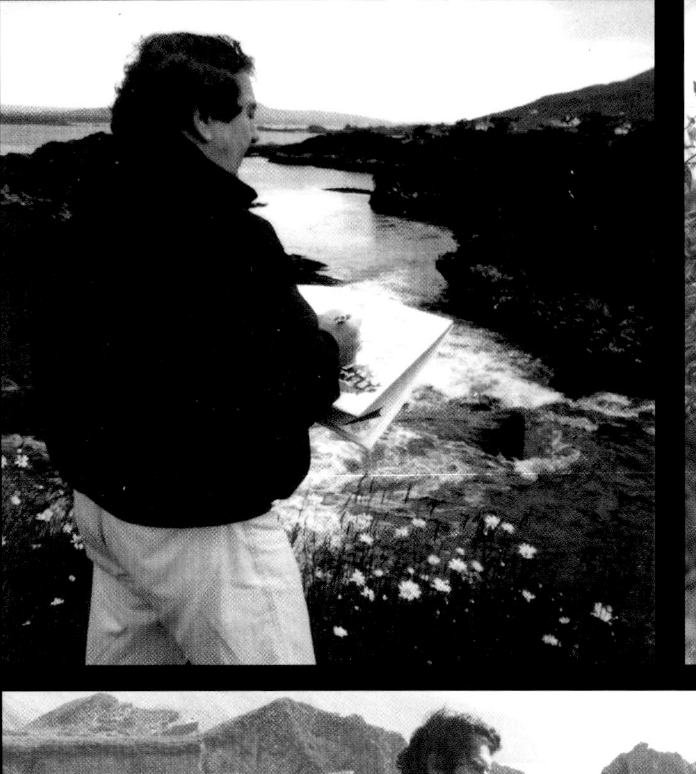

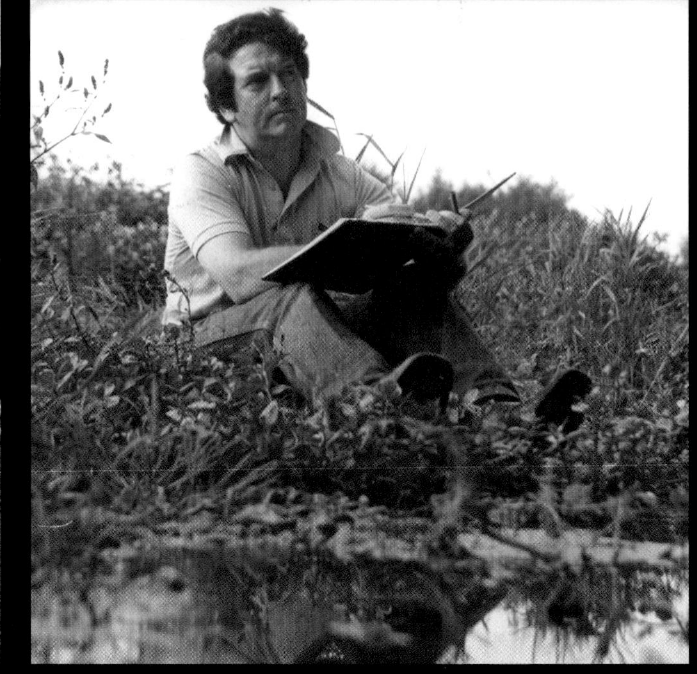

GLYN LOMAX

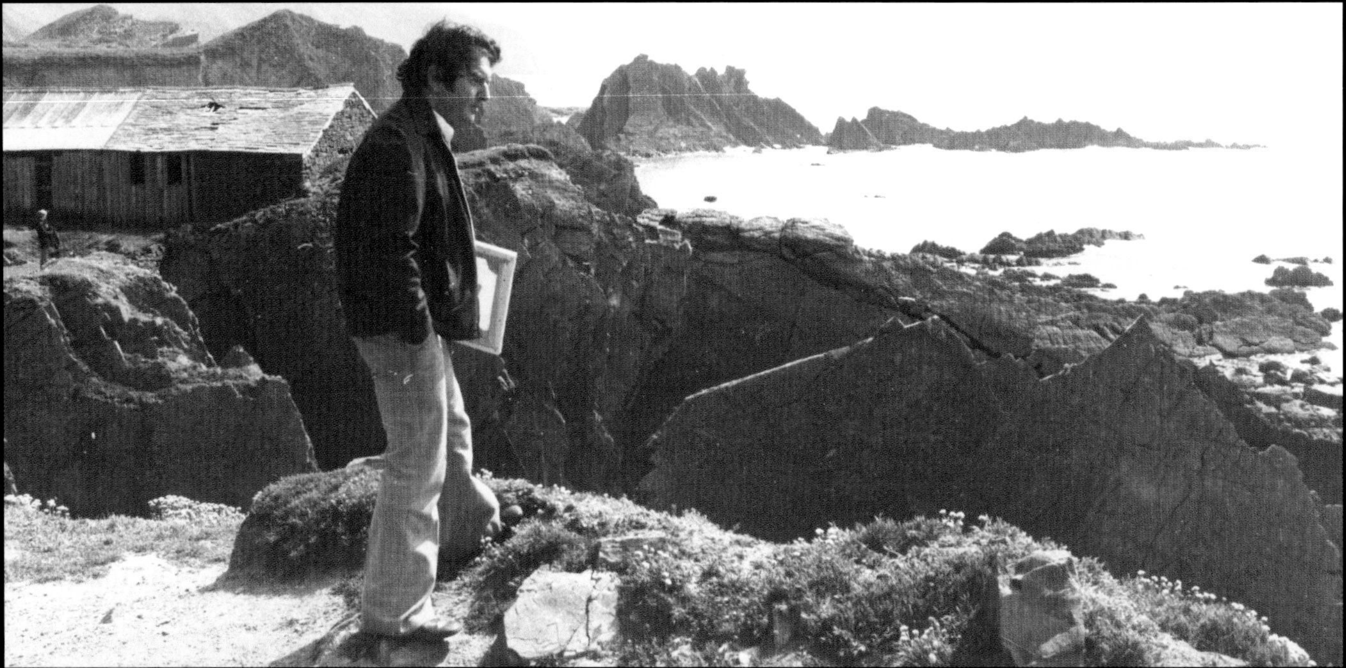

PAUL DALLAS-CONTE

'Lecturing' to students might give him more time to do his own work. He would, however, need further qualifications.

In 1966 he moved with Pat and two small children to Devon to do Exeter University's Advanced Diploma in Education. This was an idyllic year for the Cotton family, particularly for Alan who responded warmly to the lush Devon countryside. After completing his diploma he seized the chance of the job of Senior Lecturer in Art and Design at Rolle College in Exmouth. At first the family lived in rented accommodation because, despite selling their cottage in the Forest of Dean, Devon house prices were so high that they could not afford a house with added studio. Eventually Alan spotted an advertisement for an old farm site in the village of Colaton Raleigh. The site was steeply situated on the side of a hill and covered with semi-derelict buildings. Economic necessity dictated that Alan dismantle the ruined buildings and build the house and studio himself. It took a year of his life, but it was a year he has never regretted. He worked on the site almost single-handedly, digging the initial trenches and laying the foundations, putting in the drains and raising the walls, learning different skills as he progressed. Alan did no painting in the year it took to build the house, with its integral studio, all his creativity going into making a viable family home. He still takes great pride in his home and derives huge satisfaction from developing it further, as he does from creating new 'rooms', on different levels, in his romantically arbour-filled garden.

Around his home in Devon there were many motifs for Alan to paint. The river Otter meanders through pastureland at the end of the lane where the Cottons live, and Alan painted many versions of the river at different seasons and in different lights. Cows returning from their pastures at milking time were a favourite early theme. After looking up into the skyscapes of the Forest of Dean, Alan found himself looking down into gently folded valleys and into reflections on river and pond. The morning sparkle of the river and its satiny sheen on calm evenings inspired many lyrical paintings.

When he needed a change from the soft estuarine landscape of south Devon, he explored Devon's north coast. He found an exciting new subject in the rugged cliffs around Hartland Quay. Here was a subject that was not only exhilaratingly wild but also perfectly suited to his method of applying paint. Using painting knives he found that he could lay each sweep or block of paint onto canvas in the very shape of the rocky land it represented, 'building' the landscape with paint in a new way. Returning to Hartland again and again, he immersed himself in the history and folklore of the wind-blown coast, notoriously dangerous to shipping. He studied the land in depth, beginning his practice of getting to know everything possible about the places he paints.

The monumental paintings of Hartland that Alan Cotton began to accumulate caught the eye of many collectors. His Hartland paintings were acquired by the City of Plymouth Art Gallery and the Royal Albert Memorial Museum in Exeter for their permanent collections. In Exeter classes of schoolchildren were asked to choose their favourite painting from the museum's collection and they chose Alan's. They were encouraged to write essays about the work, and many wrote personally to Alan. Later, a box containing Alan's drawings, mainly of Hartland, an original painting, and a filmed interview, was commissioned by the Royal Albert Memorial Museum for the Art Angle Project, to travel around all of Devon's schools. Hartland was deep in Alan's psyche. Many years later Alan returned to see if the original thrill of the place was still there. He found that it was. In an exhibition at the Walker Galleries in Sidbury, Devon, Alan's later Hartland paintings showed him using paint with even greater freedom. In the accompanying catalogue, entitled *Return to Hartland*, he described his feelings about the place. 'My love affair with Hartland began in the mid1970s, not long after my arrival in the Westcountry… I remember with great clarity that first mind-blowing experience of coming down the hill to Hartland Quay, standing on the cliff edge and looking along the coast. It was a stormy day and as I watched that great solid mass of water constantly hitting the coastline, with such power, fragmenting on the rocks, I knew that what I was observing would provide the springboard for large dynamic paintings. Drawing and painting amongst the rocks, I began to use the images that so inspired me for a series of large 6' by 4' paintings. Back in my studio, working at this scale using painting knives, I used my muscles and a lot of energy to try to reconstruct my impressions and feelings in paint. I dragged great quantities of pigment across six feet of canvas, almost sculpting the image into life.' In an article in *The Artist* (August 2007) he discussed the reasons why he found this landscape so exhilarating. 'I have always been interested in the way that the cliffs form a kind of barrier that the sea is constantly trying to erode and undermine, so there is a constant drama at the cliff edge determined by the mood of the sea, which can be violent or, at the other extreme, benign.'

His Devon home, and the community in which he lives, has given Alan Cotton and his family a great deal. He feels privileged to be able to spend his life painting and to sell his work well, but he is no ivory tower artist. It is important to him to be able to mix with anyone and to share his enthusiasms, as his wide circle of friends would affirm. Alan says 'I like ordinary people and I want my work to be accessible to ordinary people. I can't bear pretentious art – I find it embarrassing.' The years of teaching in Devon have given him useful insights into how other people relate to art, and help him demystify it for them. In the book *Learning and Teaching through Art and Crafts* (BT Batsford 1975) that he

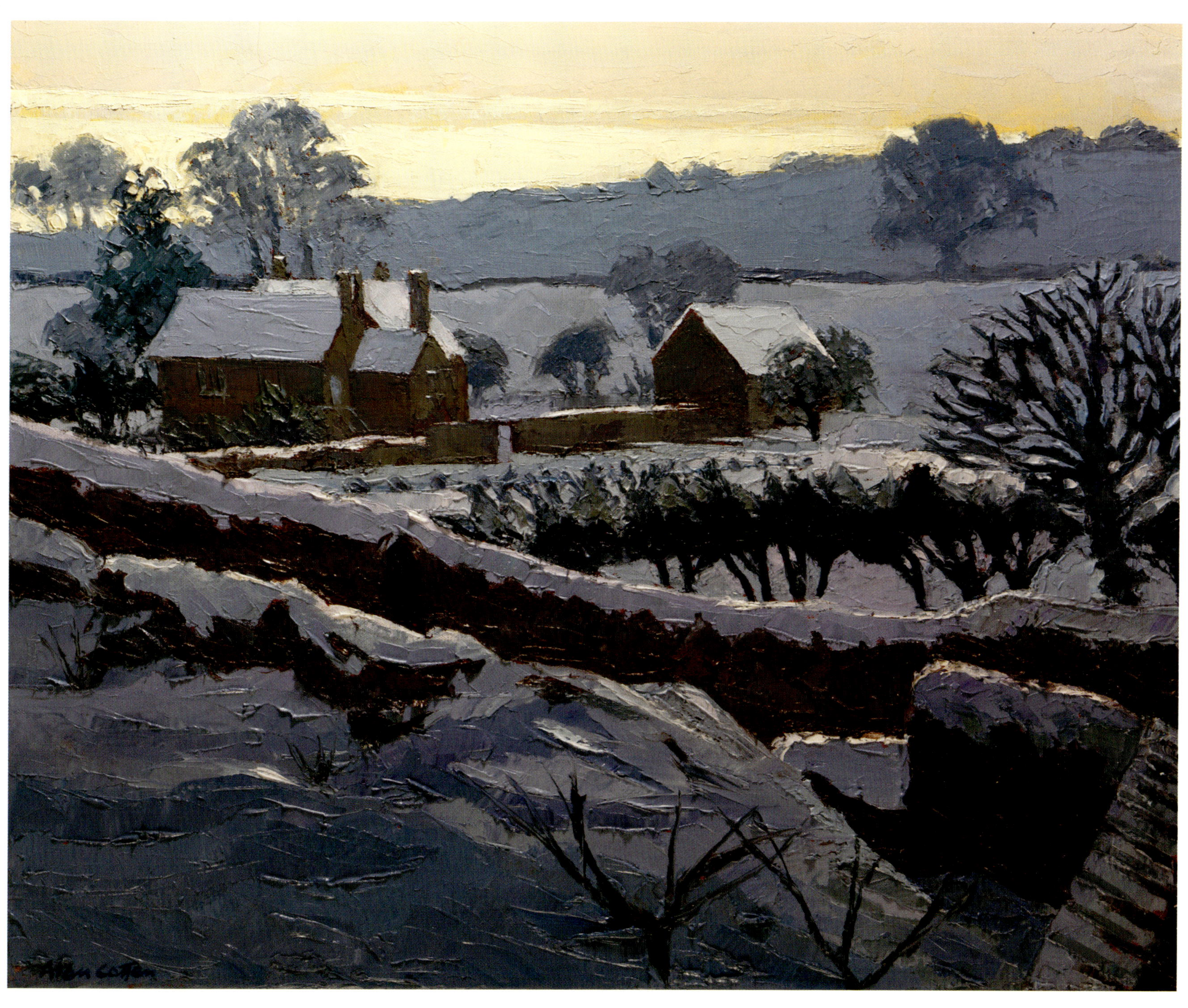

Colaton Raleigh, Devon – Winter Snow through the Artist's Window, 2010
oil on canvas 20 x 24 ins

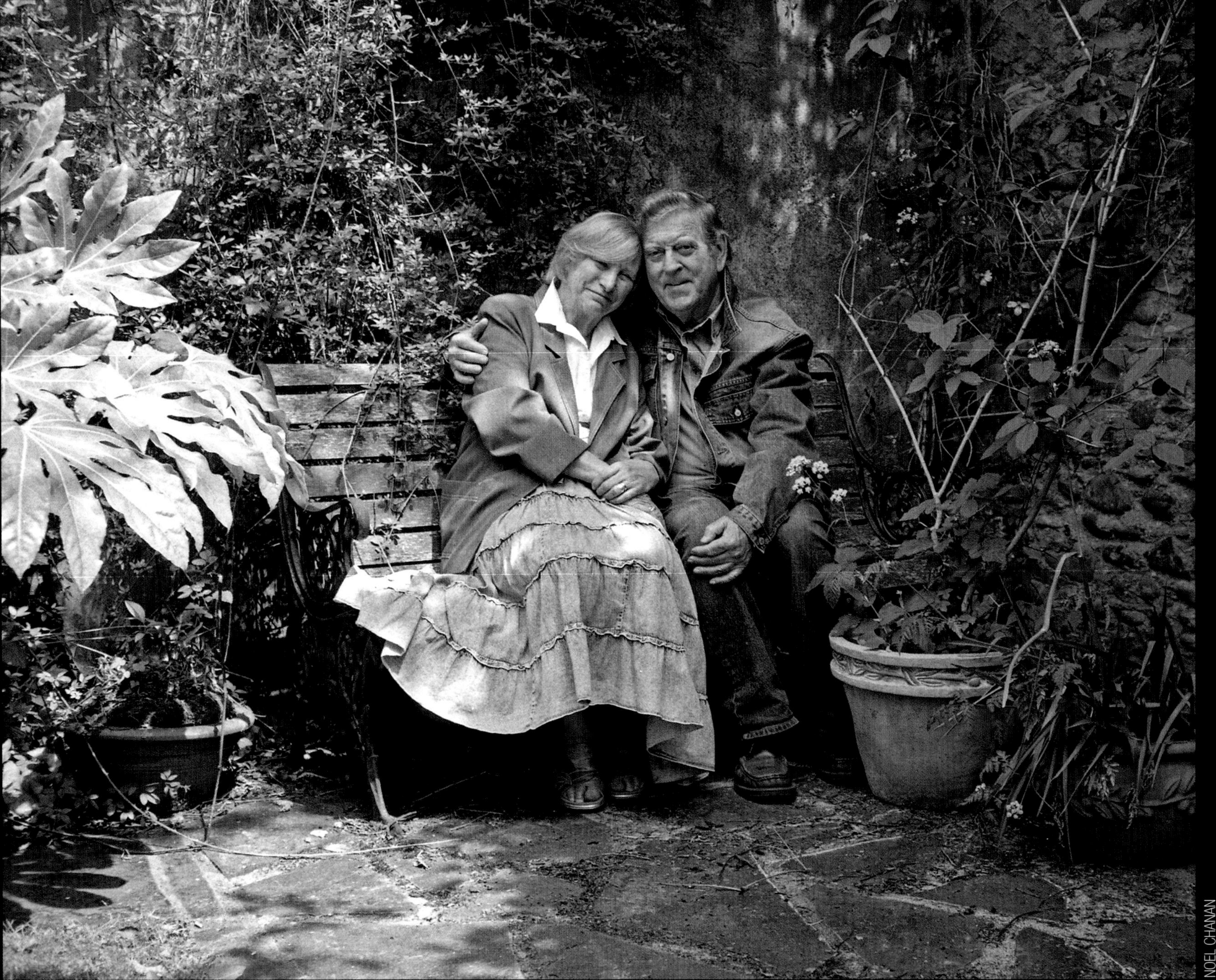

NOEL CHANAN

Alan and Pat in the garden at Brockhill Studio, May 2010.

wrote in conjunction with Frank Haddon, he stresses the importance of creative learning by looking at other work as well as making one's own. 'Art education, as well as developing children's expressive urge to communicate feelings and thoughts and extending their powers of observation, should also help them to develop a sense of discrimination and visual awareness… making art objects alone is not enough. One important area of investigation is the study of the great art of the past.' In this very practical teaching manual Alan quotes the painter Frederick Gore: 'A work of art is not a reality; it is a model of reality. It is a play on reality. It is a toy. We are able to play with it; we are able to play around it with ideas; we come to understand it and through it to understand reality'. With Gore, Alan firmly believes that art can be both educative and fun.

Besides teaching, Alan has done a tremendous amount in promoting art in Devon, as Judi Spiers, amongst many others, would testify. As she recalled, she met Alan through Television South West 'when Kevin Crooks was Head of what we called Strange Programmes. I got to know him better after Kevin's death, and I had him on my programme when he was a tour artist with Prince Charles. He recently donated a picture of vines in Piemonte for Children in Need, for which we received over £5,000. I had rung him up and asked "I don't suppose you could give us a print, could you? " He said "No" and I thought, oh dear, I've overstepped the mark here. Then he said "No, but I can give you a painting." I was staggered. He's a very approachable man, where some artists are very 'gilded box'. You could see a kid saying something really rude to him and he would laugh. He loves a glass of wine, loves to have some fun, and his wife's a delight as well. When you see him strolling round you wouldn't think he was The Artist. He really does see the value of 'putting back in' and encouraging others. He has this wonderfully warm presence, and I think of him as a friend and a character, the man who paints. I always want to live in an Alan Cotton painting. I want to go down that little moonlit lane leading to an Irish cottage. I can see myself walking down to the sea. I particularly want to clamber into the Piemonte and Provence pictures. Most of Alan's painting is uplifting, as I feel all art should be.'

Alan Cotton's formidable energy finds outlets not only in his painting but also in his many other activities. He plays tennis, exercises when he can, and drives his Porsche around the county faster than he should. He is always ready to take up a new challenge, whether it is flying with the Red Arrows at the invitation of his friend Brian Hoskins, or starting up a new Society. Friends have tempted him to explore parts of the world he might never otherwise have chosen. The biggest challenge of all, however, remains keeping the momentum going for his own painting, and overcoming those occasional dark times when nothing goes right.

ON HIS FIRST TRIP to Morocco Alan spent seven weeks exploring the area around Marrakesh, a tiny corner of which is depicted in this painting. He found the light in Morocco so different from anything he had previously experienced that he needed a whole new range of colour and new ways of applying paint in order to suggest the luminosity of sunlight falling on parched land. In this midday painting the brilliantly luminous shadows become the focus of the composition, their deep colours offset by the pungent yellow and orange robes of the two figures. The shallow pictorial space, increasing the intimacy of the scene, relates to some of Alan's Venetian paintings, in which he focuses on unnoticed corners, his eye confined by the density of buildings.

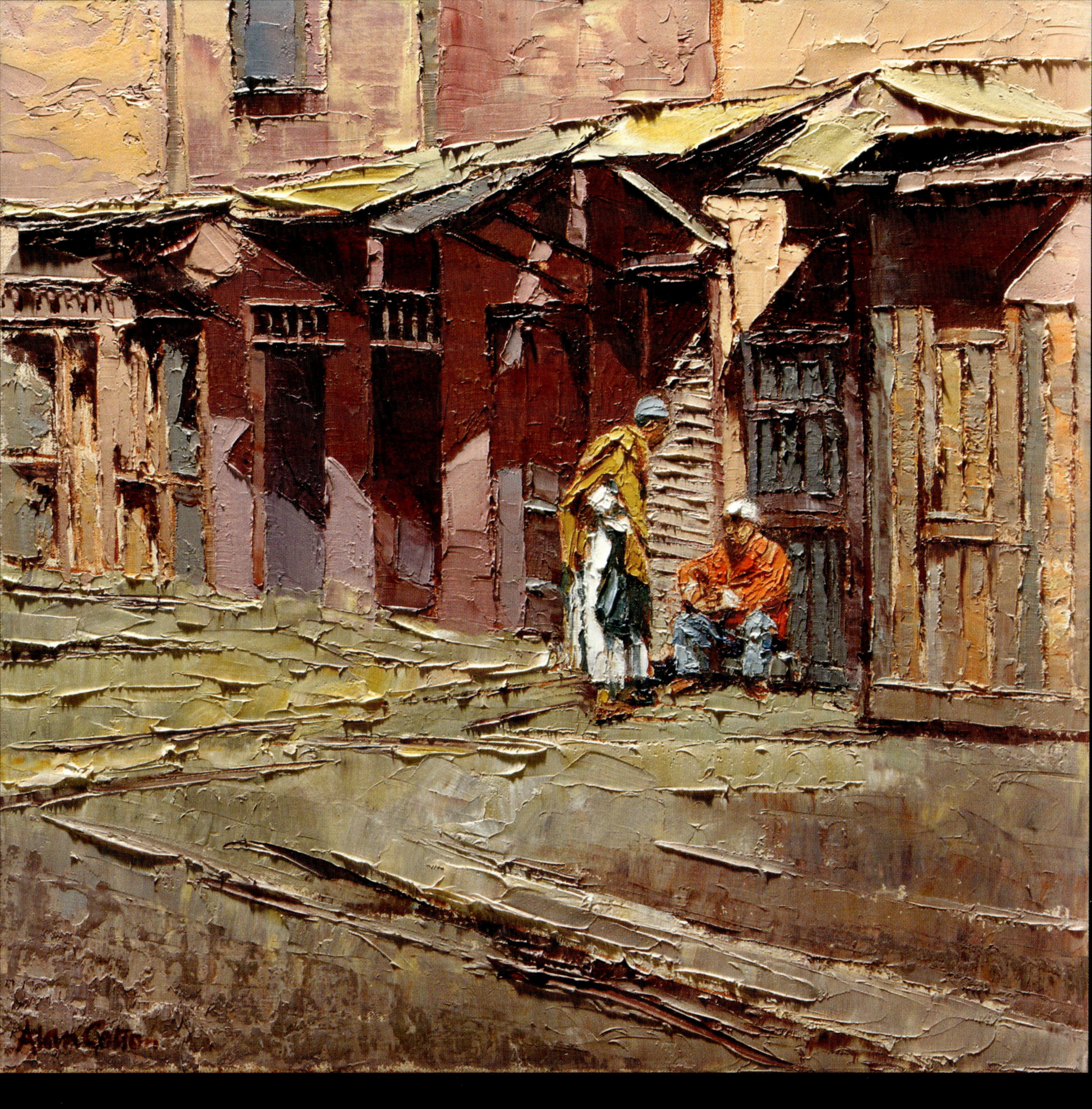

Morocco – On the Edge of the Souk, 2005
oil on canvas 24 x 24 ins
Collection John Hammond

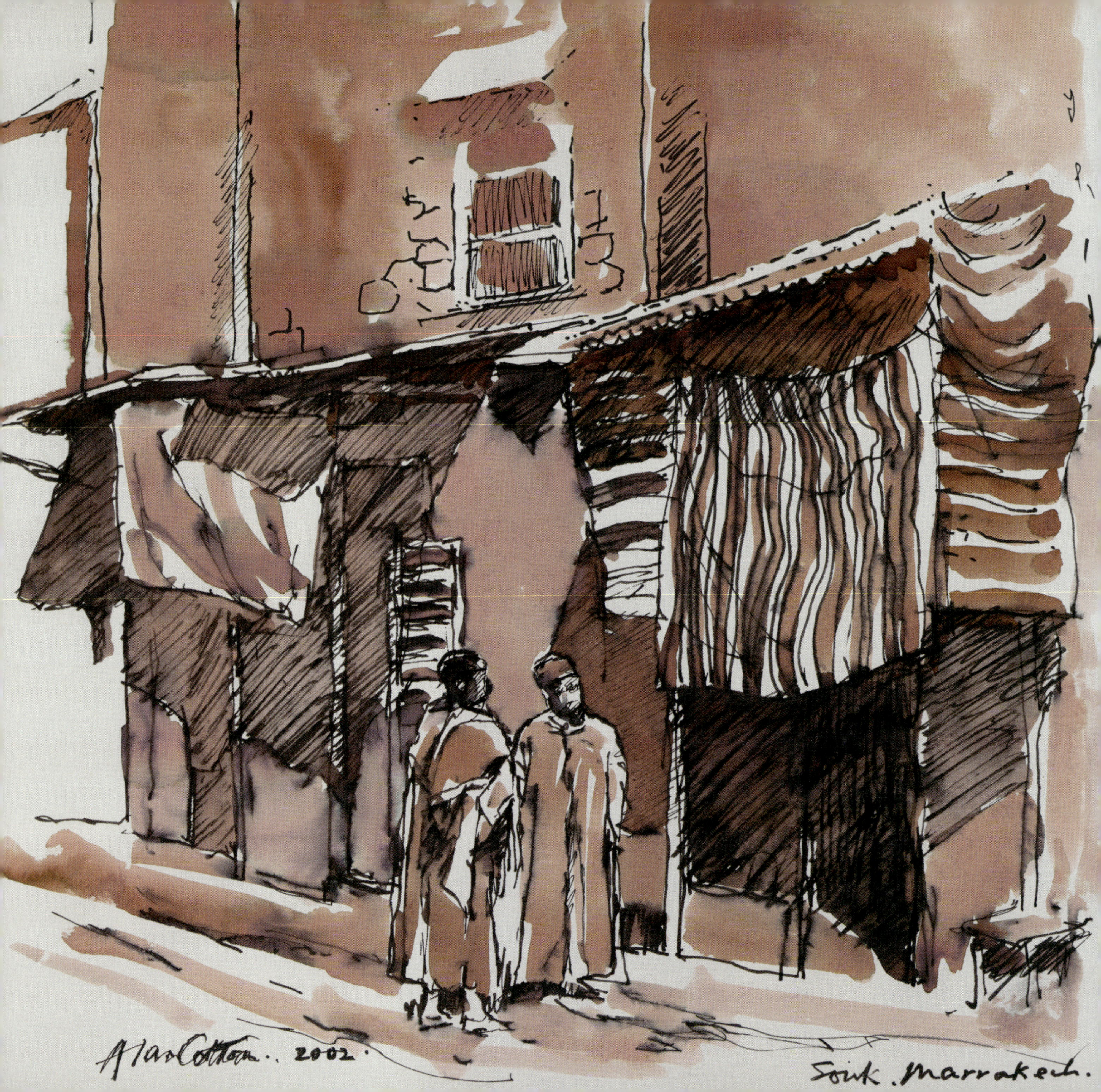
Alan Cotton .. 2002.
Souk . Marrakech.

Chapter Four

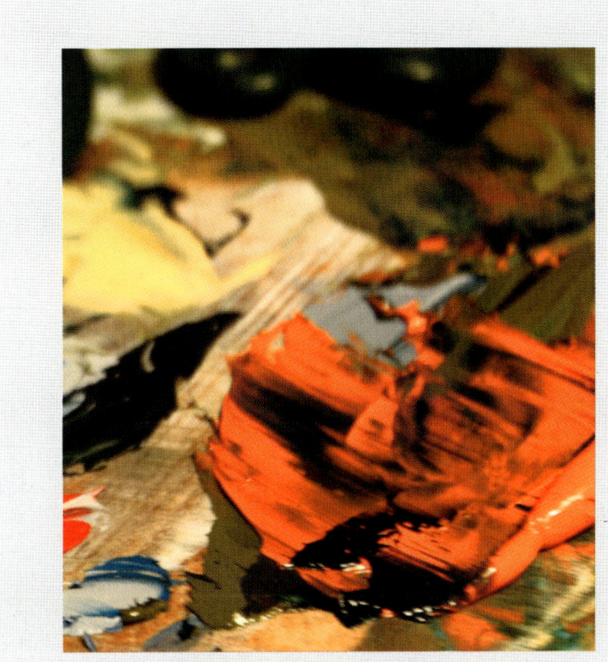

Block and Tackle

Even Alan Cotton's irrepressible optimism has not immunised him from the onset of the dreaded 'painters' block', and there have been many periods in his life when nothing has gone right. He finds those times difficult to cope with. He gets depressed, is unable to sleep, and his health suffers accordingly. Alan compares these periods of artistic block to being in a maze and unable to find a way out. As he recently observed, 'I used to get so low, but nowadays I realise that what I need is new material. Travelling is the answer. I have had many blocks over the years, lasting from a month to much longer, but now I realise that the very essence of what sparks me is being in landscape. That's what I am, a landscape painter.' Sometimes the light is too flat or the scenery too lacklustre to provide much inspiration, but even when Alan is fired up, his excitement does not always find its way into the paintings. 'A couple of years ago I did about a dozen paintings and scrapped them all. I was doing paintings that I thought were OK and I came in one day and thought "this isn't good enough". Because it's very hard to destroy paintings I just abandoned them. Upstairs I have a stack of abandoned paintings that are no good. I keep them because they are canvases and I could scrape them down and re-stretch them. I now think it is a mistake to start paintings when you are tired out. If you are going through a tired period when life intrudes on everything you are doing, problems with family and so on, and if you are a caring sort of bloke which I think I am, it affects you deeply. It is often family issues that mess things up.'

Alan's rigorous schedule of work makes self discipline and maintaining energy levels essential, but he also needs both outside stimulus and support at home. 'I am pretty disciplined, but I find it counterproductive to work when I am low. You try and paint because you must – you've got a deadline – and then it all goes pear shaped and you really struggle. As I live in a fairly quiet place, that can be a problem when you are on your own and work is going badly. I can waste a whole day doing nothing at all.'

As Alan has discovered, the way to tackle the problem of repeating oneself is to collect new material. As David Messum confirms, he does need to make new breakthroughs. 'He's not an artist who would ever bin a picture, and often what happens is that he paints the same picture again and again. They are all quite close to each other. A lot of artists do that and, seen in the studio, the paintings seem to fight with each other, but seen separated on the gallery wall they are perfectly alright. It depends on what is on his palette at the time. He doesn't clean his palette very often, and if you are having a brilliant day you use what's there. But he does sometimes need to break out.'

As Alan has learnt from long experience, the next important step, having collected new material, is to have

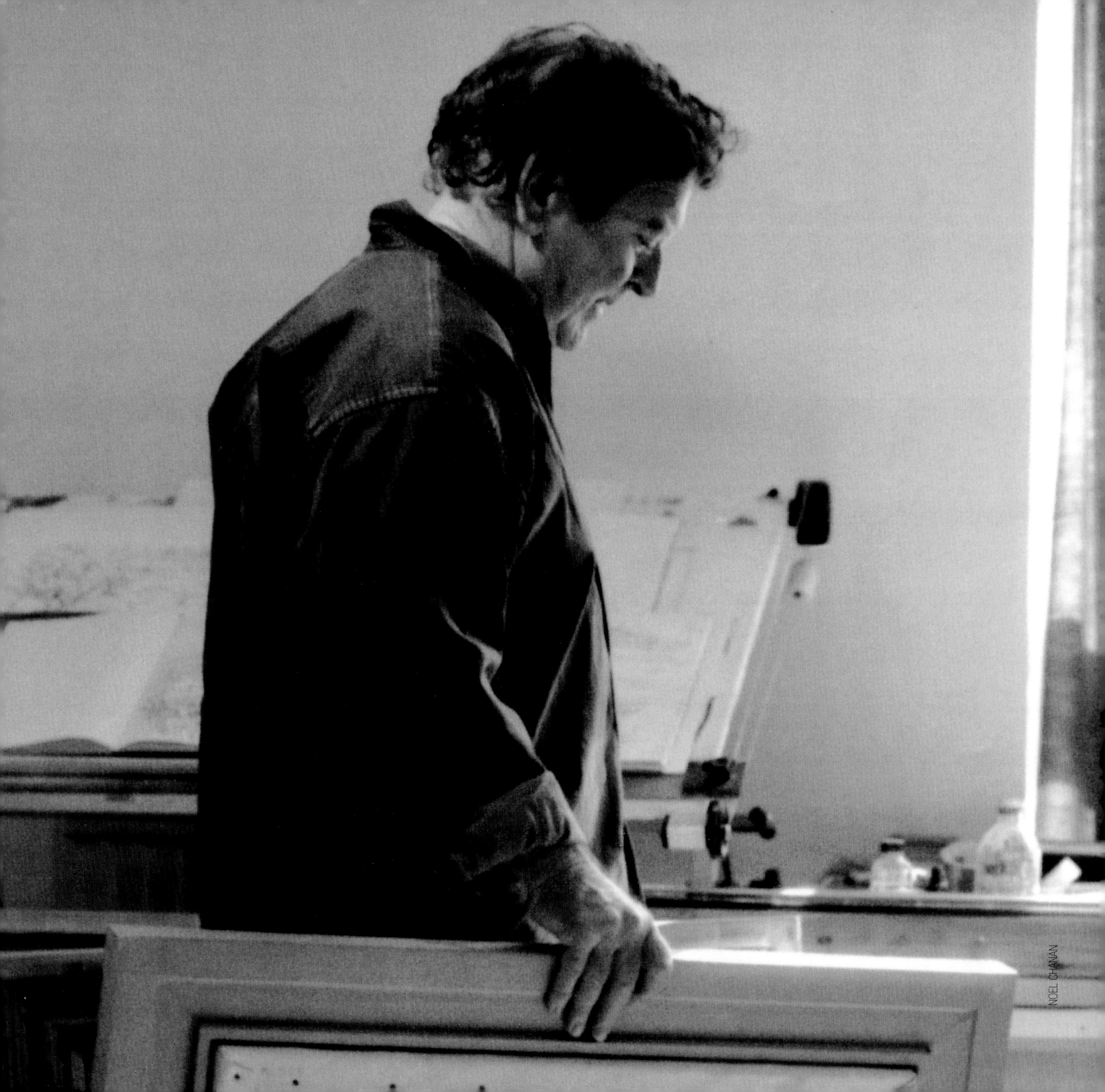

NOEL CHANAN

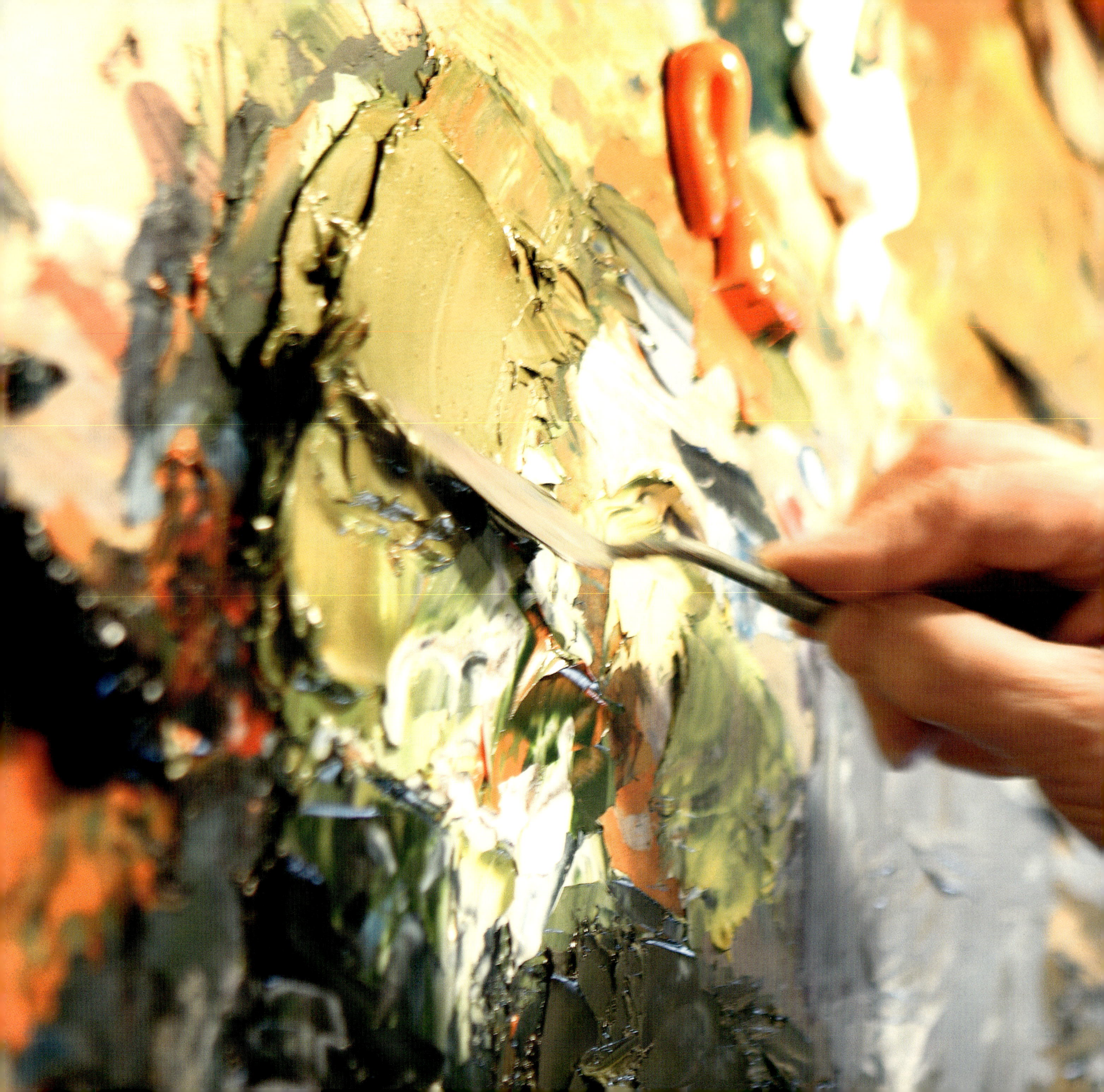

everything ready for action on return to the studio. 'The ideal situation is to have an abundance of material and a large enough physical space so that you can leave stuff around. The physical backup is important, and I have the perfect situation here. One thing that I try and do is to set up my work for the following day and put everything ready. Typically I paint for five to six hours at a go, and when a show is looming I spend more and more hours until I get physically exhausted. I have learnt to wear a hat when painting because the lights in my studio are very strong. I also need to drink plenty of water. And for me music is important – a lot of different music. You come in one cold dawn and you have got to make things happen. You put on some music and Wow! Jazz gets you going. Sometimes I can still remember the piece of music I was playing when I look at my painting. If you are listening to Puccini you are hearing the most romantic stuff. The love duet from Madam Butterfly for instance, which is the most sublime piece of music, does affect the painting. You are in that sort of mood, loving, caressing. Another time it could be Bolero, or jazz to energise you. If you are doing a big painting, that's the sort of music to play. There is a strong correlation between the music you play and what you are doing and how you do it. You can even pick up a beat and feel physically fitter and simply go for it.'

Besides the difficulty of reinventing the wheel, there is the difficulty of starting work at all. Alan is no stranger to the problem of getting down to work, and nowadays he tries to make everything ready for an immediate start the following day. As he says, 'displacement is one of the big problems for anyone in creative work. So to overcome this awful trait that human beings have, I try and eliminate excuses. One of the excuses is to pad around the studio setting out the paint, cleaning the knives, doing preparation. When you are at your best you have no fear of starting, but when you are not you fall back on those things – another cup of coffee, another walkabout. The only way to deal with it is just to engage with it.' But, having engaged with the work and perhaps painted hard all day, it can come as a bad blow when the result looks quite different from the original idea. 'Sometimes you can look at a thing and in a fit of passion scrape everything off. But that's usually a bad decision. Sometimes you get stuck and just leave it. Sometimes the danger is that you are afraid to break out of a familiar formula. Two things motivate you – internal and external. In terms of satisfying your public you can go on for ever, but in terms of satisfying yourself you must move on. I have felt at times that I wasn't moving anywhere. And I never paint as well as I would like to paint, not by a mile.'

Alan knows that, whether fired up or not, he has to get into the studio, pick up his painting knives and start work. Only when he is at the coalface can those magical breakthroughs start to happen. As he points out, 'part of what you do is craft and you are bound to fall back on craft, yet there is a freedom that I feel I haven't yet gained. I'm still exploring. Occasionally everything is right and you let go – the tightness goes and you let fly. To betray that first impulse to paint seems wrong. It's always on a knife edge between the actual experience of the landscape and the paint – that's the double whammy. Although there is a lot of abstraction in my work I can't lose the original experience that I felt in the landscape. The feeling of the place has got to be there.'

To counter the periods of 'painters' block' Alan now realises that he must find new inspiration by getting out and exploring new places. That means going drawing, and he loves drawing as much as he loves handling paint. He agrees with Van Gogh's dictum 'drawing is the root of everything'. In the catalogue to his 2004 exhibition, *As I See It*, Alan muses on what drawing means to him and how he uses it to work his way back into his paintings. 'Drawing is what I first learnt to do as a child and when I look back at my teenage drawings, without being immodest, I believe I really did draw well and it was a very natural thing for me to do. I can spend hours on some drawings, but mostly they are simply visual notes which other people simply couldn't interpret… At one time I used to make more elaborate drawings with lots of written notes, but it dawned on me over the years that more and more comes from the imagination and memory, from working on the painting in the studio, from what actually happens on the painting table, from combinations of colours and from trying to find the key to the painting. Drawing is the catalyst, so that when I'm in the studio I try to set down the bare bones of the drawing I've got onto the canvas and that gives me an abstract series of marks as a starting point which allows me to convey the idea through the use of paint. Very often the way into the painting is to find the right colour key for it and once you have the confidence of a few marks of the right colours, the sequence flows from that. So the amount of invention I put into a painting is considerable. Although I always start with something I have seen which has turned me on, what I am trying to do is to trust myself, to believe in my own memory and imagination, so that I can actually create something new which is as much about paint and the way paint is used as it is about the starting point.'

Alan Cotton rarely sells his drawings, and the extensive body of work that he has built up in his sketchbooks serves him well as a library of memories of places and experiences. For commissioned work, he has often presented the new owners with the sets of drawings from which the paintings are derived. Although he does not like to repeat himself, he does look through his old sketchbooks for inspiration. His method of drawing, from student days onwards, has been remarkably consistent. His ink drawings, made with pens of different sizes and types, including reed pens

Farm amongst the hills - nr. Barolo.
Collection of farm buildings following the contours of the hill - wonderful pattern of vines - golden ochres in colour -

Overall impression of pale gold & pale orange colours burnt oranges in foreground vines.

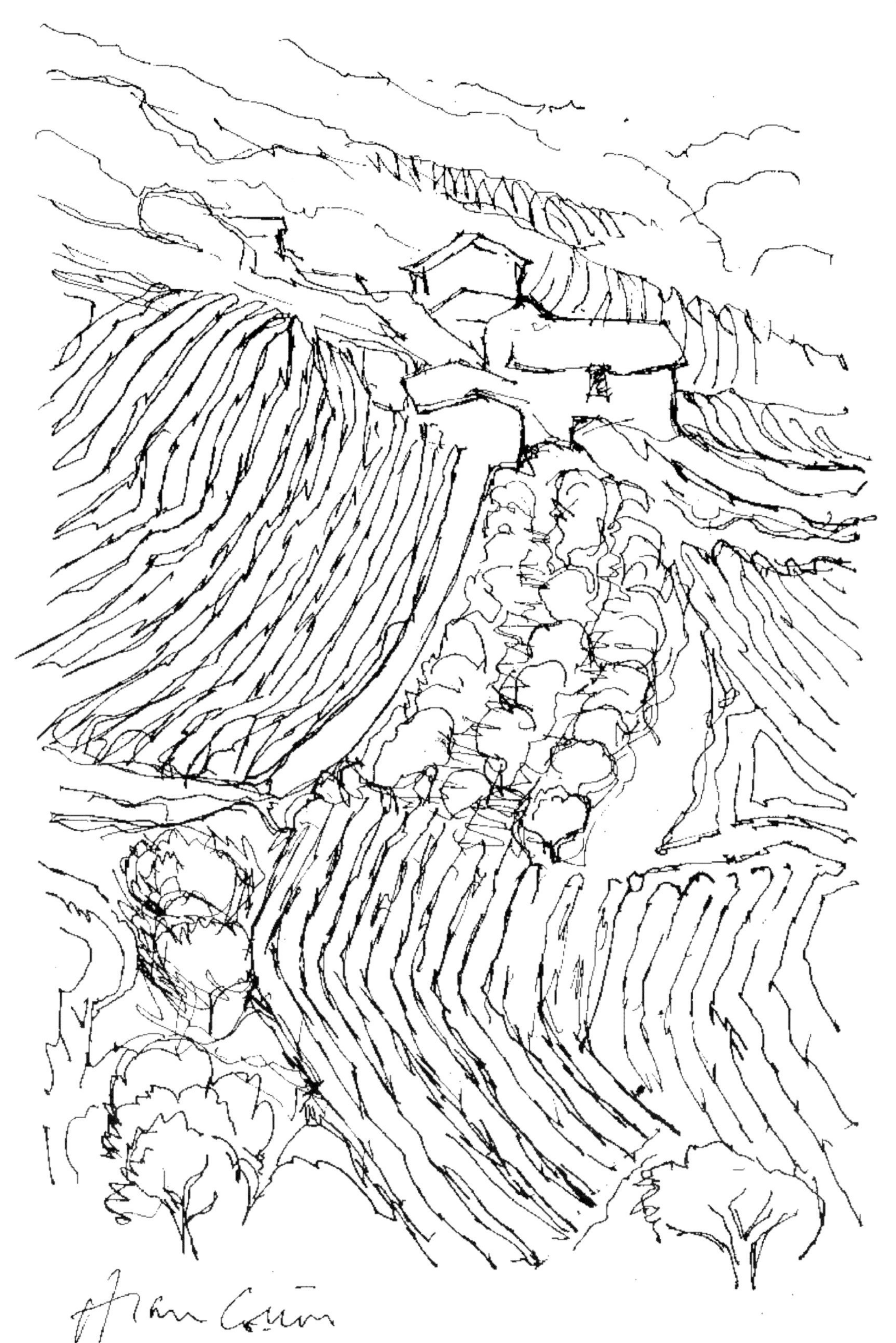

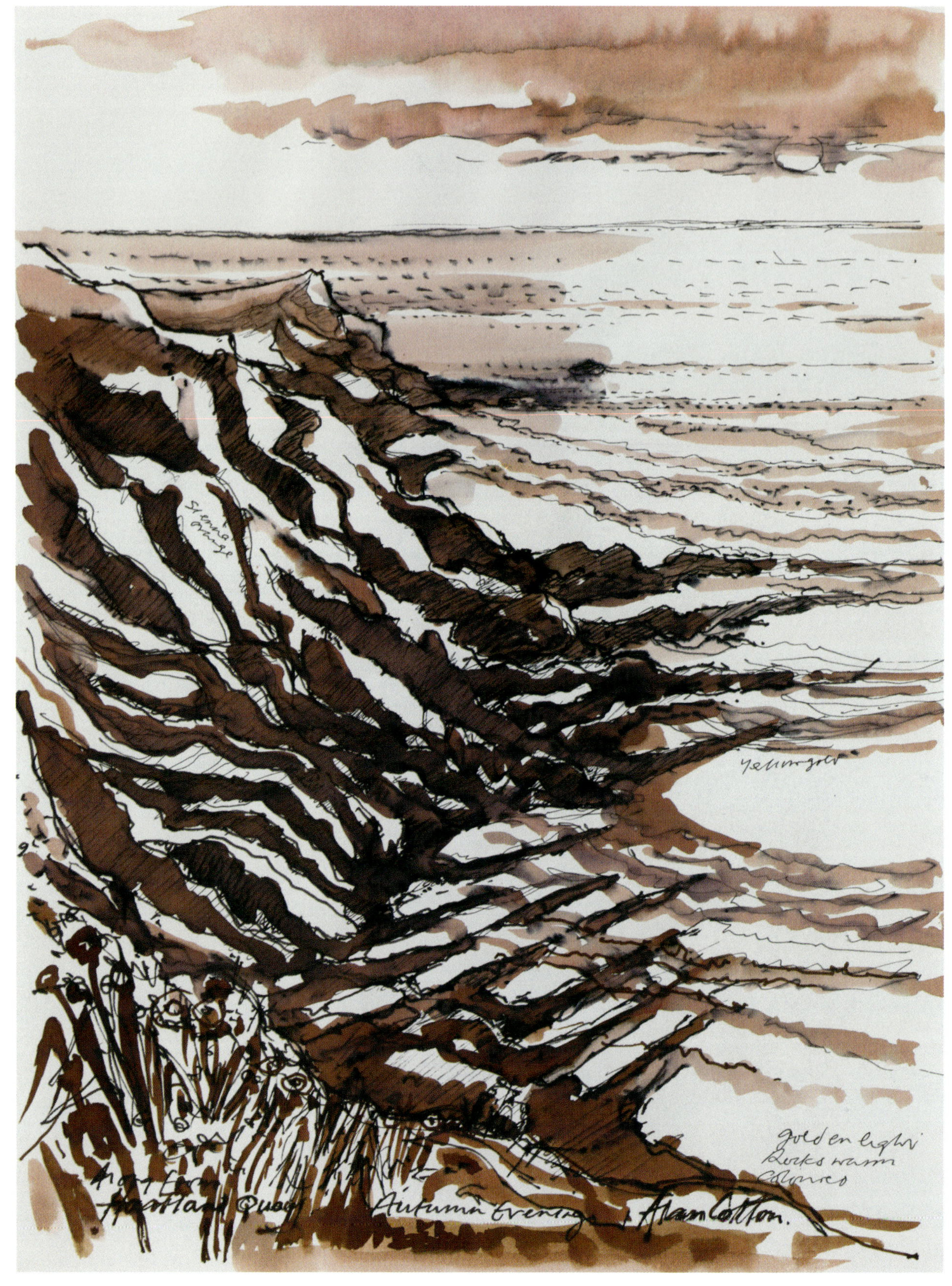
Yellow gold
Golden light
Rocks warm
colours
Hartland Quay
Autumn Evening
Alan Cotton.

and even sticks, have a flowing, cursive contour line that delineates the forms boldly and freely. Rapid scribbled marks, accurately positioned within the pictorial space, serve to represent trees, cliffs, buildings. The energy and the speed of the hand moving across the paper are clearly felt, and his enjoyment in the mark-making is tangible. Pen and wash drawings, made to analyse the tones of a subject, are equally free. There is very little colour notation, as Alan prefers to rely on his memory and invent in paint the colour chords that most suit his subject. Yet the drawings themselves are as suggestive of colour as they are of space. Although they are fairly literal depictions of the scene he observes, Alan's drawings are as far from the careful pencil plotting of forms in space so beloved of English artists, especially those trained at the Slade School of Art. They are perhaps nearer to the work of French artists, especially Van Gogh, in the freedom and variety of mark-making used. Alan finds drawing with pens more natural, like handwriting, and over time he has developed a vocabulary of marks, from thick lines to dots and stipples. He long ago abandoned the idea of working on large oil paintings on the spot because it involved lugging easel, canvases, paints, knives and other paraphernalia around. Now he travels with only sketchbooks, pens and a few watercolours. This gives him the freedom to draw in awkward places and catch that sense of the 'quotidien', the here-and-now-ness of a place. As he emphasises, 'drawing encourages looking and experiencing. A drawing will remind you of the sun on your back and the sense of place: a photograph is never as meaningful. It's immediate, and I can draw very quickly if I need to. Usually I look for a structure, very often a tonal structure, which is more use than just putting a line around something. As you draw you are taking in far more than you are putting down. The drawing is like a conduit between you and the painting. You are aware of all the things around you, the waves coming in, bird noises, the rustling of plants, all the sounds and smells around you. Somehow you need to make notes to allow you to recreate the sensations that inspire you in the first place. You often get the feeling of trying to possess the place, to own the experience. If you see something that is so amazing that you want to make a painting of it you want to get to it as quickly as you can. You are so afraid it's going to go, because these moments are so rare. Drawing is the quickest route, believe me. The imagination works overtime. You feel territorial about places, as if they belong to you. You are aware of your special relationship – "this is my place, I've discovered this". It's like being with a lover, you don't want to share the person. You feel that when you are drawing, and when you get back to the studio you try to recreate the excitement. There's an analogy with courtship. You have met someone, and doing the painting is like getting into bed and bringing it to a climax.'

For Alan drawing is the primary activity for experiencing the world. The excitement that goes into his drawings is permanently fixed, and can be recalled as the starting point for many paintings, although, as memory fades, he needs to return to the place to regain that initial passionate involvement. However, he works fast, absorbing the scene around him with enormous intensity. 'My best paintings are when I've had a Wow experience and I come back to the studio and get on with it. They have the power and the intensity. Pat has been with me when I have torn into the landscape, rushing ahead because the light is always changing, and she knows that it's as if I am high on drugs. With drawing you can do a dozen ideas in a day. I want great gobfuls of experience. Nobody ever told me at art school what drawing was for, that you don't just draw for drawing's sake, to develop a skill, but that you draw as a method of thinking through to the painting. For a painter it's far more than conveying an image, it's almost like getting under the skin of it through drawing. The moment I realised that, it was like a revelation to me and my work took off. You go for the jugular. You ask yourself what it is about this that turns you on. That's the important question. The first thing is the gut reaction – Wow! Then you ask what elements of this are important to me and what are unimportant. Being a knife painter helps because you are feeding lots of bits of information into a knife mark which can make a simple statement about something quite complicated. You don't need too much colour information because a lot of that is formed on the palette. When you start with a general idea other things happen so that the discovery is all part of it. That's the magic of painting. '

Although Alan often thinks about painting while he is drawing, he has little idea which of his drawings or parts of drawings he will use for composing paintings. Back in the studio, he juggles with the collected mass of work done on the spot, using elements from even the sketchiest of visual notes to compose his pictures. 'Sometimes I can do a drawing in five minutes, which will make a big central painting, but others I do and I actually get carried away with the drawing and I start to enjoy it for its own sake. Sometimes I spend many hours just drawing on one spot and in fact those don't always make the best paintings. I have many drawings that I have never painted because they are too intimidating, there is too much information… When I am developing the paintings back in my studio, the drawings remind me so much of the place, not just the visual sensations either, but the circumstances in which I did them, the scents and sounds, the warmth of the sun, the potency of the colours, so that the process of painting is done not only by mixing the colour on the palette, but all the memories evoked by the drawing, which all combine to make the finished painting.'

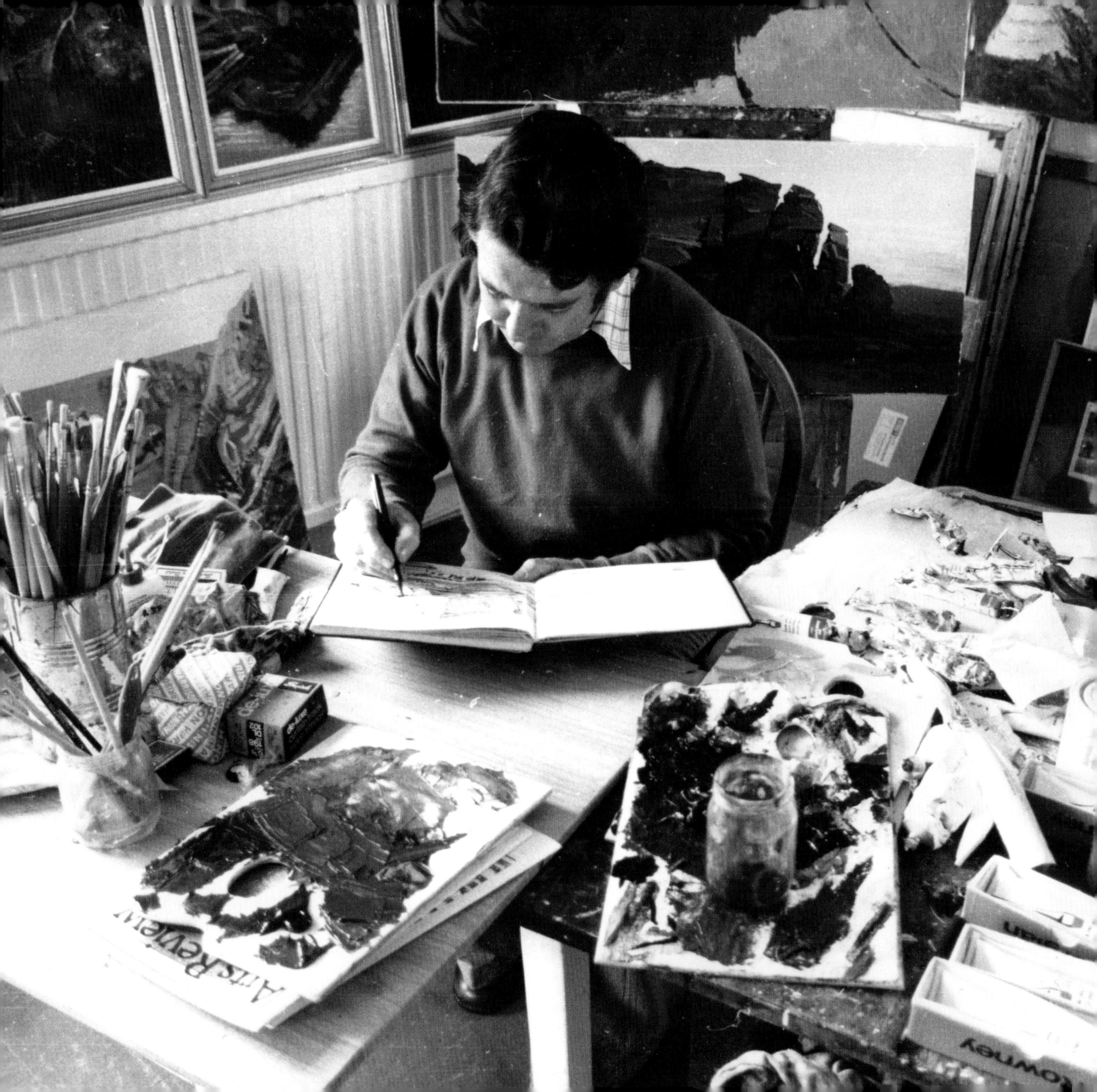
Arts Review

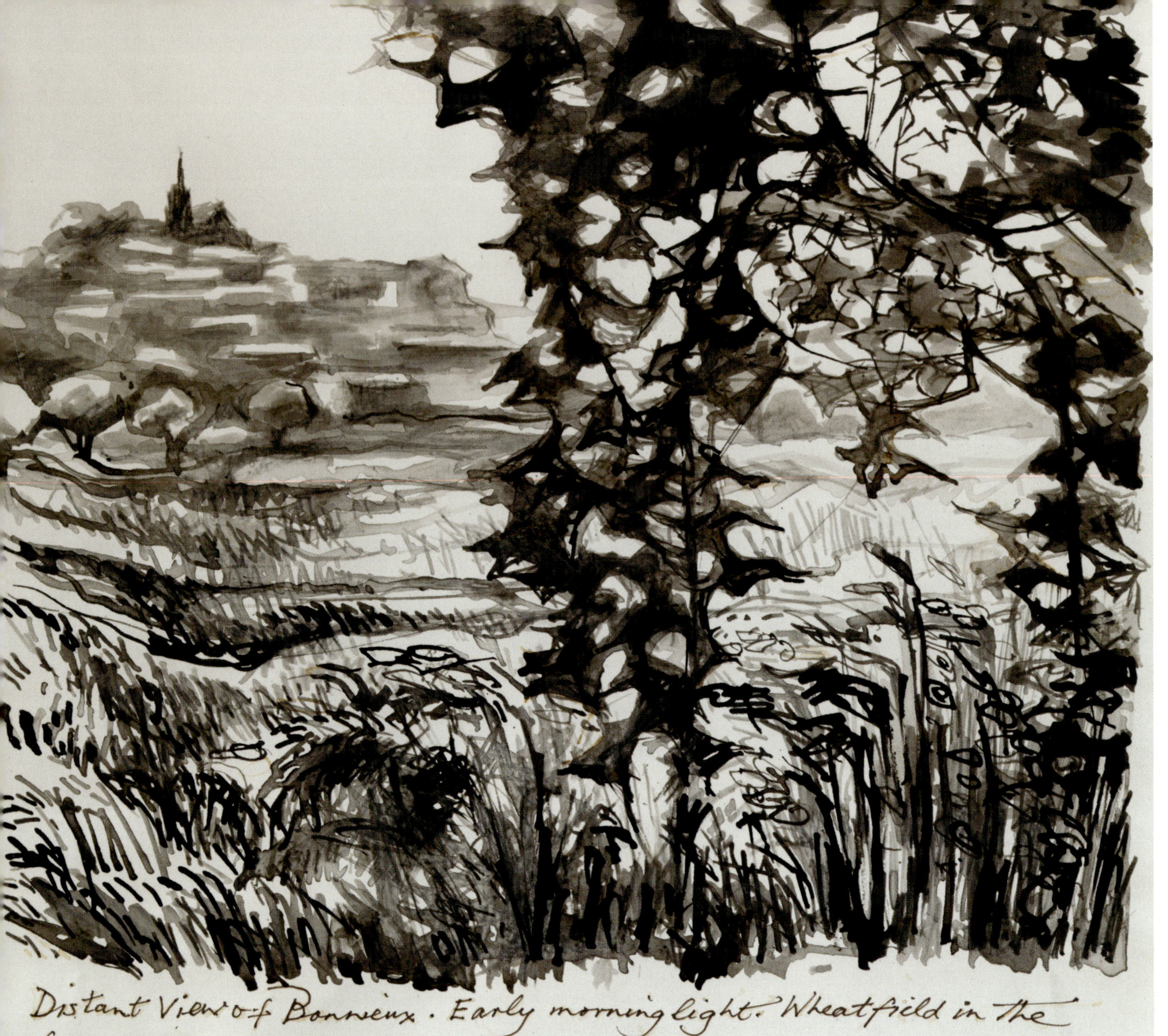

Distant View of Bonnieux. Early morning light. Wheatfield in the foreground. many complex patterns caused by movements of wind – golden colours, strong contrasts of brilliant light and deep warm shadows. What attracted me was the overhanging vines which occupied almost half the composition, much of this was in deep dense shadow, which contrasted dramatically with the brilliantly illuminated field. Some of the vines though were Punctuated with small but high key passages of light. Where the leaves appeared translucent.

A delight in drawing, Alan believes, is something that all children are born with. As he pointed out in his book *Learning and Teaching through Art and Crafts*, very young children enjoy making marks by dipping their fingers in custard or gravy and patting and pushing it around the table, long before they can scribble with crayons on paper. Later they explore making marks in puddles of water or scratching in sand or mud. In these early stages children are not making pictures but are simply discovering that they can obtain a record of their physical action. The images that slightly older children make are not usually observed things, but rather schematic symbols of their experiences. Sadly, not all children continue to enjoy drawing and painting, and many lose confidence as they grow older. In Alan's case, the early satisfaction that he obtained from making marks has never left him. He heightens his perceptions and deepens his understanding of the world through drawing, as well as enjoying the mark-making for its own sake. And he reiterates, 'you don't often start a drawing for the same reasons. You might start one as an aide-memoire for a painting or part of a painting, but you so enjoy the activity of making the marks that you spend endless time on the spot doing the drawing for its own sake. Sometimes you are chasing the light or in the rain and your drawings are very small and a bit sketchy with bits of tone on them. Then you go on to the next things. I have dozens of those – it's a different kind of drawing. I appreciate the spontaneity of children's drawings, and I would like to achieve that sort of spontaneity myself.'

Not all art lovers are aware how important the artist's unique touch, his handwriting, is in attracting the viewer. In the catalogue for his 1995 exhibition *Reflections*, Alan confirmed this point.: 'Since the time of the Impressionists, I think it has been recognised that the mark and the quality of the mark is the dynamic of the painting… For me the knife allows me to produce so many different marks that I really believe I have a fair bit of control… and the guts of the painting – the whole language of the painting – is in the marks really. People look at the images and the places, but I am as much concerned with the dynamic of the painting – the physical surface, which is very tactile and very sculptural.'

The influence of other artists' work has seeped into Alan Cotton's psyche and formed his art although, as he readily admits, it is difficult to know exactly how it feeds into the work. In his catalogue *Cotton on Canvas*, Alan discusses his particular loves. 'I gain a deep sense of joy and pleasure from the work of so many painters. Bonnard for his sensuality, Degas and Botticelli who drew like angels, Soutine and De Stael, for the rich way they use paint, and so on… Certainly I think Cézanne and Van Gogh inspired me as a young student. It was the search for their painting haunts which first took me to the south of France. I think Cézanne is a great influence on many 20th century painters because of the way he was able to analyse visual things through the formal aspects of painting, looking at composition, shapes and design. Van Gogh inspired me by his almost childlike vision. The way he used the guts of the paint, so that it stood out from the canvas and was shaped and marked and had this feeling for impasto. His work is so spontaneous and there is such joy in the sensuous use of his materials.'

Alan Cotton's output over more than thirty years has been prodigious. He has worked on about sixty major paintings every year, and the total number of paintings that are being enjoyed by collectors around the world is well over a thousand. Even those periods of 'painter's block' have not diminished his overwhelming imperative to draw and paint.

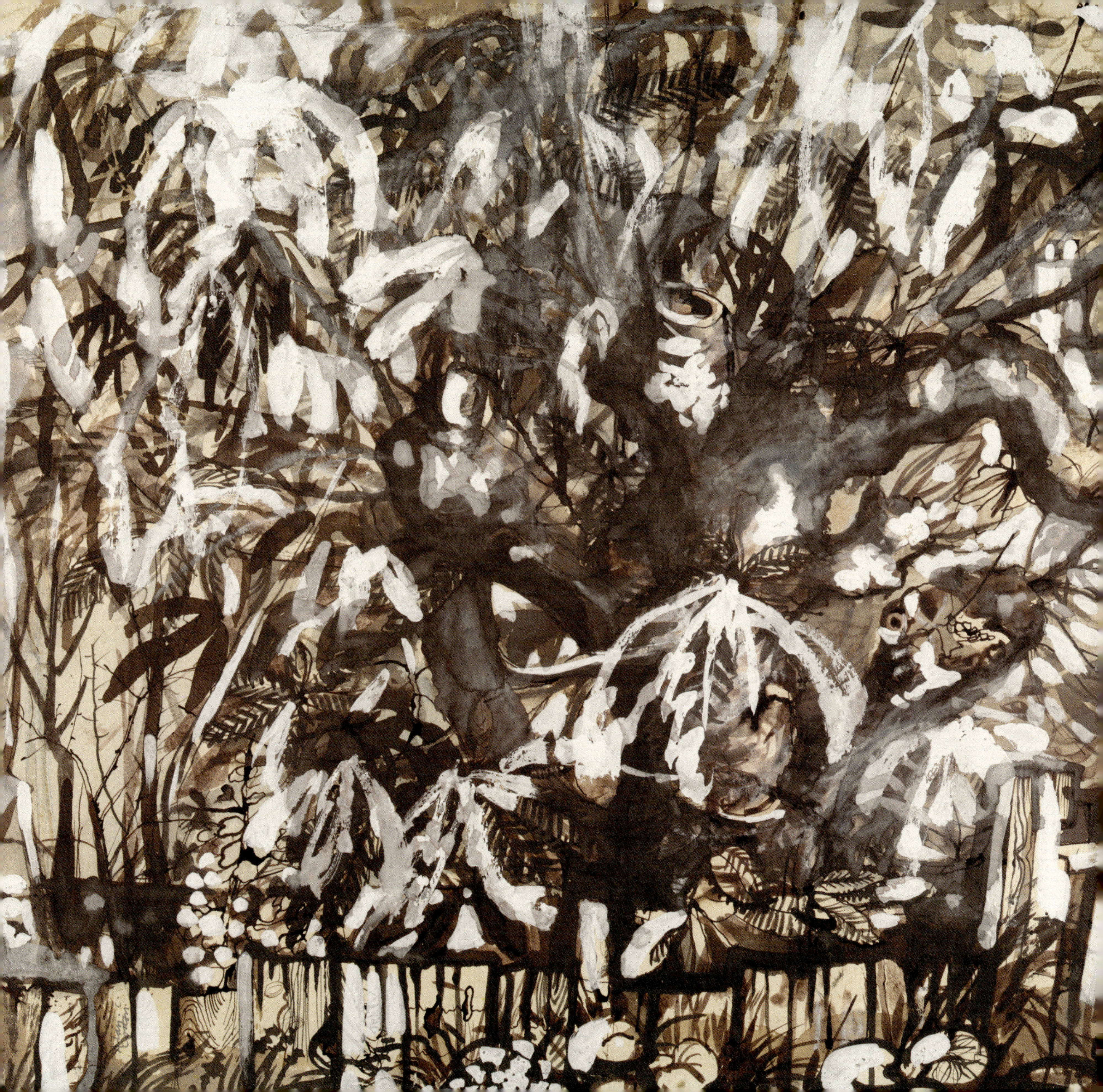

ON HIS TOUR of New Zealand Alan accompanied The Prince of Wales to the Albatross Centre at Taiaroa Head, near Dunedin, where the Prince was making a speech. Detaching himself from the royal party for a few hours, Alan made a number of drawings of the cliff edges and the albatross colony there. He was enthralled by the sight of the birds riding the wind and the waves, laced with long fronds of seaweed, buffeting the rocky headlands of this remote corner of the world. From this single intense experience he composed a series of paintings in which the wind and weather are major protagonists. The direct strength of this painting, reminiscent of Courbet, is based on the colour opposition of red and green.

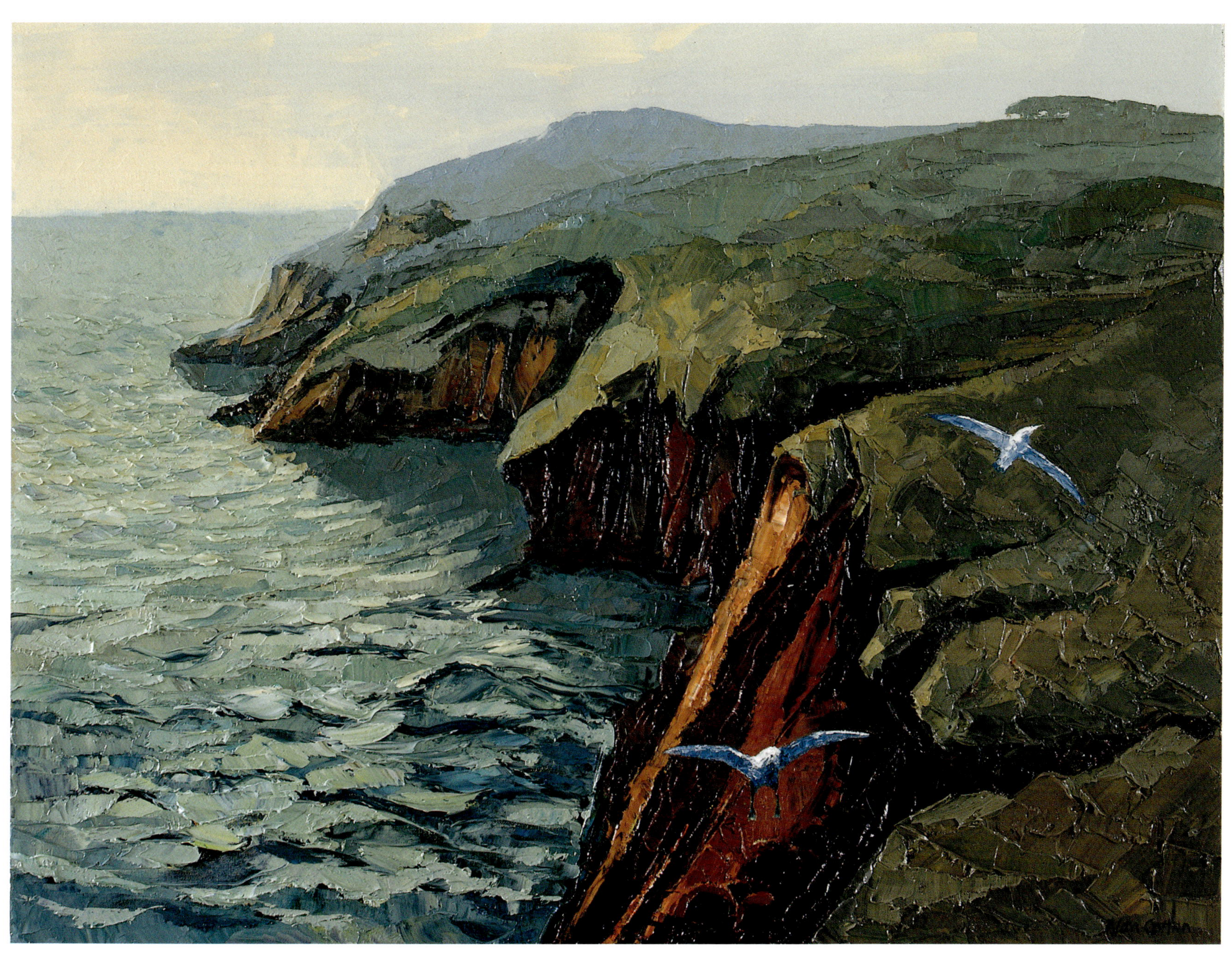

New Zealand – Albatross landing near Taiaroa Head, 2006
oil on canvas 28 x 36 ins
Collection HRH The Prince of Wales

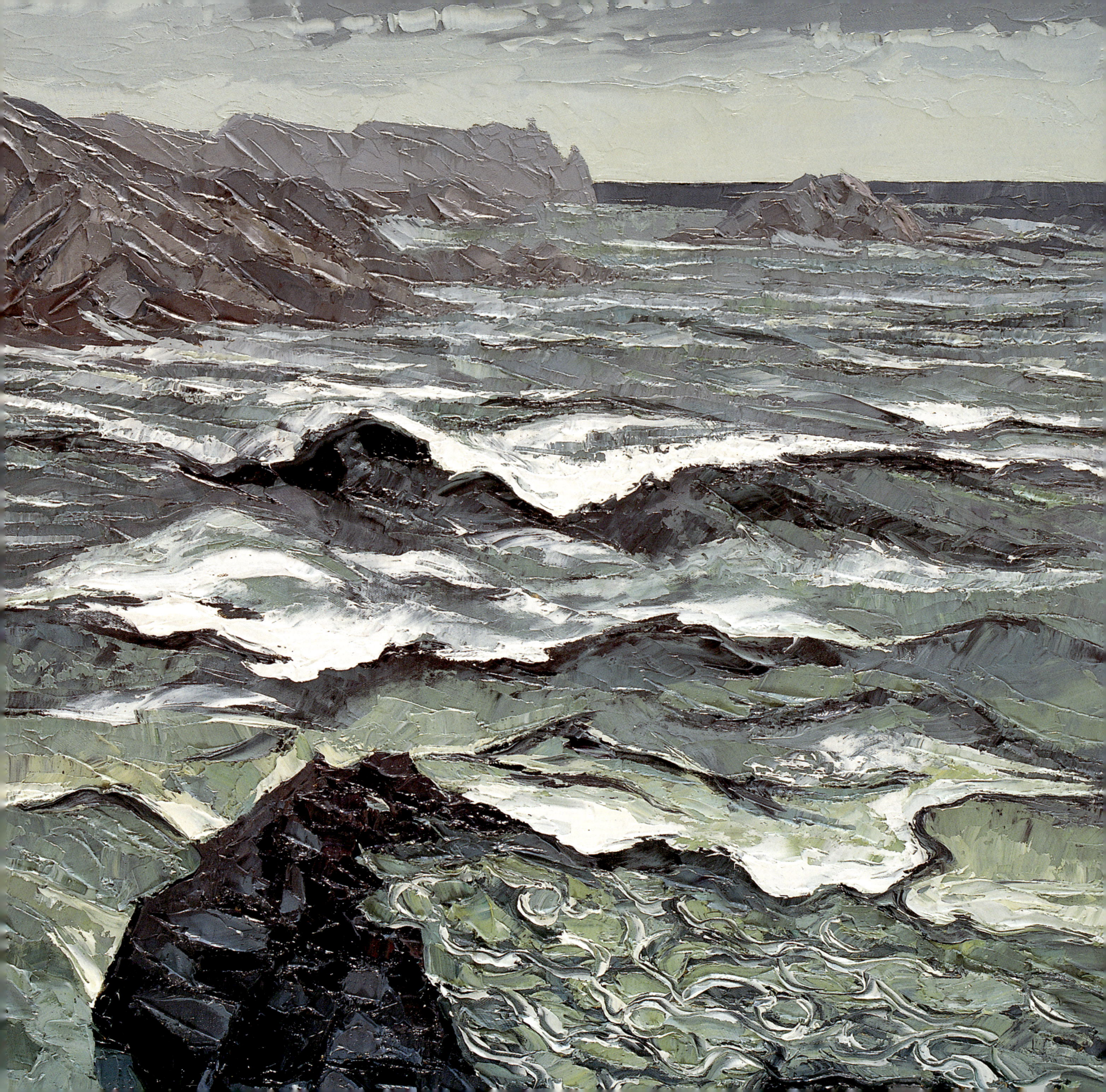

Chapter Five

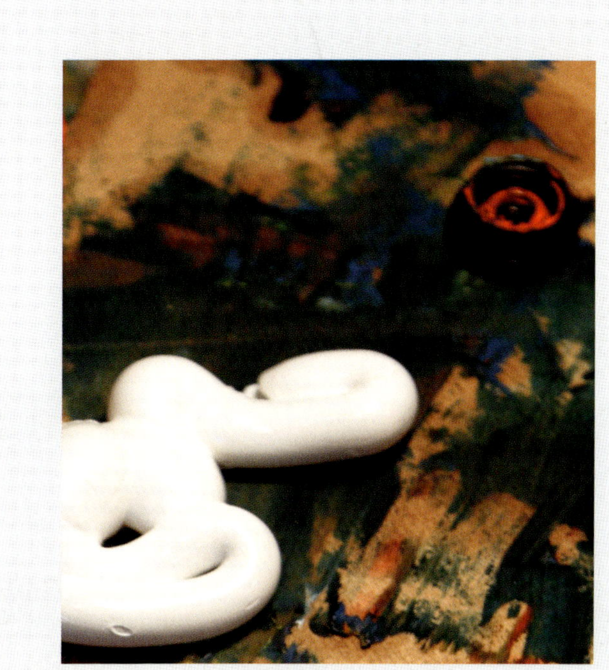

On the Move

New Zealand - Wild Seas at Taiaroa
oil on canvas 36 x 28 ins

Travelling in search of new subject matter is the surest way for Alan Cotton to deal with the dreaded 'painter's block'. Although there are plenty of motifs around his home for him to fall back on, new places energise him. In the 1970s, when he lived in the Forest of Dean, early forays into the countryside took him to Snowdonia, where the geological complexity and brooding colours of the land made a deep impression on him. His large, detailed drawings, influenced by the work of Graham Sutherland and John Piper, emphasised the darkly turbulent mood of the landscape. Both his drawings, and the paintings made from the drawings, display a romantic empathy with the dark, contorted hills and mountains lit by gleams of light. The large painting *Snowdonia*, now owned by the University of Southampton, shows Alan's handling of paint at its most vigorous, the knife marks adroitly delineating the startling striations of the land.

After moving from the Forest of Dean to Devon, Alan found further inspiration in Hartland Quay, on Devon's north coast. This wild area of rock and cliff engendered the dynamic early paintings that effectively put him on the artistic map. His 1978 exhibition, which travelled around the South West, was glowingly reviewed by Greville Poultney in the Dorset Evening Echo. 'If you marvelled at the large, powerful paintings of Snowdonia shown last year at the Dorset County Museum, then you must see Mr. Cotton's latest work. All his work bears the stamp of this imaginative artist whose style exclusively makes use of a palette knife. By this method Mr Cotton flakes paint on to a canvas to portray mountains, cliffs and rocks with vivid, natural intensity. *Hartland Quay* (now in the City of Exeter Art Gallery) is a superbly composed picture of Devon landscape, with a grey receding cliff line, shrouded in misty light and a spuming sea all around the rocks. Note the attractive sky with a patch of blue breaking through scudding cloud. Grey-greens are predominantly used by the artist in sea and mountain landscapes, with variation of tone used to portray the strength, beauty and sheer awe of the picture. The artist is moved and obviously compelled to paint strong pictures with subject material from the dawn of time.'

In his many forays to Hartland Alan set the pattern that he has followed, when possible, in all his travels. He liked to stay in the area for days or weeks at a time, getting to know the history and geography of the place, meeting the local people and soaking up the local folklore. His increased understanding of the subject helped to give his work validity. As he has often remarked, 'you've got to get right under the skin of a thing before you can paint it. It's got to be part of you. Life is an essential part of painting. I went to Ireland for many years before I painted it. Going to the pubs, listening to the music, watching the dancing and talking to people – I love all of that. It's all part of the story. You

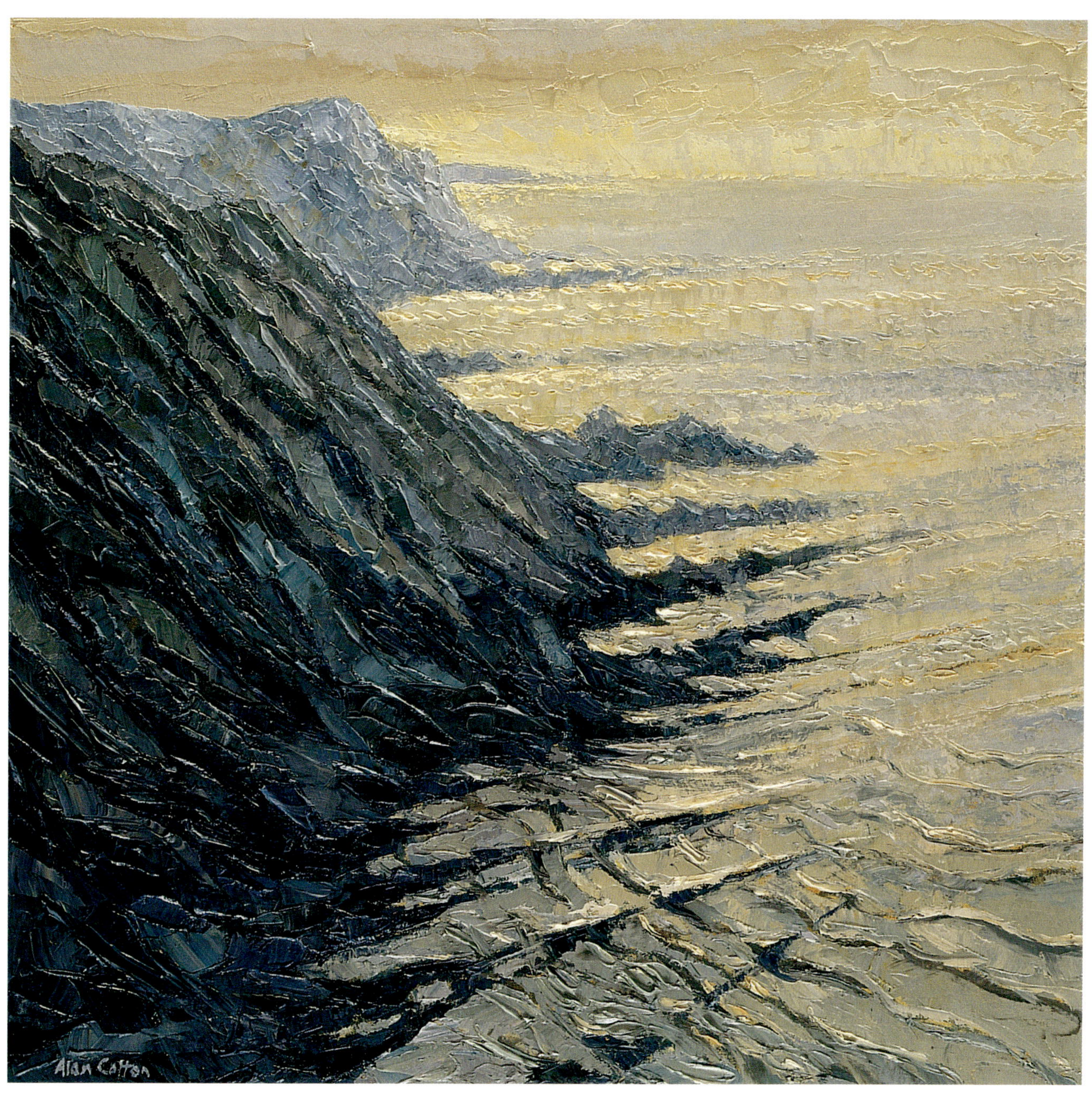

Hartland – Golden Evening along the Coast
oil on canvas 36 x 36 ins

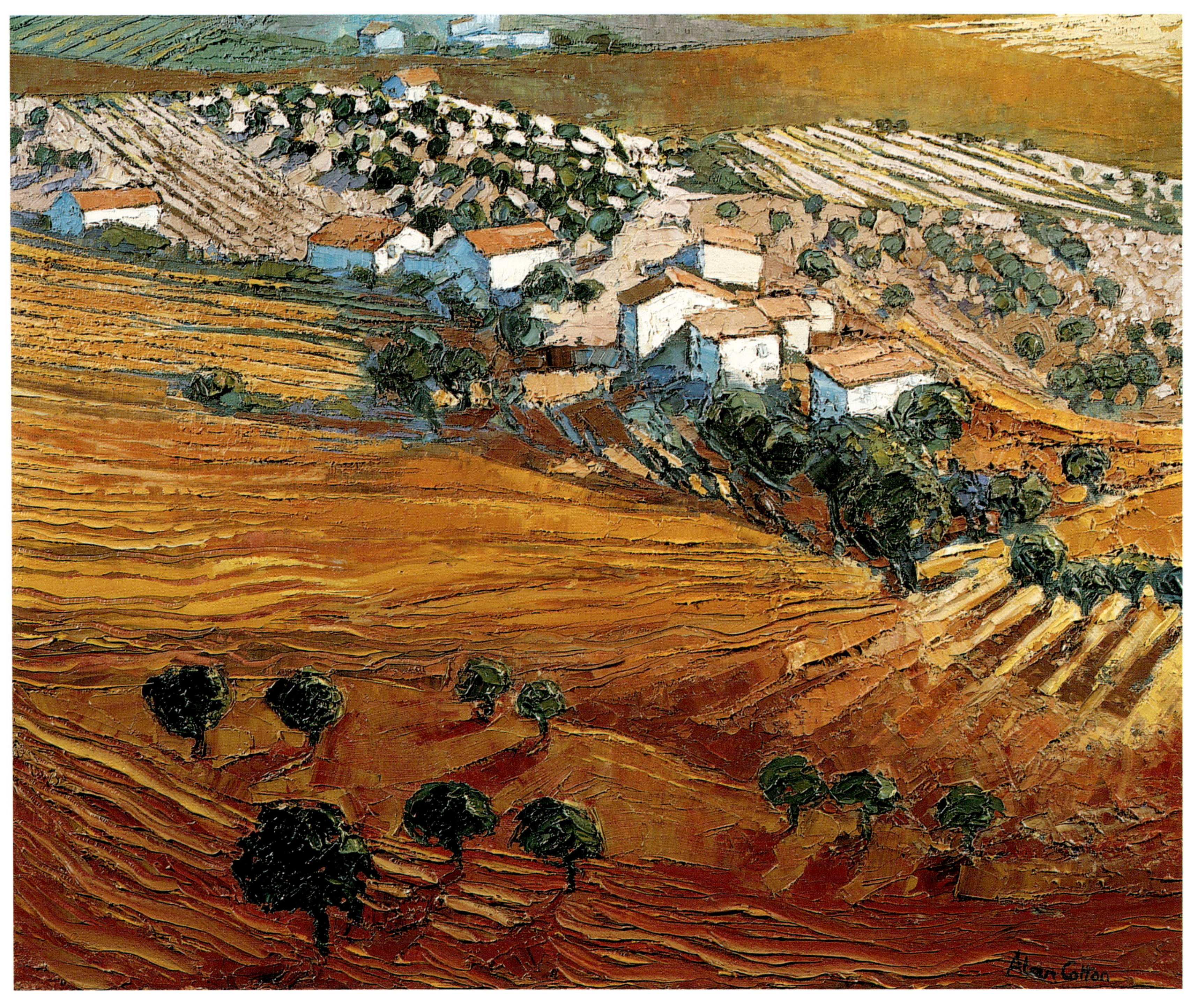

Provence – Farm in Red Landscape near Roussillon
oil on canvas 20 x 24 ins

feel you are allowed to paint it because you have affection for it and understand it. You've been there in all weathers, and then the streaks of light are utter magic. To allow you to paint, there's a bigger picture which informs you. That's certainly true of Provence and Piemonte. I have never seen a painting of Piemonte other than my own. Going into farms and vineyards with Mario, where you wouldn't normally be allowed to go, has been a great privilege. The exhibition in London when all the Piemonte people came over was a huge thrill. There is always a bigger picture – that's very important to me.'

Over a great many visits, Alan had become very familiar with the south of France. As a student, lured there by Cézanne's and Van Gogh's paintings, Provence had been something of a Mecca for him. But although Provence thrilled him, he found the well-known sites around Mont Saint Victoire impossible to paint freshly, with his own vision. It was not until he discovered the Luberon Valley with its lavender fields and orchards, the ochre quarries at Rustrel, and the hill town of Gordes, that he found subjects that he could claim as specifically his own. The orchards, particularly, moved him deeply, as he stressed in the 1992 catalogue for an exhibition of Provençal paintings. 'I think an orchard in full blossom, where you can see the light coming through blossoms against a deep blue sky or the patterns of deep shadows cast by trees is something very timeless and visually is one of the most arresting things that you can see. … To see orchards in abundance, thousands of trees, creating wonderful patterns of delicate colour, is something quite mystical.' Throughout the 1970s and 1980s Alan, still trying to make his solo way without a dealer to represent him, travelled back and forth to France, sometimes with Kevin Crooks to work on films for the BBC. One particular visit to Paris was occasioned by an American gallery that had shown an interest in his paintings. Kevin Crooks went with him, and he later wrote a spirited description, entitled *Forget Paris*, about their joint visit.

'" Monsieur, 'ere is your package."

The Chef de Bagage gestured toward our precious parcel with the generosity of an eighteenth century courtier. We were standing in the luggage hall at Charles de Gaulle Airport, racked with worry. Had Alan's four paintings, lovingly packed at Bristol, survived the rigours of Air France? … We need not have been concerned. In French eyes, the legend 'Original Works of Art' comes a close second to Brigitte Bardot….

…The American gallery owner did rather well for herself. The sunlight in a quiet leafy road off the Champs Elysées dappled the front of a nineteenth century stone façade. A tough looking security guard waves us through the front door and into the echoing hall. Madame received us in her first floor office. Her head was barely in view over a customised white console. At any moment she would reach for the diapason and sink through the floor whilst playing the theme from Phantom of the Opera… Employing the American habit of cumbersome expression, Madame spoke: "We should documentise this meeting". Suitably placed on the record, we launched into a discussion. Alan's articulate and lively discourse took him into a world of colour, line and composition. The role of the artist, the passions, the interpretation – the whole panoply of British painting. A procession of quotes, ideas and arguments moved through the room like a skein of twinkling stardust … over Madame's head and gently through the open window. … There was a pause. "Well I guess we should see the paintings.".

The package lay between us on the black leather settee like a spectre at the feast. As we struggled to release the canvases, Madame started the opening address of her fourteen-part correspondence course on how to be a super power salesman. Were we in harmony with the purchaser? What did we understand about marketing? What image were we trying to sell? What is your statement of purpose?…

We were interrupted by a slight commotion at the door. A stocky man wearing a Wall Street suit was backing into the room shouting instructions to an unseen minion in the corridor. "I have about half an hour before the limo picks me up" he said…. Hi Dean, good of you to join us. Dean here represents us in North America. He's the finest salesman you'll ever meet – can this guy sell paintings! …Madame delivered this information without taking the slightest pause for breath…

We carefully lifted the second painting from its wrapping. Alan gave a detailed description of his work at Hartland Point and how the condensed atmosphere of the North Atlantic storms gave the receding headlands a myriad of subtle shades in blue and grey. He took care to explain the effect of impasto as the folds of rock were laid with shards of paint. All of life's drama shone from the canvas with sparkling clarity.

"Kinda neat" said Madame, "but Alan, I have to tell you – these are simply not this season's colours."'

For Alan the lure of France was eventually superceded by other foreign attractions. The discovery of new places to paint often came about through the insistence of friends, keen to see what Alan could make of the places they loved. This personal pressure proved doubly valuable in providing fresh subject matter and also helping Alan to get 'under the skin' of a place. Several trips to Cyprus were instigated by his friend Brian Hoskins, the Red Arrows pilot, during his appointment as Station Commander at RAF Akrotiri. Alan's initial visit was a disappointment because the land was so dry that all the colours were bleached out. But on his second visit, in June 1990, he experienced the full

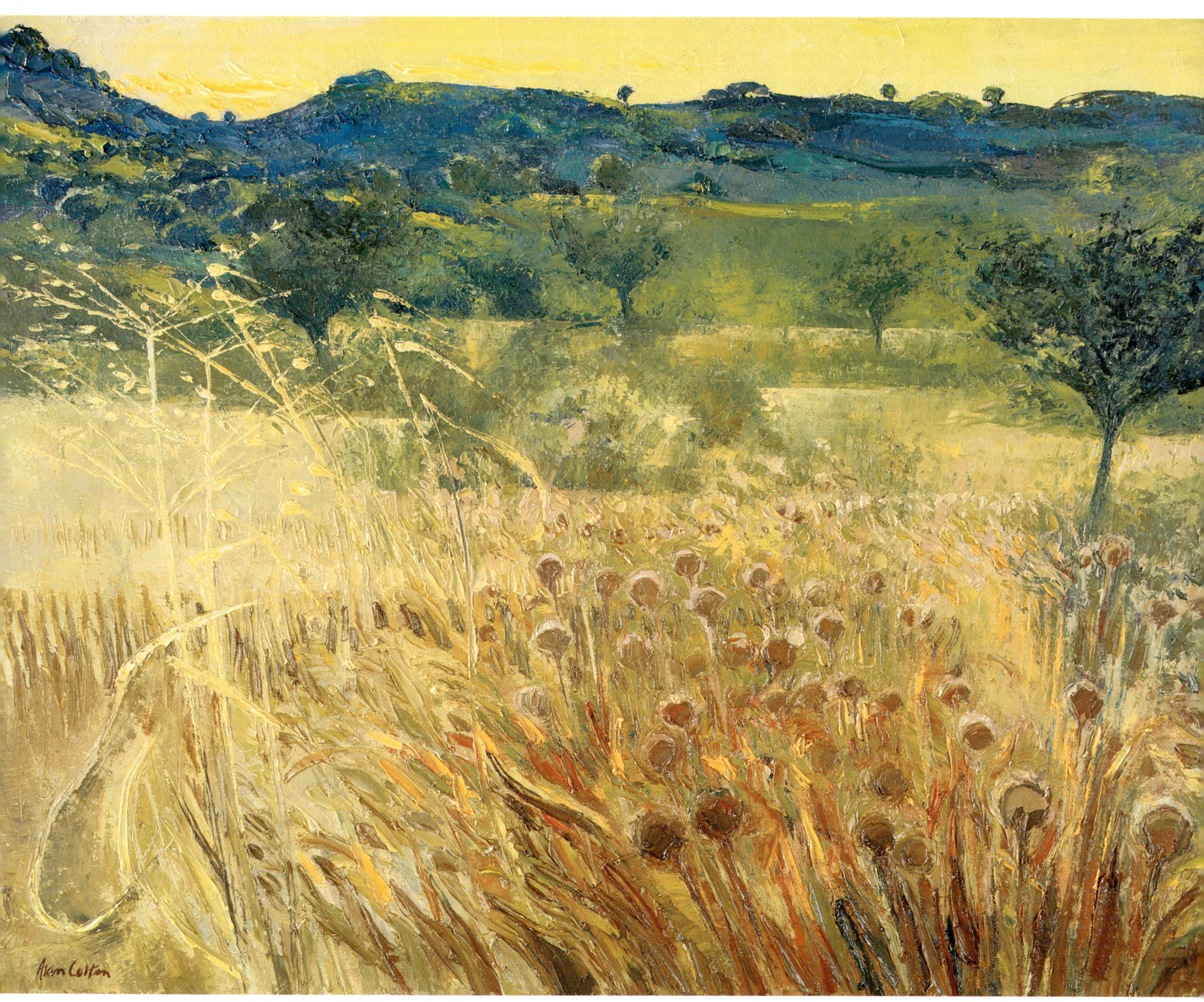

Cyprus – Crops and Olive Trees, Evening Light
oil on canvas 24 x 30 ins

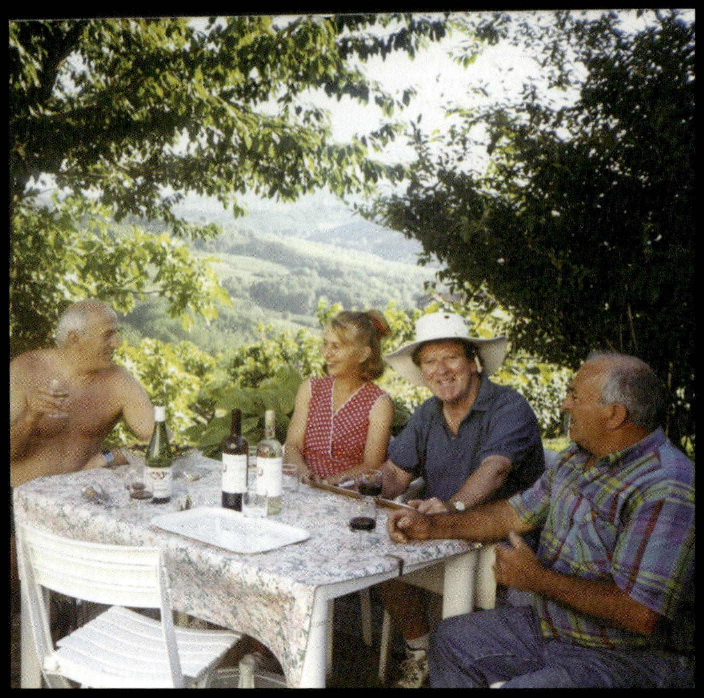

Mario Gerlotto, Caterina, Alan and Gigi, Piemonte

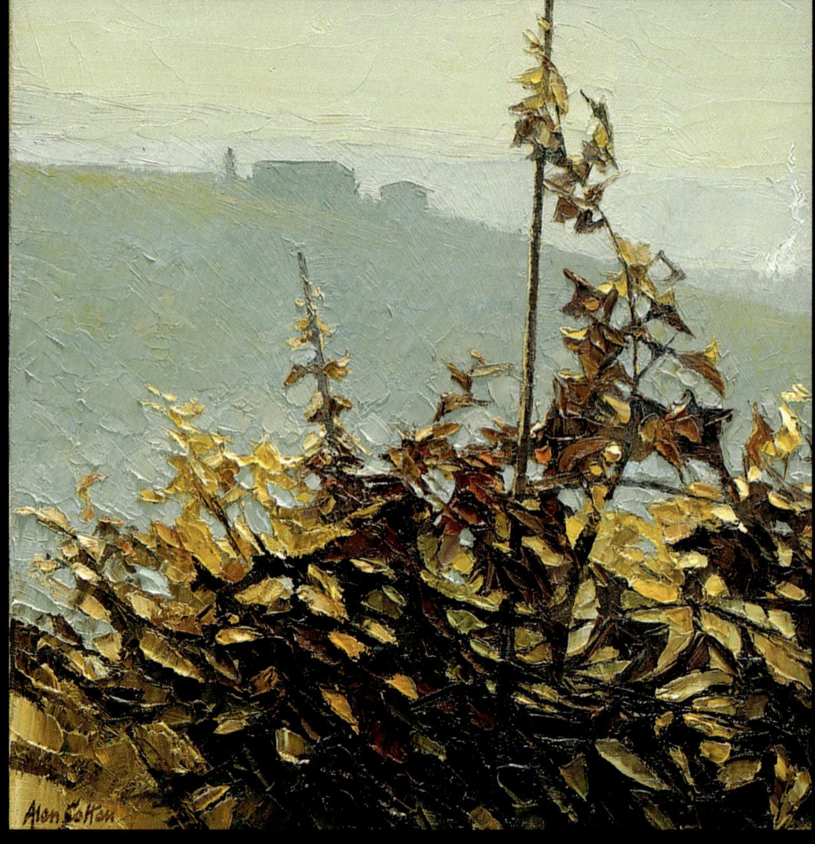

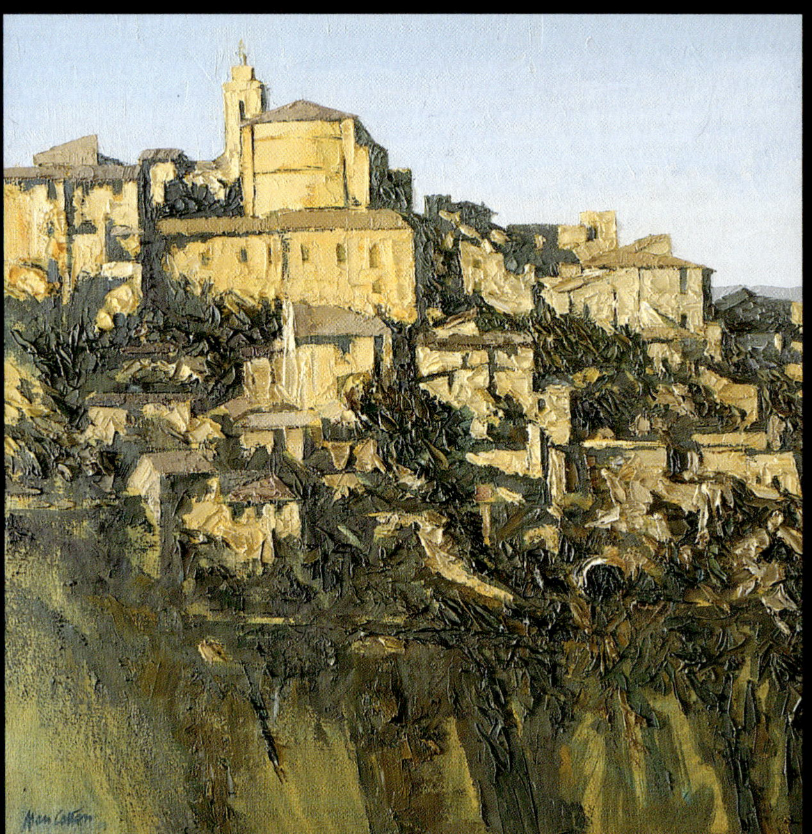

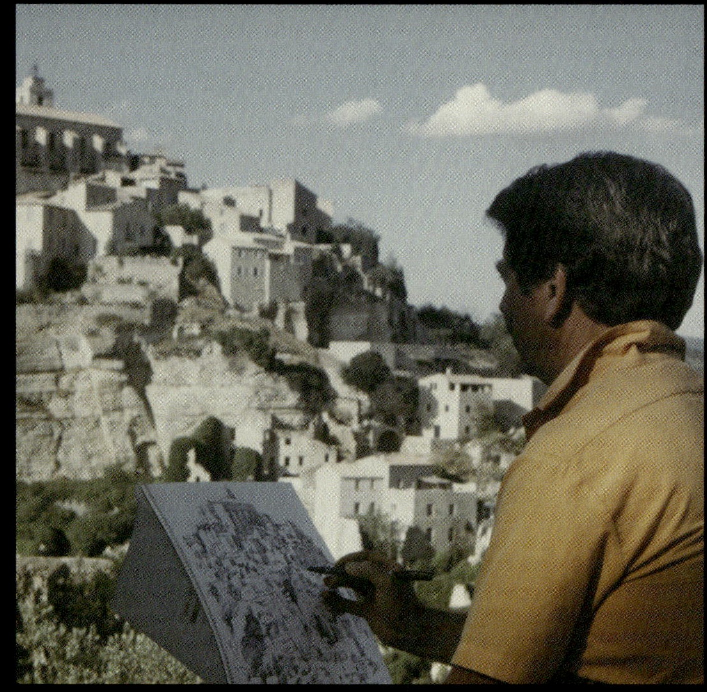

Gordes, Provence

range of colour in the landscape, from pinks and ochres to terracottas and purples. The fertile land at the base of the Troodos mountains produced plants with exceptionally vivid colouration. Brian Hoskins sent Alan up above the Troodos mountains in a helicopter and flew him around the Cypriot coast, where hidden temples could be seen beneath the water. Cyprus gave Alan both a higher colour key and a more rhythmical landscape than the geometric shapes of Provence. He was so fired up by images from Cyprus that, back in the studio, he quickly made eighteen very large paintings. With plants in the foreground set against distant fields and hills, these pictures related compositionally to his important early painting *Barley Field with Teasels and Thistles*, painted under the influence of Alan Reynolds, but showed a new confidence in structuring vast receding tracts of land, from immediate foreground to the far distance. It was two glowing, golden paintings of Cyprus that so enthralled Martin Bralsford and started him off collecting art.

The Piemonte region of northern Italy has become another of Alan's favourite painting haunts, giving him yet another new colour palette. It was at the insistence of his friend Mario Gerlotto, a local Devon restaurateur, that Alan first travelled to Piemonte. Sensing that Piemonte might provoke an artistic breakthrough, Mario Gerlotto had for years tried to persuade Alan to come and see the hills and vines of his native region and of his home town, Serravalle Langhe. Finally yielding to pressure, Alan accompanied Mario to Piemonte. There he was introduced into a community that became, over time, almost a family circle. He got to know all the locals, who followed his progress with interest and pride, delighted that their beautiful countryside was being celebrated in paint. For the opening of Alan's exhibition, *Predominantly Piemonte*, many Piemontese came to London to see the finished work. The mayor of Serravelle Langhe, who contributed a foreword to the exhibition catalogue, described how truly he felt that Alan had captured the essence of the place. 'His works of art are a canticle of our hills, they are the ecstasy of warm autumn colour diffused by the tenuous mists which embrace our small villages.' In his commentary in the catalogue Alan described his fascination with this little-known part of Italy. 'I love particularly the patterns of the landscape. This is a wine-growing region, the region of the renowned Barolo wine, where the vineyards of the nebbiolo grape create wonderful rhythms, following the contours of the hills. In the autumn… the intensity of the warm colours was something that I had never experienced before. The colours with the light through them appeared fluorescent – burnt orange, purple, carmine, through to viridian to the palest lemon.' Piemonte became the inspiration for several series of paintings in which Alan depicted aerial perspective as never before, finding soft new colours to describe the layered hues of rolling hills and valleys as they disappeared into the misty distance.

Alan thrives on contrasts, and needs a balance of different landscapes to keep him motivated. Often when painting Mediterranean scenes in his studio, he finds himself longing for the cool colours of Ireland, and vice versa. To contrast with the hot colours of the South of France, Ireland provides him with the necessary cool tonalities. Paintings of Ireland call for subtle mixes of blues, greys and greens, and compositionally the land presents new challenges. Whereas in Provence Alan takes a bird's eye view over large tracts of land, in Ireland the constantly changing skies that dominate the landscape tend to push his painted horizon downwards. As he noted in his catalogue to the exhibition *A Sense of Place*, 'the more I painted in Ireland, the more I became aware of the sky, and in my latest series of paintings the horizons have dropped lower and lower, the landscapes have become less important than the skies. The clouds themselves are fantastic shapes. Dark foreboding clouds have brilliant light glinting from behind them.'

Going drawing in Ireland seemed to be all about waiting, and this made it both frustrating and elusively attractive. Where a Mediterranean landscape spread out unchangingly and invitingly, the Irish countryside could only be seen in brief bursts of light and needed patience and persistence to discover its special beauty. In his exhibition entitled *Paintings from Ireland and Elsewhere*, Alan described in detail the extraordinary appeal of Ireland. 'The clouds always seem to be coming in off the Atlantic and creating wonderful contrasts of light and shade. The landscape can be incredibly sombre and it seems almost like the end of the world – the lighting is flat, the rain's coming down and then suddenly the mists all move away and you get great streaks of light across the landscape like a spotlight illuminating it and there's all the magic, the magic of colour, the magic of form. I love the simplicity of the landscape, the way that the lanes seem to cut a contour through it and create all these sorts of walkways and the cottages are very simple, very elemental, very basic and visually dynamic. Always you are aware of the people, even those long gone. Derelict cottages stand abandoned, but the walls surrounding them, the old outbuildings and rusting implements all tell a story. I can imagine the way in which people had to combat against the harsh conditions. I think it's all these ingredients put together which makes for a very dramatic landscape tied in with its history as well.'

In his zest for exploring remote environments for new subject matter Alan frequently gets into scrapes. In a recent trip to Donegal a little farm track leading into the hills tempted him onwards. He and Pat proceeded along it in their hired car, high grass between the deep ruts beginning to brush the underside of the car. As Alan drove around a bend

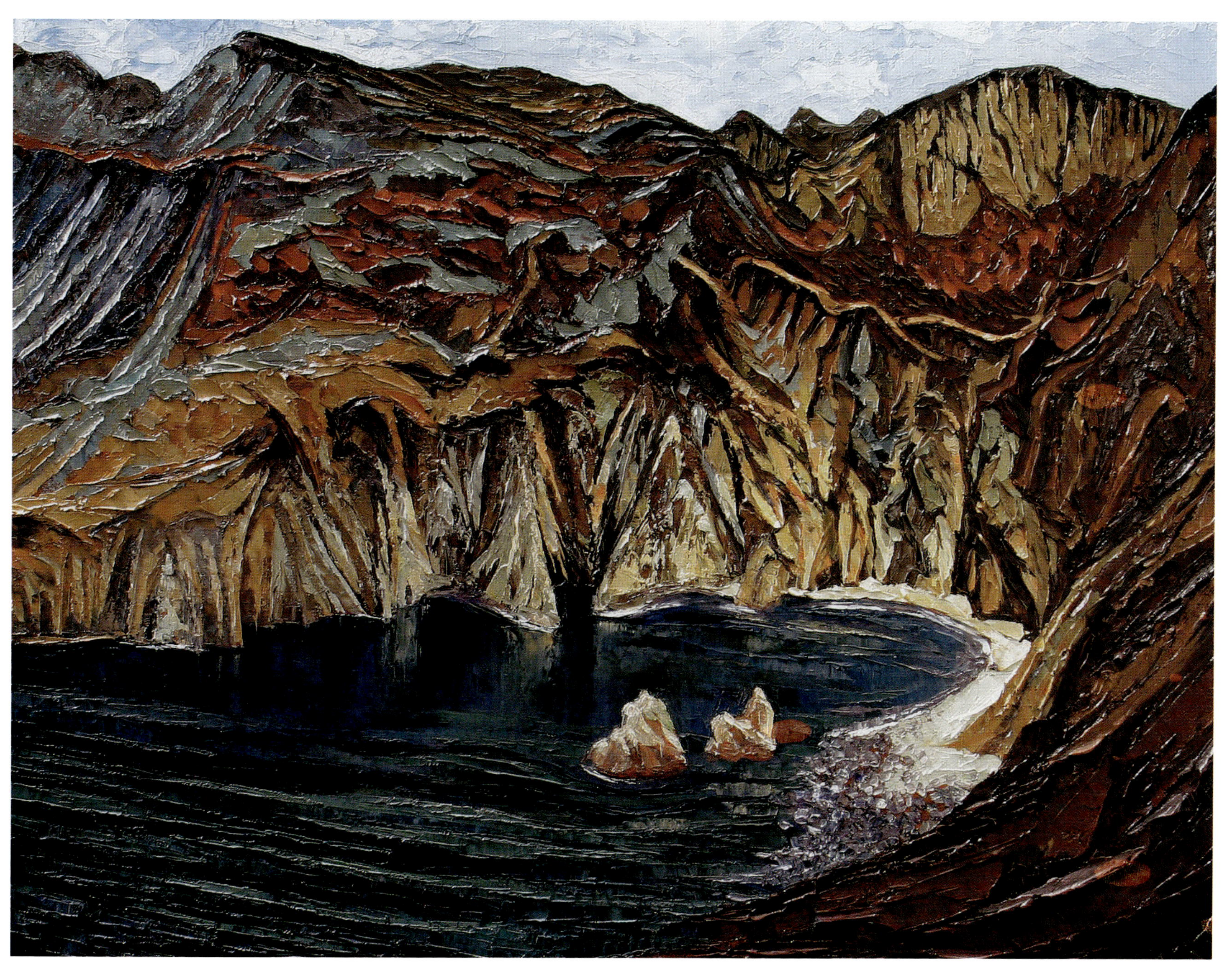

Co Donegal – Slieve League in Evening Light
oil on canvas 40 x 50 ins
Collection University of Exeter

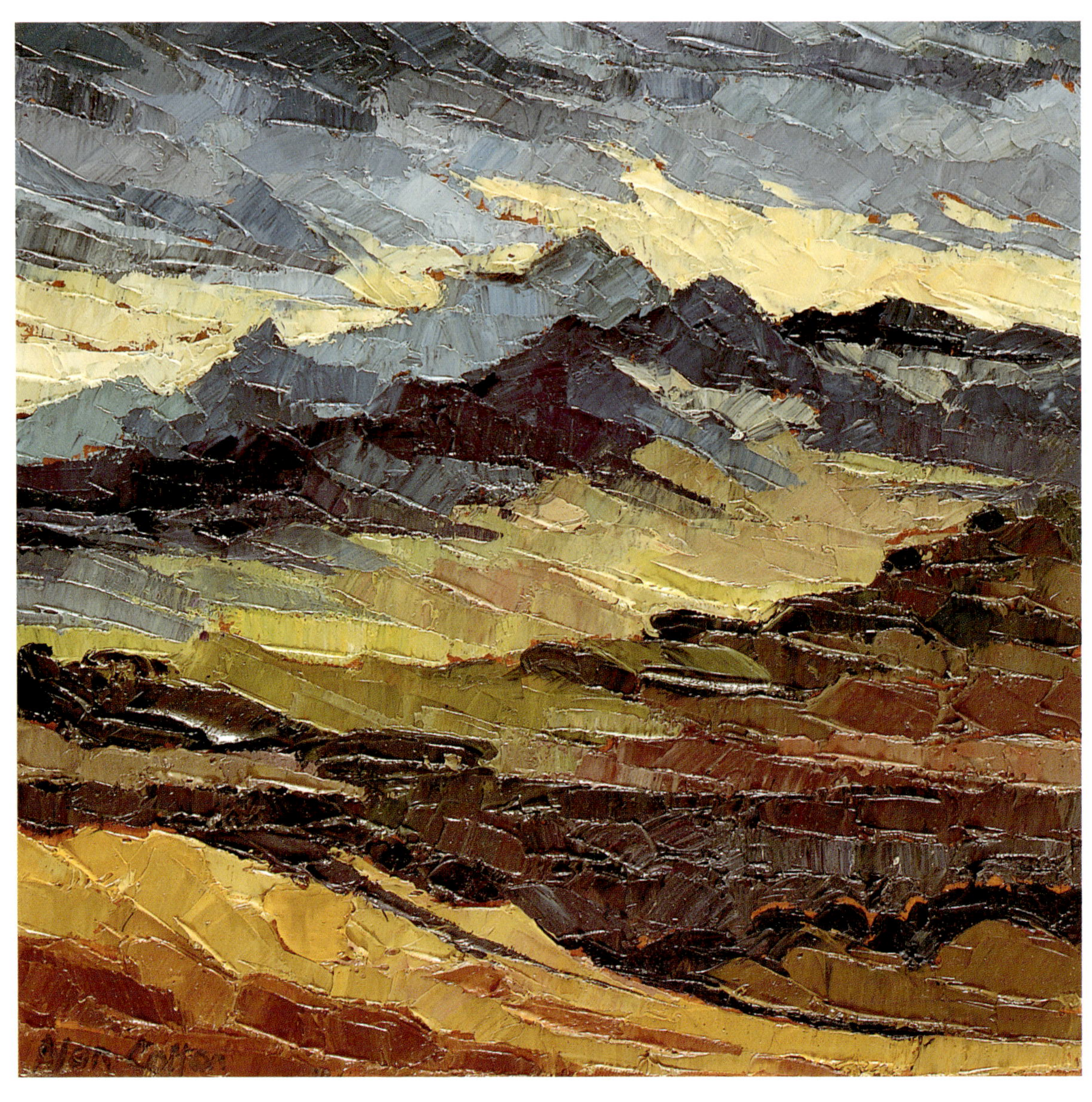

Fiji – Stormy Skies Over Viti Levu
oil on canvas 36 x 36 ins
Collection HRH The Prince of Wales

he could see water lying in what he thought were deeper ruts, but suddenly the car flipped nose down into a bog. It was firmly stuck. Alan took off his shoes and trousers and spent an hour and a half carrying rocks and dropping them into the bog, while Pat collected branches, to lay something firm under the wheels. As Alan related, 'it was just like a comic film. When we had improvised some sort of firm base, I knew we had only one shot at getting the car out so Pat did the driving while I tried to lift it, and all the mud shot out and covered me from head to foot. We had no luck at all extracting the car, and it was late afternoon and there was no mobile phone reception, so I persuaded Pat that we should walk on and try and find someone. There was nobody around so we started walking back and came to a house, but it was derelict. Another house had nobody there so we walked on, beginning to get very tired. Finally we came to a farm where a young chap was doing something to a tractor. I told him 'we have a bit of a problem – we're stuck in a bog.' He said 'I'll call my brother – we'll take the tractor and try and get your car back. Meanwhile sit in the house.' An hour went by and nothing happened, but after an hour and a half we saw our little jalopy coming down the track followed by the tractor. It was covered in mud and the man asked "how on earth did you get down there, we had a right job getting it out?" I told him that I was a painter and that's why I went down the track. They were amazingly kind and wouldn't take any money for their help.'

Perhaps the most unusual chance to explore new painting places came when, in 2005, Alan Cotton accompanied The Prince of Wales on his tour of SriLanka, Australia, New Zealand and Fiji. Alan had been at a Private View at Messums' when a telephone call from Clarence House came through. The Prince had seen and liked Alan's work and wondered if, when a suitable occasion arose, he would care to go on tour with him. For a long time nothing happened, and then came an urgent invitation, necessitating hectic last-minute preparations. As well as drawing materials, there were suits, ties and evening wear to buy for a tour of two and a half weeks. Alan met the Prince for the first time as they embarked for the flight at RAF Lyneham. The royal party flew directly to Columbo and proceeded by helicopter up the SriLankan coast, where the Prince talked to people who had suffered and visited the aid agencies that were dealing with the after-effects of the tsunami. Throughout the tour Alan participated in all the events, meeting people with the Prince. Because the Prince was so busy there was very little time to draw or paint, and any discussion of painting was in small snatches of conversation. Alan's hope that they would sit down together to draw never materialised. His problem was trying to get any of his own work done. It was difficult to detach himself from the constant round of activities such as the tour of the Royal Perth Hospital's Burns Unit. And when he could sneak a few moments, neither the Governor's gardens in Perth nor the Botanical Gardens seemed inspiring subjects. Although Alan enjoyed the various visits and all the accompanying ceremonial, the same proved true of Melbourne, Canberra, Sydney and even Alice Springs where the temperature was over 40 degrees. It was when the royal party flew to South Island New Zealand that for the first time Alan found his subject, in the albatross colony around Taiaroa Head, near Dunedin. He was able to detach himself from the other activities and draw. Unfortunately, sitting drawing in a suit on a cliff tore all his trousers. The result of this short but intense day's drawing was a fine series of clifftop paintings, in which he almost seems to evoke the wind. He remarked that he was 'aware of a musical experience, almost like a symphony, while I was doing the drawings.'

The Prince of Wales wrote a foreword for the catalogue of Alan's 2006 exhibition, which featured many paintings resulting from this trip. In it he mentioned that 'among the memorable spectacles he has captured is the colony of Northern Royal Albatrosses at Taiaroa Head in New Zealand, and the dramatic coastline that provides a setting for them. He has managed to evoke very powerfully the evocative sight of the albatrosses, majestic in flight, soaring on the updraughts about the cliff edge. Other paintings are of the wild seas, pounding the coastline around the headland. In Fiji Alan told me that the people, events and landscape provided him with a tremendous source of inspiration. He was able to travel up into the mountains at a time of rapidly changing weather, where the dark clouds and brilliant passages of light gave him the material for a series of smaller, but dramatic paintings, all done with consummate skill using a painting knife.'

In his commentary in the catalogue to this exhibition Alan mused, 'Painting is such a thing – it's no good trying to force it. If you are massively turned on by something, that's when you want to paint. From that one experience at Dunedin and those few hours of drawing came this series of paintings, made in the studio. You work from memory, from your first-hand material – the drawings – and you certainly work from the palette. As you mix paint you are creating the colour memories of the day and the time and the light.'

A lightning trip to Fiji inspired a number of paintings. The visit to Fiji was so short that Alan had to concentrate very hard. As he said, 'usually I like to spend a lot of time getting to know a new place, but on a tour like this you have to work really hard in a short time.... When we were in Fiji in the mountains, very remote, it was a marvellous time of great storms with threatening skies and rumbling thunder and lightning... We visited some strange individual buildings made from wood each with their own animal that the locals milked.' For the Fiji paintings Alan worked on

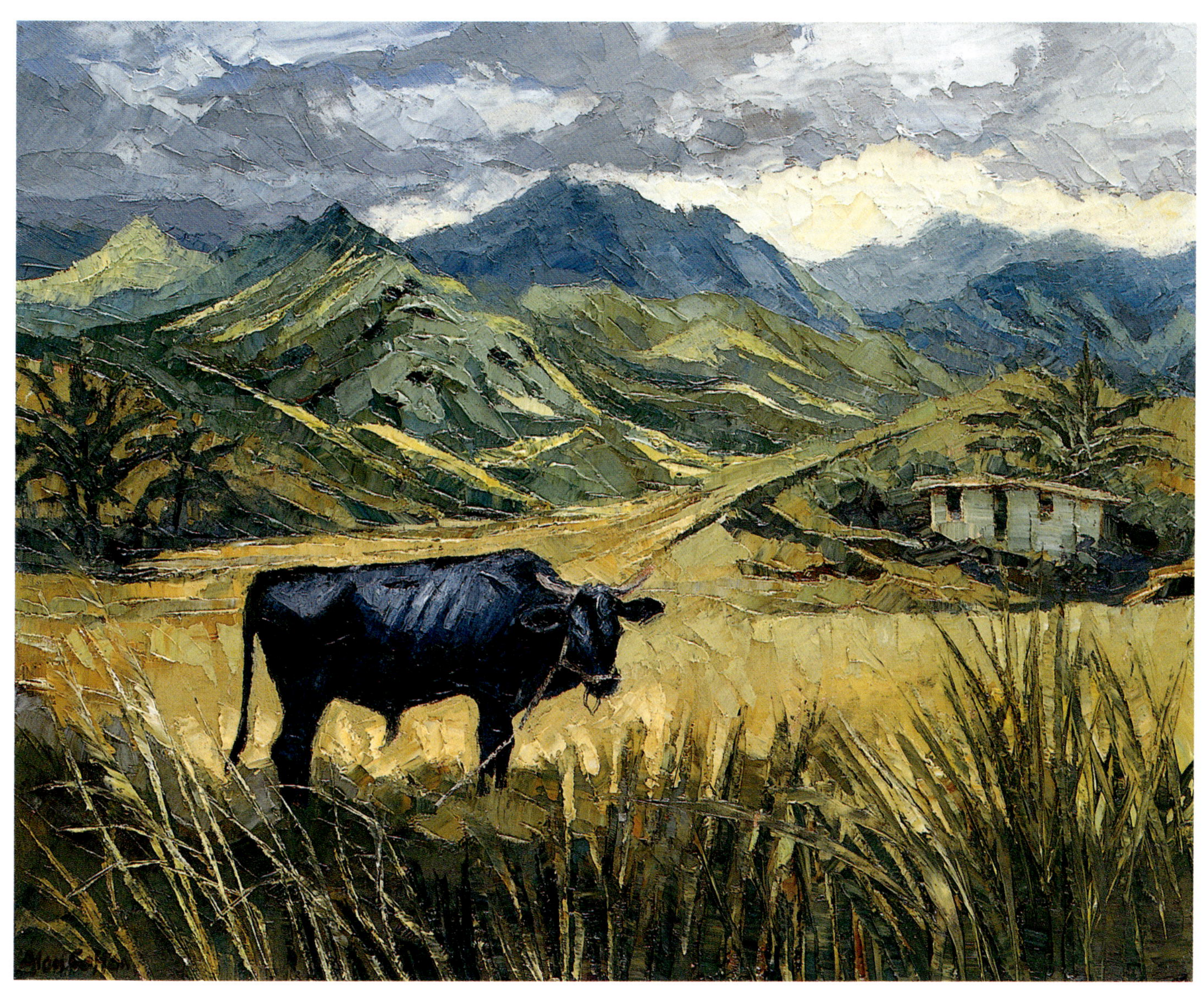

Fiji – Tethered Ox
oil on canvas 20 x 24 ins
Collection HRH The Prince of Wales

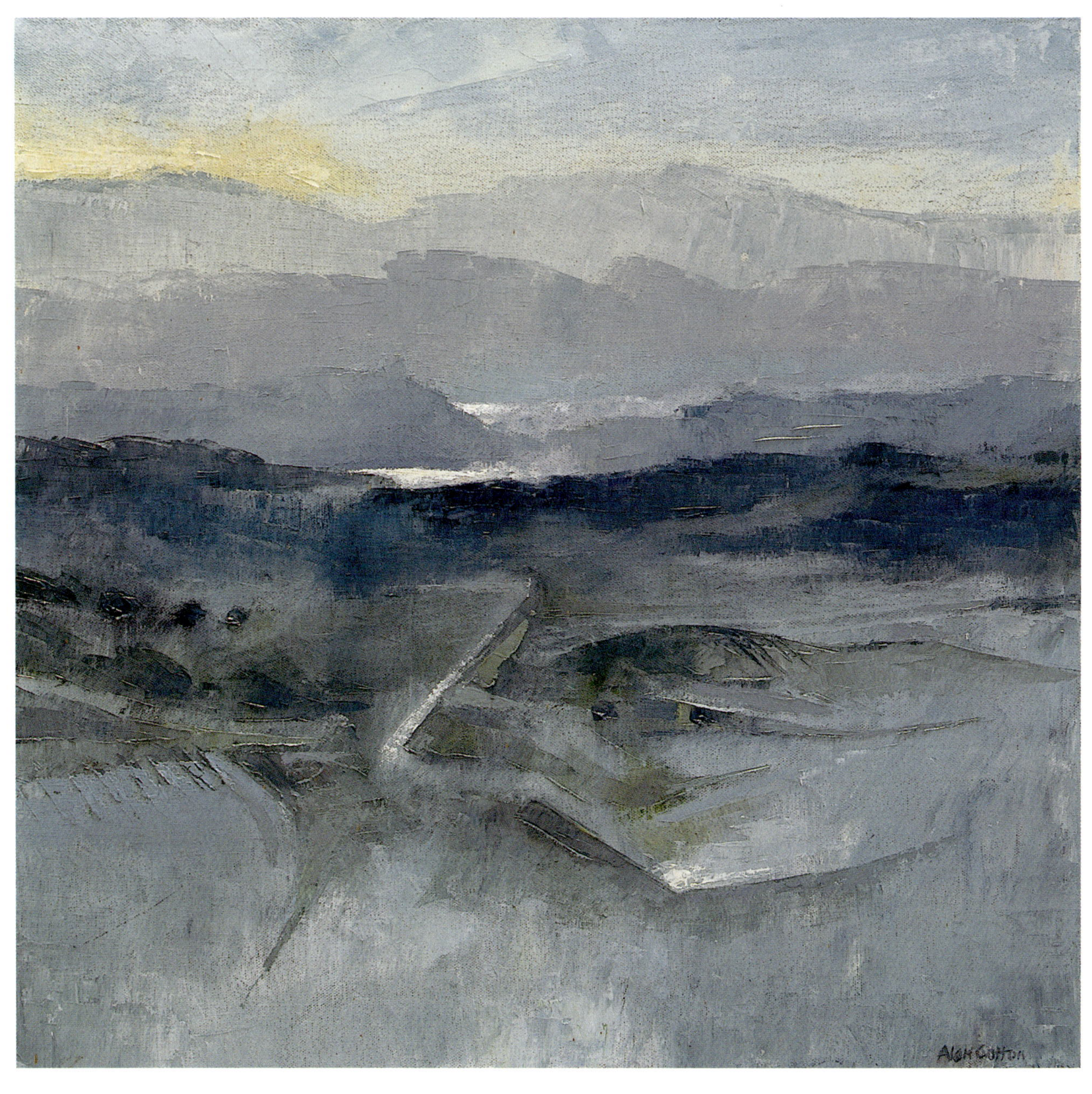

Sri Lanka – Dawn Flight through the Valleys
oil on canvas 20 x 20 ins

smallish square canvases covered with a red ground and, contrary to normal practice, laid down the lighter colours first. The chinks of red ground showing through the dark areas of paint give these pictures a jewel-like quality. They have a very different mood to his dream-like aerial views of SriLanka, and as he said, 'the mood you are in really shows in the painting… We had flown all night and it was about two in the morning our time and I was very sleepy. From the helicopter everything looked very strange. The dawn was beginning to come up and there were mists in the valleys and passages of canals.'

All these new experiences serve to stock Alan Cotton's treasury of images for painting, and at the same time open important new pathways in his life. In all his excursions abroad – to the south of France, to Venice and the north of Italy, to Cyprus, Morocco, Ireland and the Antipodes – Alan has befriended new people who have enriched his life in many different ways.

ALAN CAN NO LONGER REMEMBER the number of times he has been to Ireland to draw and collect material for paintings. He particularly loves the evenings on the west coast, where haloes of light surround all the objects in the landscape and turn the distant hills into silhouettes. This glowing composition, based on the subtle opposition of lilacs and yellow-greens, is one of several series of paintings of the Dingle peninsula.

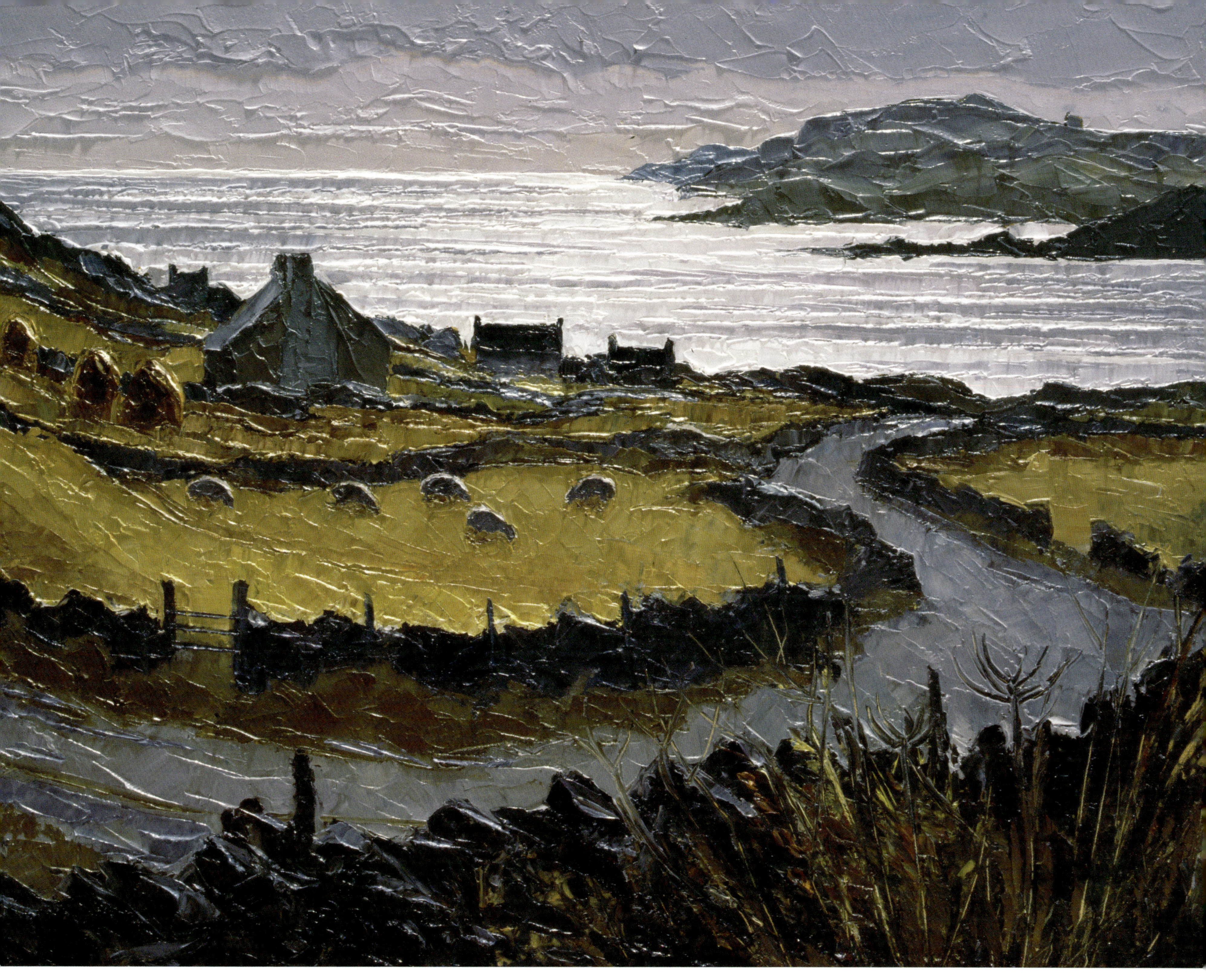

County Kerry – Grazing Sheep at Dingle Bay, 2007
oil on canvas 28 x 22 ins
Collection Tim Jones

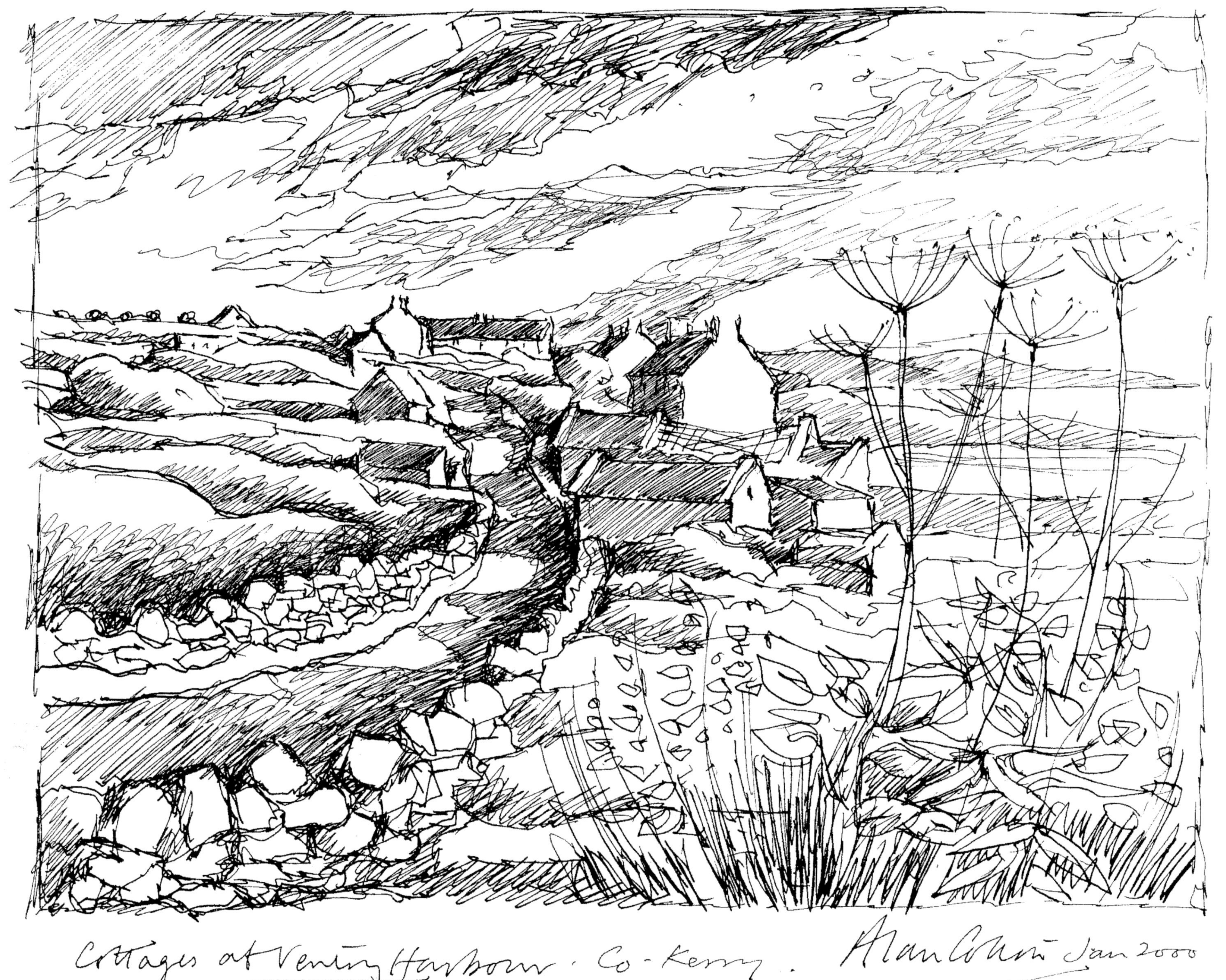

Chapter Six

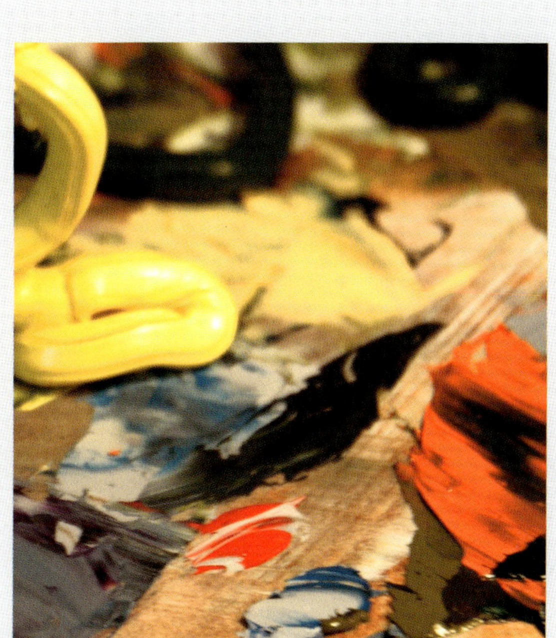

Give and Take

The Cotton family motto is 'you don't just take, you give', and Alan Cotton has been an indefatigable giver of his talent, time and energy throughout his life. From student days, when he seized any opportunity to impart his enthusiasm for art, through years of teaching amateur painters, lecturing in school and college, and setting up charitable organisations for the promotion of art, he has given a great deal. The happy result of being a 'giver' is, as he concedes, that you end up by gaining more than you give. Certainly the friends he has made along the way have broadened his experience and enriched his life, as a result enriching his work. Collectors such as Martin Bralsford, Howard and Mary Frank, Bill Holland, Brian Hoskins and Art Malik have shared their own passions and deepened Alan's understanding of the wider world. The Prince of Wales has brought him into contact with a world that Alan, as a working class boy, never dreamed existed. His art has enlarged his world, and his talent, energy and persistence have been amply rewarded.

On his home patch in Devon, Alan maintains a wide network of friends and neighbours who regularly visit him at home and appear at his studio exhibitions. Although he has lost Kevin Crooks, the closest friend he made during his filming years with BBC South West, he still keeps in touch with the BBC through Crooks's colleague Judi Spiers. Since arriving in Devon he has been involved with the affairs of the University of Exeter and even painted a portrait of a previous Vice-chancellor, Harry Kay. He has been assiduous in supporting art within the university, as Gina Cox, Curator of Art at the University of Exeter, testifies. 'Alan's heart is one hundred per cent into art, art promotion and education. He is always looking for the educational aspect of art promotion. He is not confrontational, but looks for consensus. He is patient and thorough, articulate, and a good and interesting speaker. I wish more artists were like that.' Gina admires him both for his courtesy and for his art. She sees the five paintings of Hartland in the University's collection still looking as fresh as when they were painted, and, as she says, 'the visual depth in his work encourages the viewer to step into the landscape and enjoy with him that visual experience'. Gina Cox asserts that the university was as thrilled to make Alan an Honorary Doctor of Letters (D.Litt) as Alan was to receive the award. At an award ceremony in July 2006 he received his Honorary Doctorate from Floella Benjamin OBE, Chancellor of the University of Exeter.

It was his friend Michael Morgan, former principal and chief executive of the Froebel Educational Institute in London, who was the prime mover in recommending Alan Cotton for an honorary degree. He nominated Alan on the basis of his important contribution to arts promotion in Devon and his wide network of influential friends in the

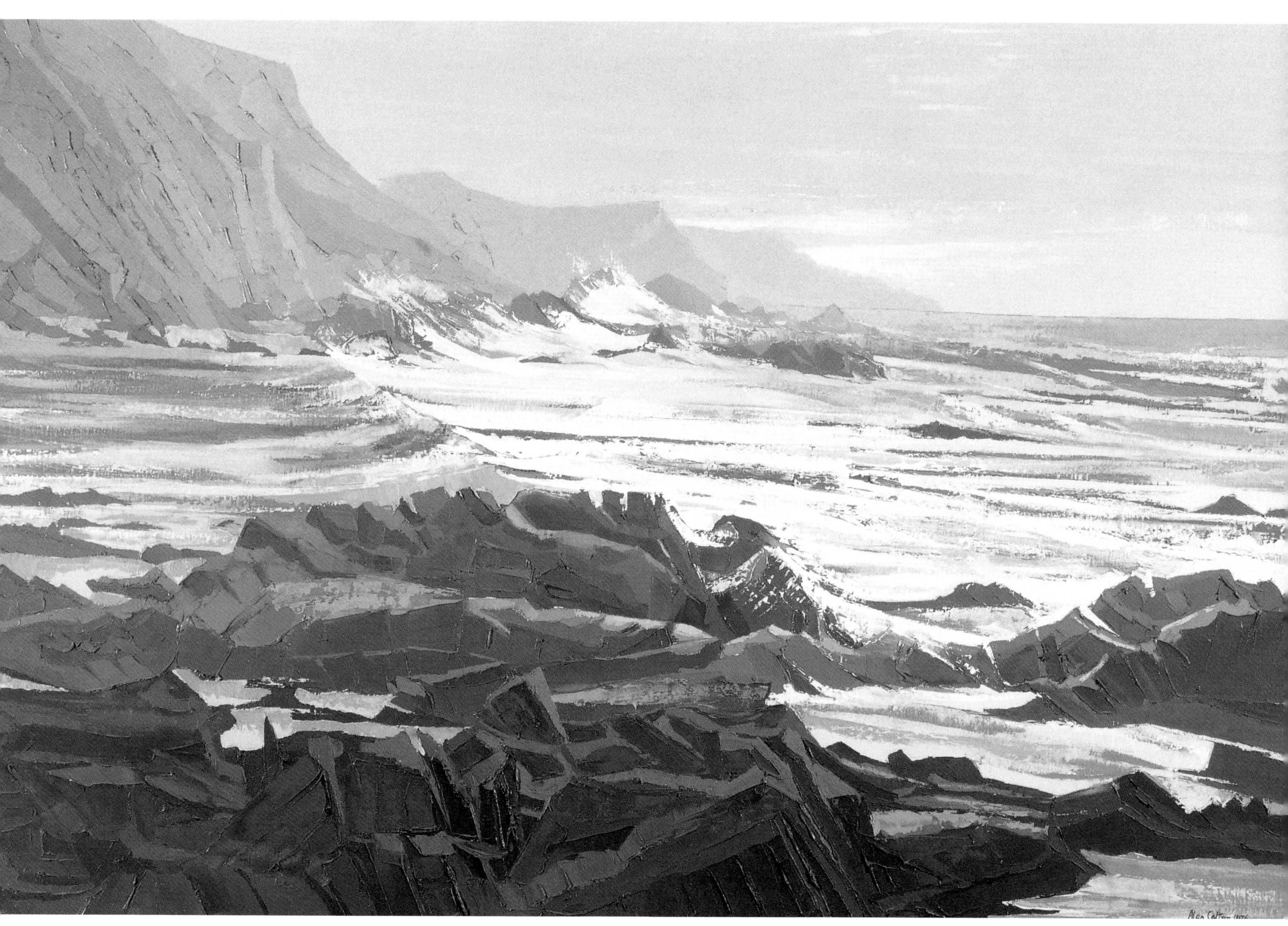

Devon – Hartland Quay, 1976
oil on canvas 40 x 60 ins
Collection Royal Albert Memorial Museum Exeter

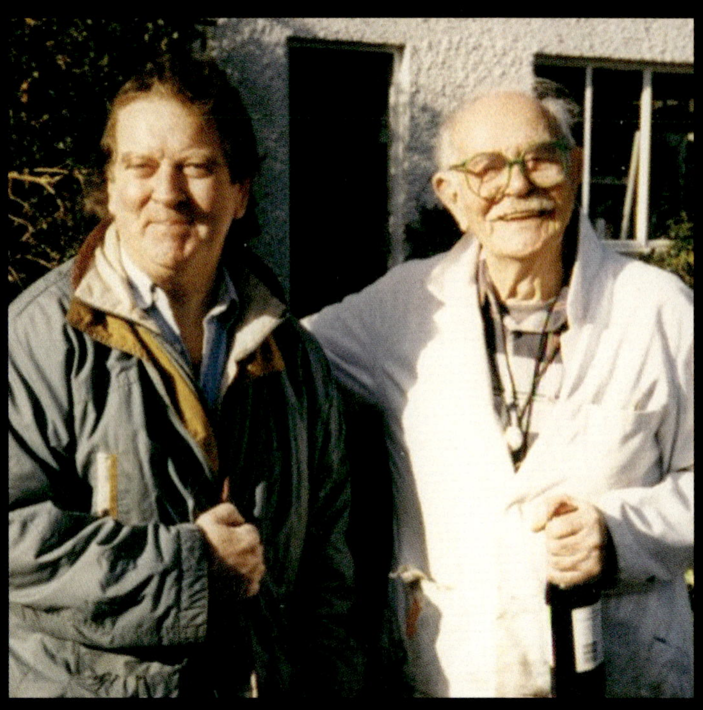

Above: with Sir Terry Frost at his studio in Cornwall.
Right: with Sir Peter Blake CBE RA

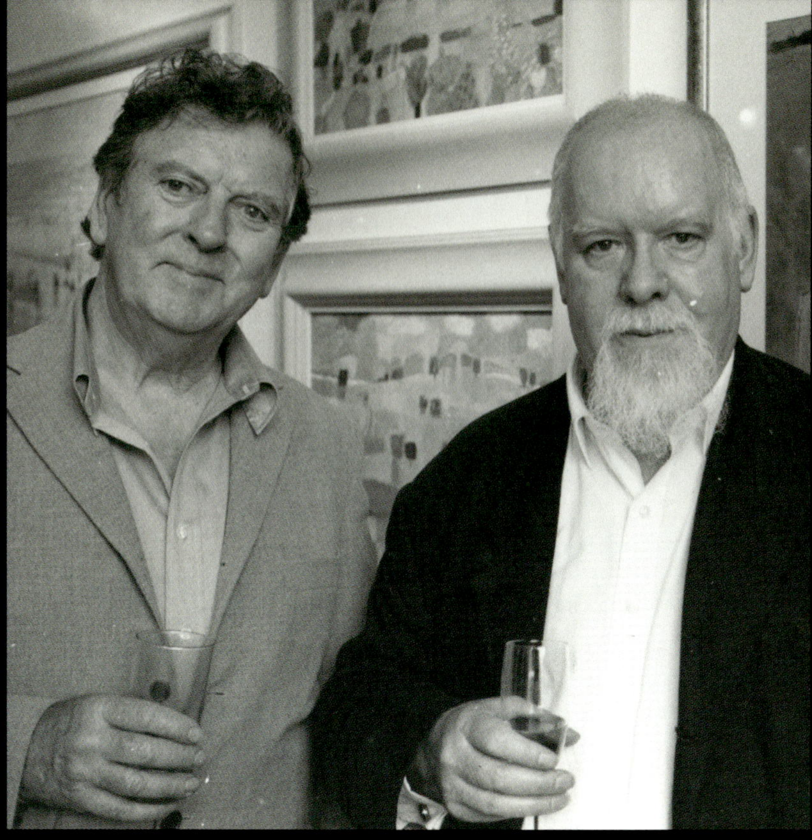

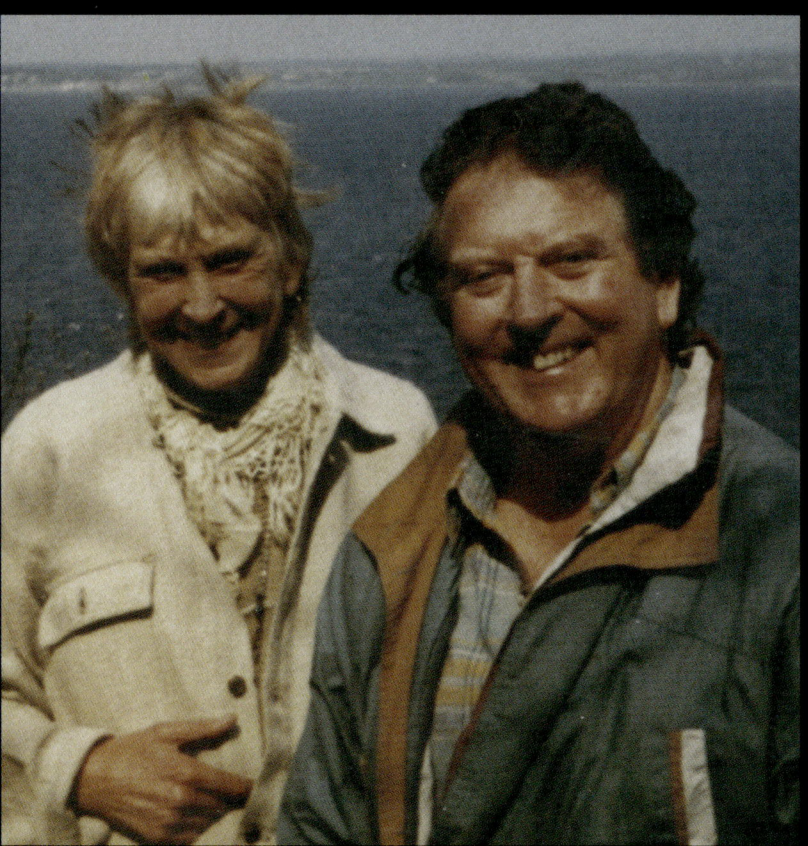

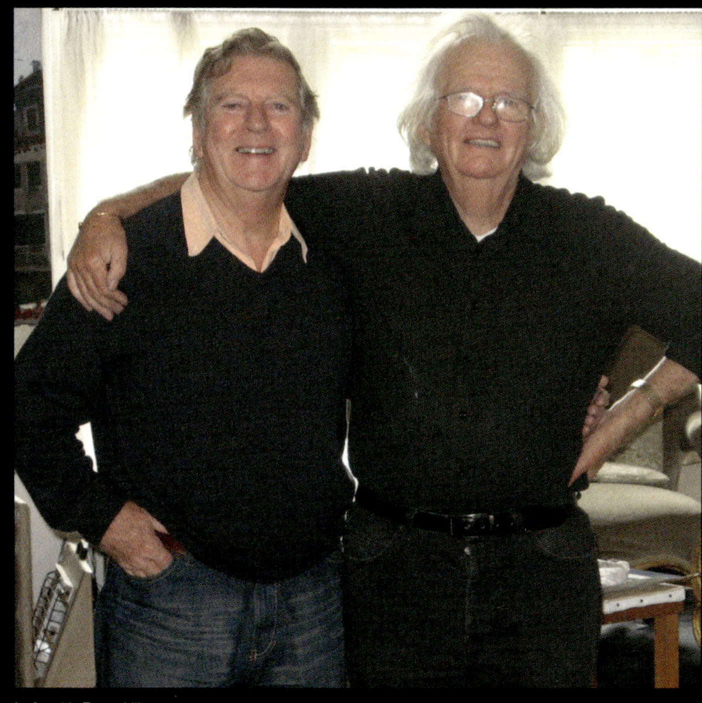

Left: with Rose Hilton
Above: with Ken Howard RA, 2009

art world. The fact that he had also been a graduate of the university, having done a Masters degree there, was a clinching factor. And at the time of his nomination Alan was President of the South West Academy, which he had helped to found, at the suggestion of the Devon auctioneer Brian Bearne. Alan became the South West Academy's first President, and with Michael Morgan and a group of distinguished artists, including Terry Frost, Peter Blake, John Miller, Robert Lenkiewicz, Alan Peters, Peter Thursby, Graham and Annie Ovenden, helped to bring the Academy into being.

Michael Morgan first met Alan at Gordon Hepworth's gallery near Crediton. After retiring to Devon Michael had taken up painting and had been invited by Gordon Hepworth to exhibit some of his work. Alan came to his Private View and commented on a painting: 'That's a very interesting piece of work and it is pursuing a new line of thought.' Michael Morgan, who was only just beginning to learn about the world of art, found Alan unstintingly helpful. As he recalls, 'Alan gave me the courage to think that I was better than I thought I was. He was the first proper painter to see my work and say "hey, hadn't you thought about…?" and to make me think differently about what I was doing. He was generous, very much an 'enabler', and keen to get me to show my work in London.'

Alan Cotton and Michael Morgan found much common ground, and when Brian Bearne, disdainful of the artistic snobbery dividing Arts from Crafts, mooted the idea of founding an Academy to bring Arts and Crafts together, they both agreed with enthusiasm. During the early stages, when Brian Bearne died unexpectedly, Alan worked day and night to get the Academy up and running, using all his formidable powers of persuasion as well as providing the initial funds. He and Michael Morgan together set up the rules and formed the constitution for the Academy. For five or six years the Academy soaked up a great deal of their time. Its educational function, laid down in the rules, was essential, and during these years the SWAc held numerous workshops, lectures and children's exhibitions. If most of the work shown in the major annual exhibitions was skewed towards figuration, the Academy stuck to its brief of being accessible, out of obligation to the departed founder who, as Michael Morgan says, 'was adamant that our purpose was to rejuvenate and make more accessible the work of professional painters as well as maintaining very high standards.' Alan inveigled his network of friends to award annual prizes for the best work in various categories, and David Messum presented an annual prize for painting.

Under Alan's presidency the South West Academy had a glorious first six years, with an annual exhibition of children's art and a well-subscribed, carefully selected annual Open Exhibition that attracted painters and craftsman

Provence – Cherry Orchard near Roussillon
oil on canvas 20 x 24 ins

from all over the South West and further afield. This was accompanied by a good quality fully illustrated catalogue, involving a great deal of editorial work. Although he has now stepped down as president, Alan still maintains a keen interest in the Academy and is still involved in its current efforts, post recession, to survive. He is still struggling to revive the Drecki lecture as an annual event, in memory of the remarkable Polish refugee Zbigniew Drecki, who bequeathed the Academy £40,000 in his will. In 2010 the photographer Noel Channon will give a lecture entitled The Poet and the Artist, describing the relationship between Ted Hughes and Leonard Baskin. As Alan recalls, 'we had huge ambition for the Academy, and what we achieved was tremendous. And it gave an extra dimension to the way I live. Because I've always been disciplined about painting, starting early so that by 2 o'clock I've done a day's work, I do have time for other things.'

During the early years of the South West Academy's life, however, the pressure on Alan's time was immense and it took its toll on family life, although, as Michael Morgan recalls, 'during those years he very skilfully managed to get his painting done'. Alan's out-of-studio time was taken up with meetings and negotiations. When his Presidency came to an end he relaxed a bit, but involvement with other charitable institutions have taken the Academy's place. Charity work of some sort has always been part of his life, and over the years he made opening speeches at hundreds of charity exhibitions, as well as giving dozens of paintings to charitable causes. He has donated a painting as well as funds to the charity *Peace One Day*, with which his son Richard is involved. Through Richard Alan has got to know *Peace One Day's* founder and director Jeremy Gilley. For a number of years Alan has also been involved with The Children's Hospice South West and is a huge admirer of the work its staff do in heart-rending circumstances. More recently he has become involved with both the University of Exeter and the University of Bath in their plans to augment the arts within their institutions and build dedicated arts complexes to house them. These charitable interests necessitate many meetings, as well as many enjoyable lunches and dinners with various grandees. Alan, ever gregarious, enjoys both the ceremony of these events and the extra piquancy of a man from his background being a part of it all.

Perhaps the grandest of the ceremonies he has attended are the fund-raising 'Icons Dinners' in support of the Duke of Edinburgh's Award Scheme. He described his first Icons Dinner, held at Windsor Castle. 'Pat and I were invited with all these celebrities – Roger Bannister, Bruce Forsyth, David Jason, Xandra Rhodes, Duncan Goodhew, Des O'Connor, David Shepherd (the other artist invited), Moira Stewart, Germaine Greer, Matthew Pinsent and so on.

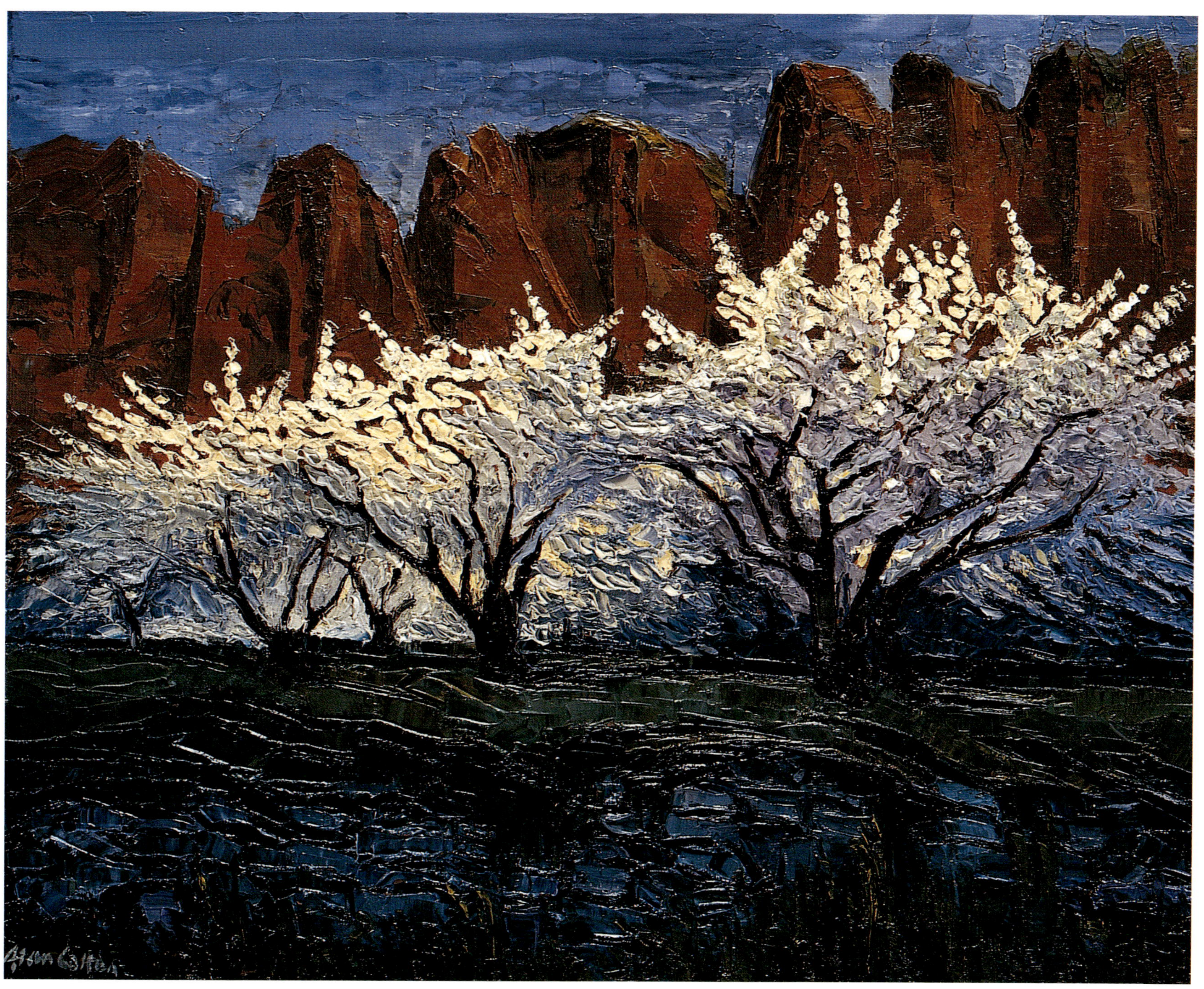

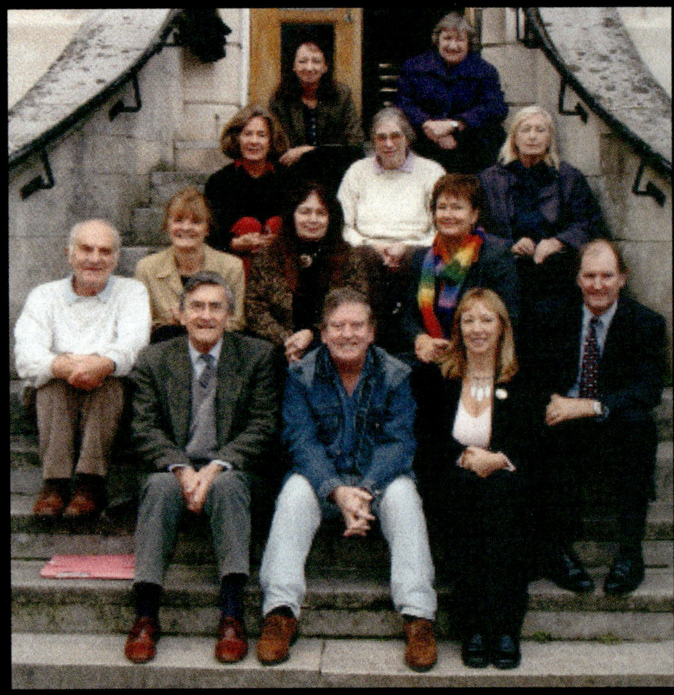

Alan (centre front) with the Trustees and the Council of the South West Academy of which he was President from its formation in January 2000 until 2006.

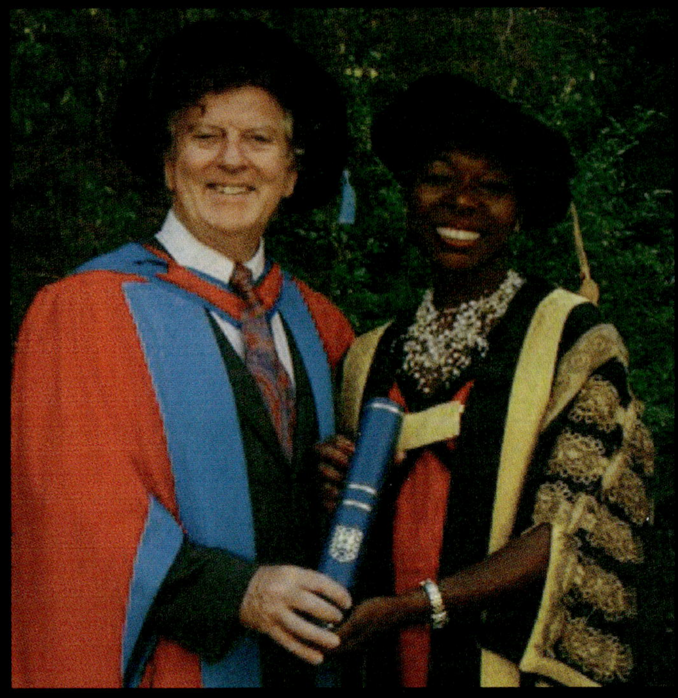

Alan receiving his Honorary Doctorate from Dr Floella Benjamin OBE, Chancellor of the University of Exeter.

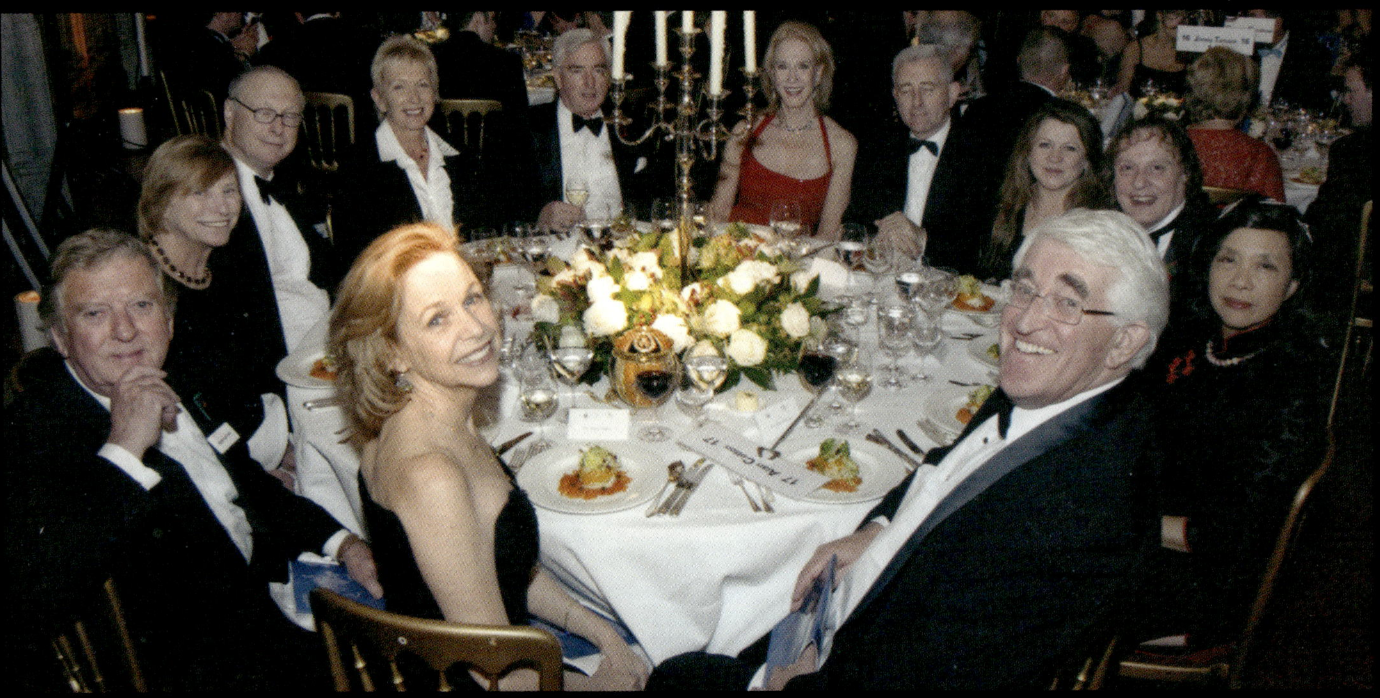

Alan (nominated as an Icon) hosting a dinner with other Icons at Windsor Castle in 2008 to raise money for the Duke of Edinburgh's Award Scheme.

Some were invited for one night, some over two nights. We met for an hour before the paying guests arrived, and were photographed beforehand. Then the Icons walked in to the Great Hall where all the guests, each of whom had paid £1000 to attend, were assembled. I walked in with Jimmy Tarbuck saying, "Jimmy, I'm not used to all this stuff" and he said, "Come on Alan, smile at everyone and walk on". 'At the dinner each Icon presided at a table for ten people, with twenty-seven tables in all. The Earl of Wessex gave an introductory talk and then former young offenders spoke of what the Award Scheme had meant to them. Because the gold and silver awards were so hard to get, one guy had gone in for the Bronze medal, and for the first time in his life someone tapped him on the shoulder and said "Well done". He went on to get the Gold medal, get out of prison, get a job and marry and have two children. This young offender was followed onto the stage by two girls who explained how the Award Scheme had changed their lives. Although you need all this celebrity stuff to raise the money it is actually about real lives that are totally changed.'

As well as with the Duke of Edinburgh's Award Scheme, Alan is also involved with the Prince's Trust, and is keen to help with raising money for its ventures. He suggested to Andrew Baker, the head of Duchy Originals, that a gathering of the tour artists might be able in some way to contribute. The Prince of Wales has taken artists on tour with him for thirty-three years, paying for them privately, and there are a good number of them who are still painting. A possible auction of donated paintings seems a promising project, which Alan would be glad to promote in return for the opportunities that the Prince of Wales has given him. His involvement with the Prince's Trust has brought him a whole new circle of acquaintances. As he says, 'These new connections have given me new experiences. Whatever you are as a human being is based on your experiences. I was utterly fascinated to be on tour with the Prince of Wales and was very impressed by the role he plays and how hard he works. My mum was a great royalist and I was brought up that way.'

For Alan Cotton, a rich texture of life away from painting is important. He is sociable and enjoys the company of others, especially when he can help people to achieve their goals. As he stresses, 'painting can be a lonely, introspective business and I'm not like that. I love being with people, helping them.' This generosity of spirit spills over into his paintings.

THIS JEWEL-LIKE SMALL PAINTING, composed on the square format that Alan particularly favours, owes its singing colour to a cleverly balanced opposition of blues and oranges. It gives an intimate view, through a frieze of bushes and trees, of the Provencal hill town of Bonnieux, where the painter Frederick Gore lived. There are echoes of Cézanne in the depiction of the pine trees in the foreground and the simple, block-like symmetry of the buildings beyond.

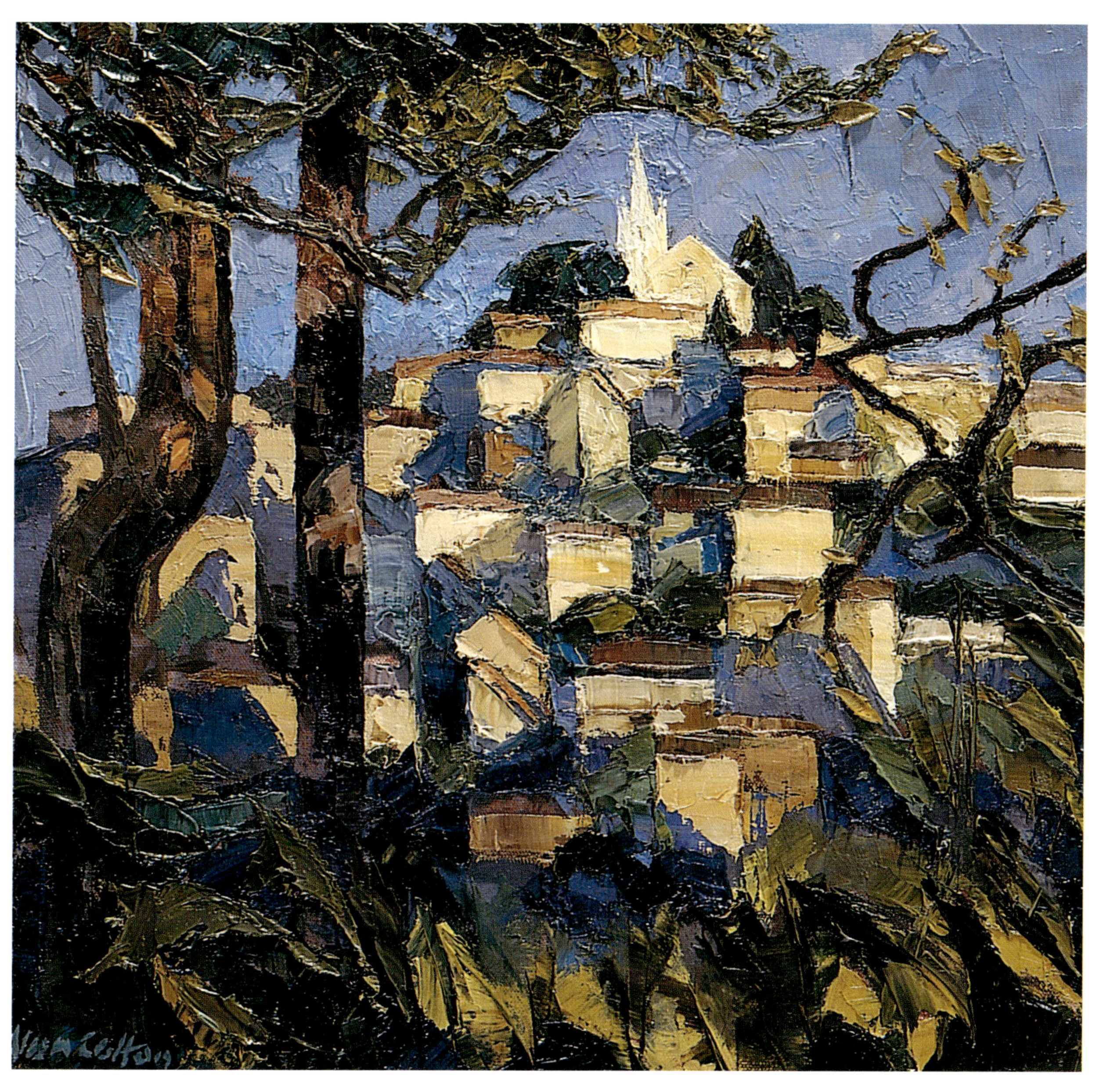

Provence – Bonnieux from the Coppice, 2008
oil on canvas 14 x 14 ins
Collection Sheila Hancock OBE

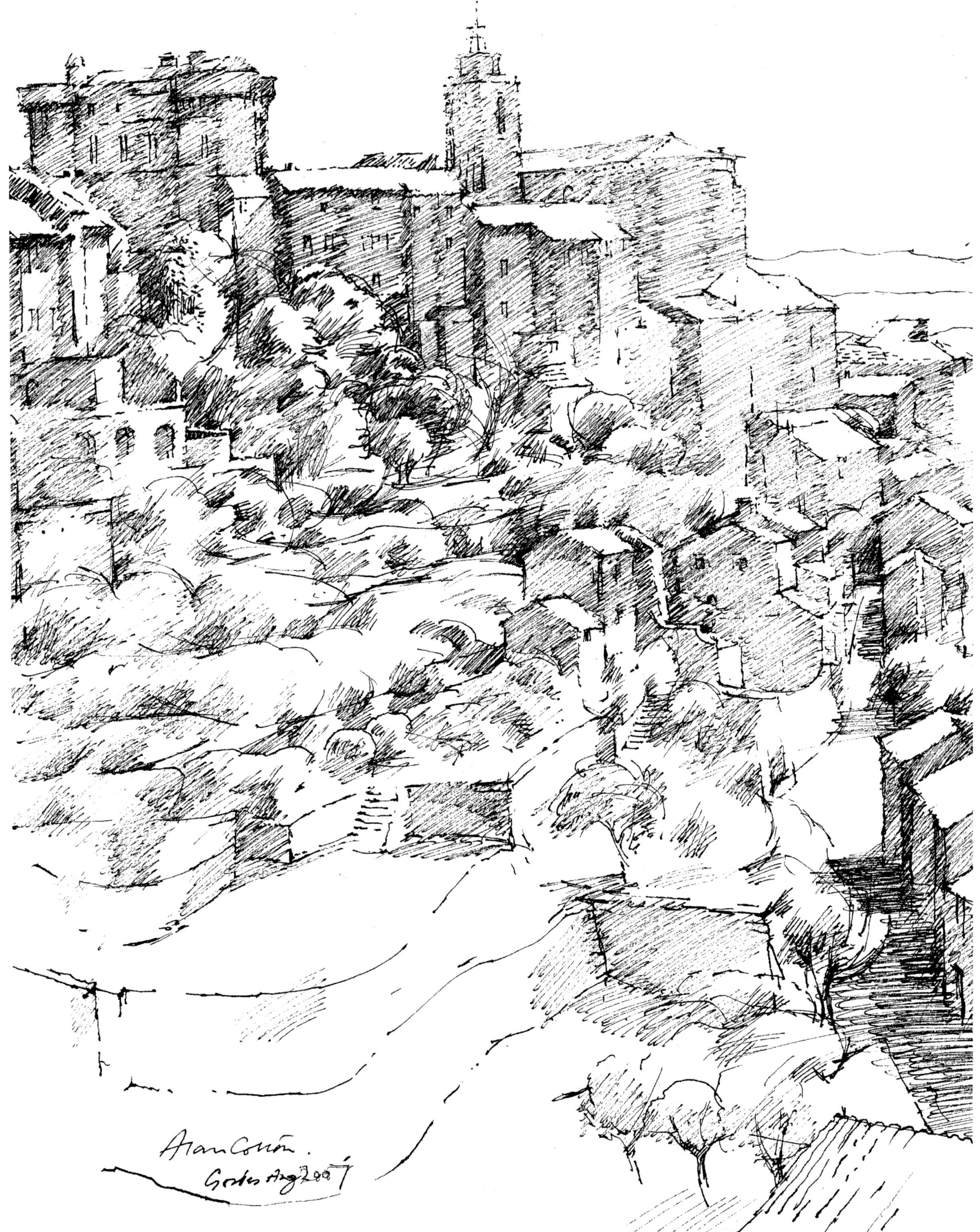
Alan Cotton.
Gordes Aug 2007

Chapter Seven

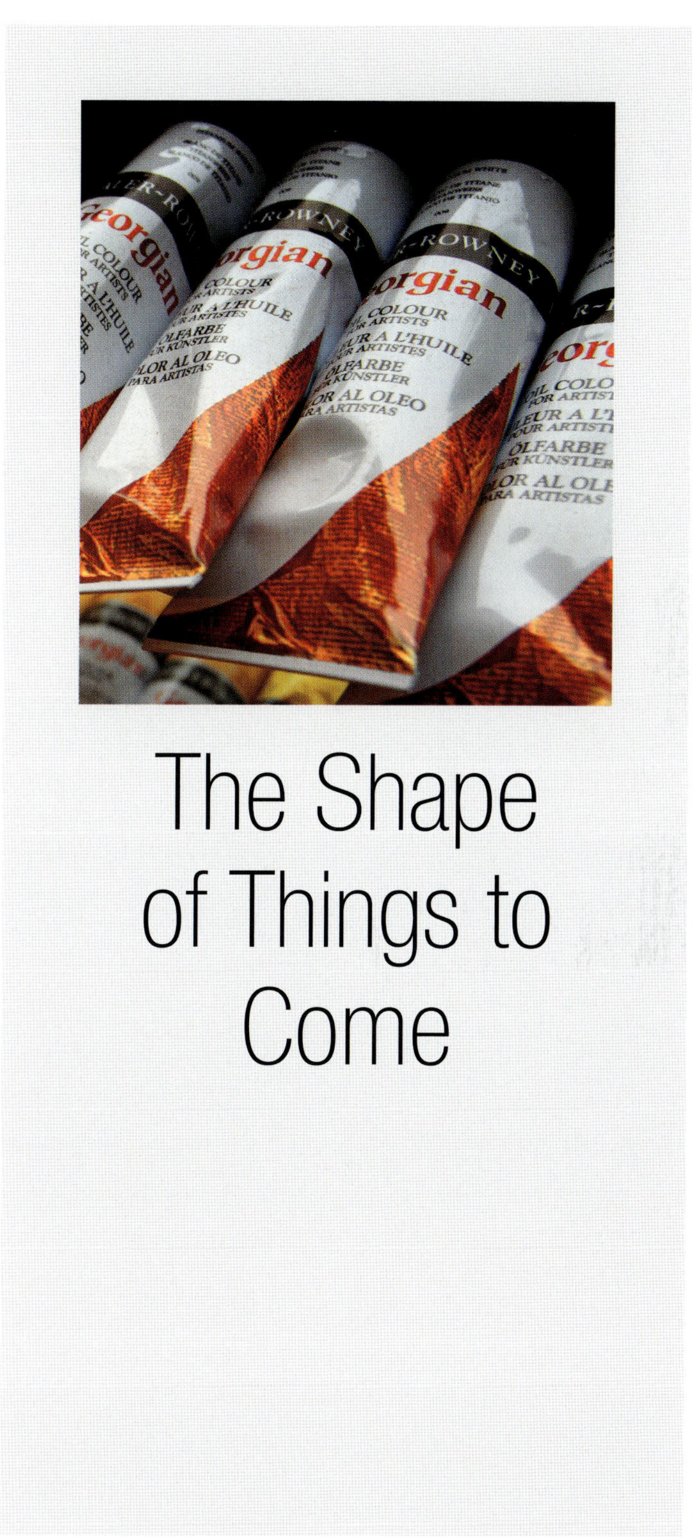

The Shape of Things to Come

With an exhibition looming, the time comes for Alan Cotton to prepare. After months of working alone in his studio, the outside world moves in and the studio becomes the hectic centre of operations. Canvases lean, drying, against the studio walls. Other canvases, already framed, are stacked in the hall. Sheaves of drawings cover the studio floor, and sketchbooks lie piled in corners. The easel holds a painting in progress. Alan is still working furiously in order to produce a fully satisfying mix of subjects to display on the gallery walls. He keeps all the current work around him until the last minute, finding that one painting can start or resolve another, or indicate the need to move in another direction to a contrasting set of images. 'At the moment I am working on these Irish paintings in very cool colours, and I am enjoying letting the red ground show through the thick paint. I'm on a roll and have painted several small, quick paintings. At these times it seems so simple, but underpinning the simplicity are all the things you have done before which allow you to do that. It's quite a decision to leave a painting, to know when to stop. The discipline is to leave the mark alone when it goes down and looks right. Some subjects suit simplification more than others. The drawings for these paintings are terribly slight and it's mostly done from imagination and memory, and a few colour notes.' The lowered horizons of his Irish paintings, with broken light appearing through massed clouds, allow Alan room for invention. These skyscapes are amongst the most abstract passages in his work.

In the studio a painting table, encrusted with mounds of dried paint, serves Alan as an extra-large palette. He has never lost his appetite for mixing oil paint. He loves the stuff of oil paint, and likes to have an abundance of it around him. Shelves full of large tubes in a great variety of colours line the studio walls. The enjoyable, 'playtime' activity of mixing paint takes him right back to his childhood and his early delight in playing with colour, seeing how the colours relate to each other. Now a lifetime of experience informs the colour choices he makes. When he looks at his drawings he has only a vague idea of which colours to squeeze onto the palette to start with, often changing his mind as he paints. 'You invent colour by mixing on the palette. The joy is to invent the colour as you go along. I like the ochre range very much, yellow ochre and raw sienna. Prussian blue is so lively that a tiny bit can tip the balance. I use titanium white and I don't use black very much. When you start squeezing this lovely sensuous material out on to the palette and start to mix it and find yourself getting into it, that's when the discovery happens. The mixing of colour is a very intuitive thing. I learnt a lot from Walter Sickert in that regard, because he has a wonderful way of pushing the colour down tonally, so that the light marks really resonate. The light that catches the figure on the top of a breast or a shoulder in his Camden Town paintings is absolutely amazing. Bernard Dunstan is in that tradition. His are quiet

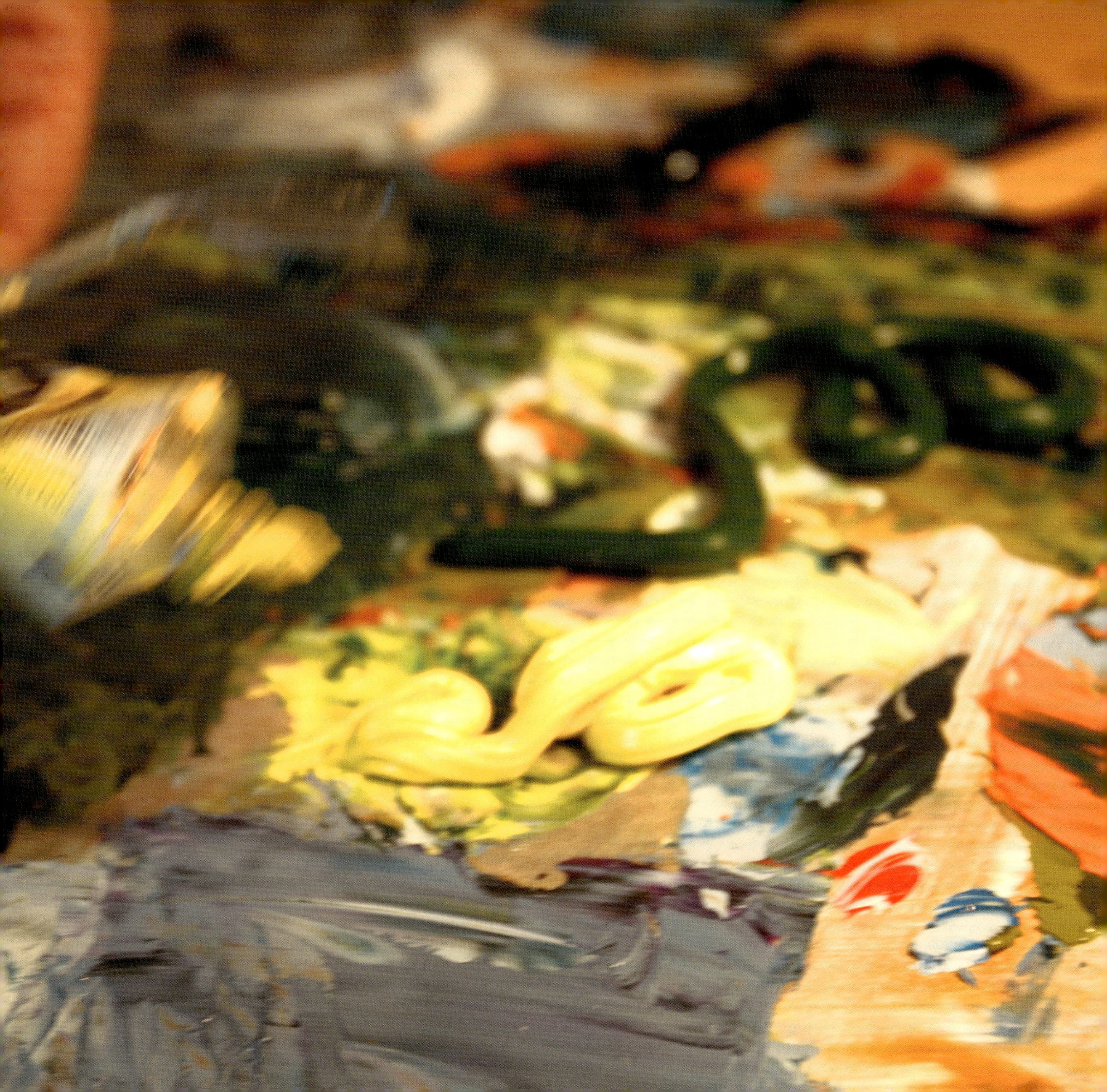

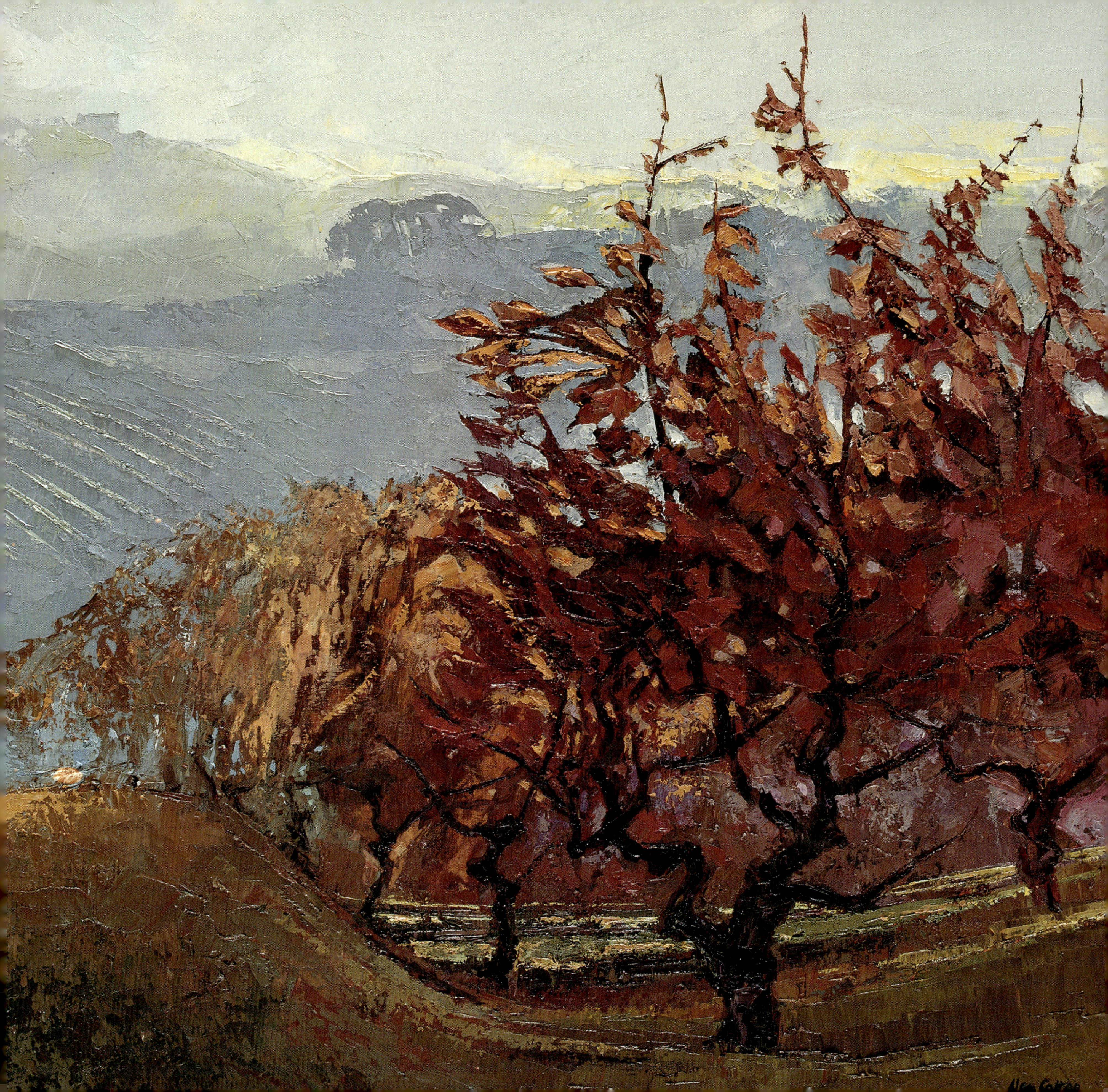

Piemonte - Fiery Vines against a Hillside
oil on canvas 40 x 36 ins

paintings, discreet, but I get enormous pleasure from them. For me the finest draughtsman is Van Gogh. The marks he made with a reed pen for foliage and fields are the same as the marks made with paint. But I believe the greatest draughtsman of all time was Degas. His drawings are so sensitive, so subtle. I love the Degas pastels in the Musée d'Orsay in Paris – it's a room full of miracles for me.'

With an exhibition a few months away, the necessary preparations begin. Writers for the catalogue are already engaged. Messum's sends a photographer to Alan's studio to record all the paintings and drawings for the catalogue, and also to take studio and location shots of the artist at work. The gallery's policy of allowing the public to glimpse the man behind the paintings helps to explain the work and boost the sales. The highly technical business of photographing the paintings takes time. In Alan's case it is vital that the photography picks up the impasto on each canvas, as this is a hallmark of all his work. For this reason the lighting is adjusted and readjusted to catch the marks of the knife edge. Although Alan lays his slabs and sweeps of paint on the canvas intuitively, in instinctive response to the nature of the land he describes, the edges of the knife-worked paint cast shadows that become an integral part of the image. Because he works in his studio under overhead lights, the shadows that fall below the ridges of paint begin to take part in creating the final image. Painted waves or cliffs hold shadow below in the same way as waves or cliffs in a sunlit landscape. And, because the finished paintings are generally seen lit from above, the impasto shadow on the canvas remains constant for the viewer. Although Alan does not plan how the impasto shadow falls, he is aware of the added depth it can give to the pictorial space. He also knows, however, that it is not to everybody's taste, recalling with amusement the comments of a man who had tried knife painting after hearing Alan lecture on the subject. When asked how he had got on the man replied 'Very well indeed. My only problem was all those nasty little wispy edges of paint, so I got a pair of scissors and cut them all off.'

As the paintings multiply around his studio walls, Alan begins to consider what mixture of imagery might enliven his exhibition. He prefers a mixture of subjects to a single theme. 'At the moment I am really enjoying the Irish work, but then I want to change completely. Another part of me says 'you used to paint in Provence and Italy – where's all the sunlight? I did go to the Turkish part of Cyprus last year, where the fields were full of golden, glowing crops and all those beautiful yellows and golds. I am getting to the point where I want to be surrounded by that in my studio. I am also thinking about Piemonte and those gentle people in Italy. Do I want an exhibition theme? Seeing some of the shows I've had where one side is a whole group of colours from Ireland, moody and dark, and the other side the colours are incredibly warm, is good. The gallery responds to that and hangs the show like that. Messums hang exhibitions so well.'

David Messum is an unorthodox dealer and his gallery is unusual in staging such a number of back-to-back exhibitions every year, producing fully illustrated catalogues for each. When he first moved to Cork Street, David was apprehensive about the hierarchical crew of dealers in the street, aware that his approach to selling art raised many eyebrows. Active promotion and overt publicity and promotion were definitely frowned upon, and this was made clear to David who was told 'my dear boy, advertising is not necessary'. All the galleries in Cork Street used to combine to hold an annual street party, and on one occasion Carol Tee managed to interest the BBC in filming it. She was firmly put in her place with the stricture 'we don't want those sort of people here'.

Messum's gallery has broken the Cork Street mould, with every exhibition both well advertised and meticulously planned. Alan Cotton's exhibitions have become cornerstones in Messum's calendar. The planning begins with discussions between Alan and Pat Cotton, David Messum and Carol Tee, after which the gallery team takes over. As David says, 'Carol always comes with me for the initial meetings, because, apart from being a nice person to have about, she takes over the organisation and processes all the contracts. Alan is unusual because he never has a contract, and he gives all the money to Pat, who looks after it all. She is a huge power behind the throne and does absolutely everything for him, quietly making his appointments, sorting out his photographs and running his life. Alan literally does not carry money on him, which is rather endearing.'

As the exhibition approaches, the whole gallery team swings into action. The outcome of each show is anticipated by all with a mixture of pleasure and trepidation. As Alan says, 'increasingly we have done well. For the gallery's sake you want each show to do as well or better than the last. You never quite reach what David would like, but nevertheless you do aspire to do well financially for the gallery. But the driving thing is the work, so that when you walk into the gallery you feel you have given it your best shot. All artists are so vulnerable, and you really worry about it. Somehow you are never quite sure, so reassurance is important. Nowadays I sell from my catalogues and I like the reassurance of knowing that I have sold a lot before the Private View. Now I would worry if I don't sell from the catalogue beforehand.' With expert photography these catalogues have become extraordinary ambassadors for Alan's work, tempting buyers from around the world. They are beautifully produced mini-books, as informative as they are visually dynamic.

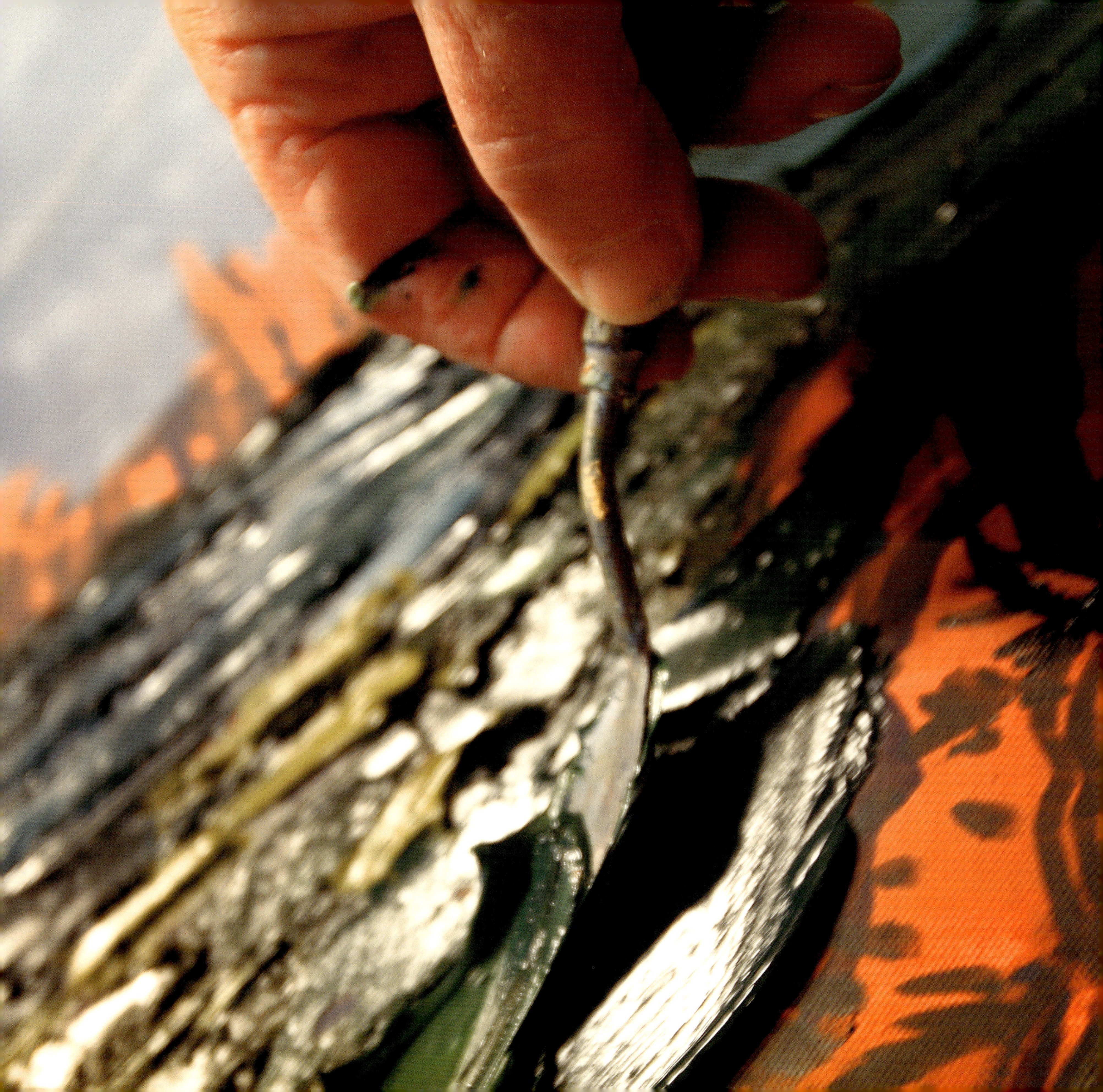

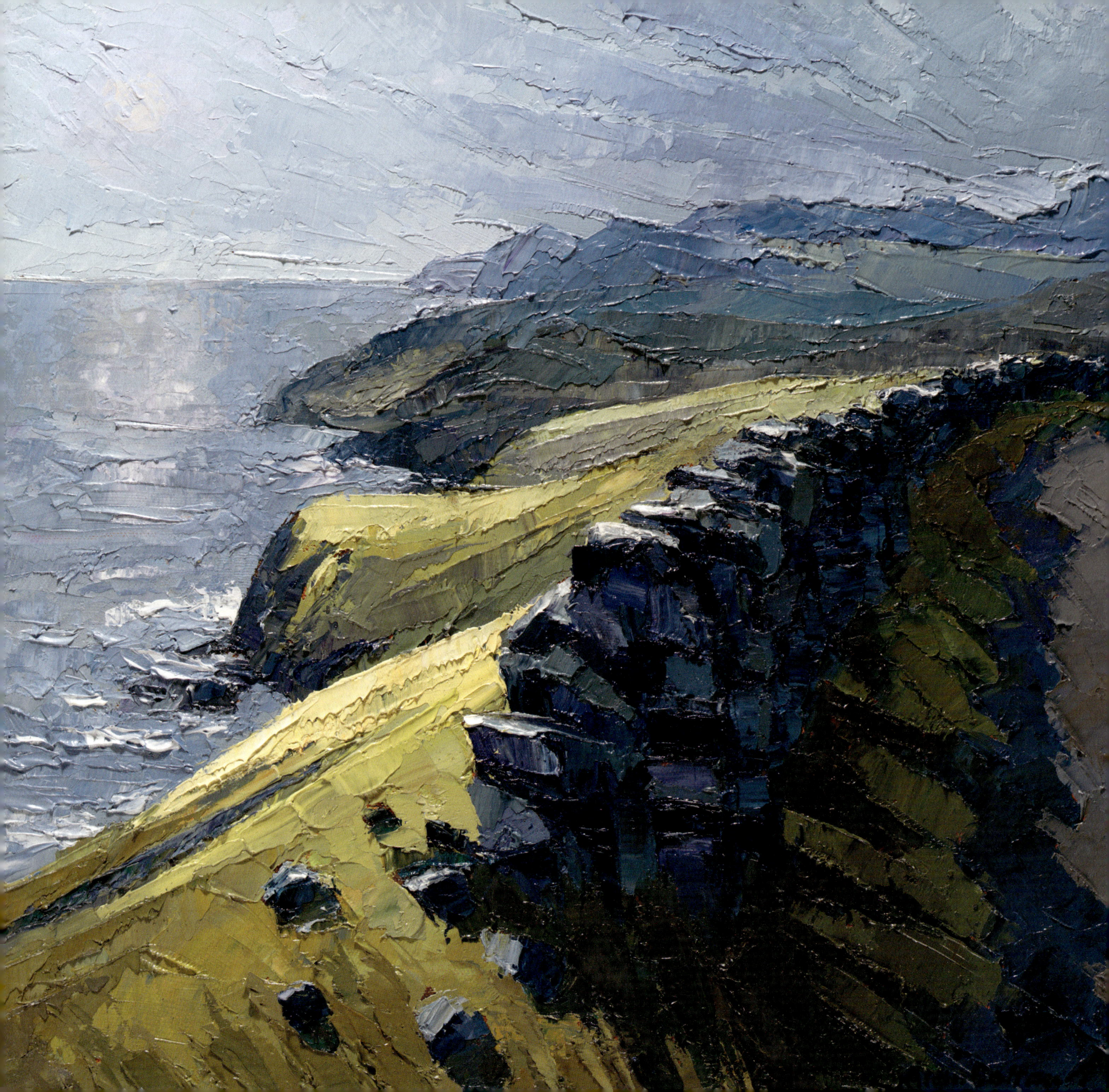

Donegal – Broken Wall along the Coastal Edge
oil on canvas 14 x 14 ins

The current show for which Alan is working is centred around his new paintings of Ireland. 'The time I had there recently was very wet and cloudy, so these paintings are all about the skies and I paint them quickly to try and capture this feeling of changing light. The land only occupies about a third of the paintings, which are about the skies and this terrific churning movement of the wind off the Atlantic. I am trying to recapture those ideas of dark, threatening skies, almost like the end of the world, and the breathtaking passage of light across the middle. The warm and cool colours are reversed, as normally landscapes have the cool colours in the distance. I am still using a red ground, and it is getting redder. It really does something for the cool colours, making them sing.'

The harder he works the more Alan finds he is learning, discovering new ways of applying paint. 'The paintings this year are more energised with the paint. Each mark I use contains a lot of information within it. Some painters might take an hour to cover the area that I cover with one mark. I'm trying to reduce it to all kinds of metaphors using different densities and urgency. The urgency of the mark is important because an action is recorded there for all to see. A slow mark, a sweeping mark, an energetic mark – all these things are there to see as a record of physical action and the painter's mood. You are trying to make a simple statement about something that is complicated. That's what I am trying to do, often subconsciously because I work intuitively. I want to paint a range of things so I need to use a variety of marks because there is some information you cannot convey broadly – it's too precise, too specific. Because it's fashionable to paint broadly, the push is to work only with big slabs of paint. I don't feel the need to be fashionable because I want to paint a wide range of things, from vast rocky cliffs to the tiniest of seedheads.'

After several months of working for a show, Alan finds that the latest paintings become more fluent. 'I don't revise much. Sometimes you get stuck and leave it. The big painting I am working on now is ninety percent finished and I'm in fear of finishing it, for two reasons, (a) it's an important painting for me, and (b) there's so much paint on it I'm afraid of disturbing the surfaces so I'm letting it dry. For me painting is a balance between the physical paint and the inspiration which started me off in the first place. I am not really an abstract painter, the work is abstracted by the way I approach it. It is hard to start and get back into painting without new ideas. It is always more exciting to do new work when I don't know if I can pull it off. In Ireland I am always chasing the light and I work really hard and get high as a kite. With Morocco I struggled to get the luminosity of the light and I treated the paint a bit like watercolour and let the white canvas show through. I don't want a limited range of marks. It would be so easy to do formulaic paintings but I don't want to do that. I have had to find my own way through.'

When asked if there are new places that he would like to explore in the future, Alan mentions India and also mountains, but with the same breath says that he really longs to go back to Piemonte, where he feels at home, as if he were part of the family. He likes to belong to a place as much as he likes it to belong to him. His old painting haunts still hold a special magic for him.

Being 'part of the family' in familiar painting grounds reflects the central importance of his own family in Alan's life. He and Pat are at the core of a family that now extends to nine grandchildren. They all meet often and share big family holidays. Alan likes to have his grandchildren staying and working with him in his studio, and has started painting with a couple of his granddaughters who show real talent. The grandchildren energise him, and Pat maintains that 'Alan will never slow down'. Alan confirms this. 'The last decade has been the most vigorous of my life. I have no concept of age being a factor. There is so much to discover. I feel that my best work is still to come.'

For Alan Cotton the future looks richly inviting. A new association with Coriander print workshop has led him into printmaking, and there he is working with Brad Faine on screenprints of some Irish images, using a multitude of colours to generate the nuances of paint and suggest the impasto shadow. He is intrigued by the techniques of colour separation, and intends to continue making prints alongside his painting. He is also deeply involved with charitable work, especially with the University of Bath's designs for a new arts complex. The suggestion that he might stage a retrospective exhibition in their new galleries offers a stimulating prospect. He is also a prime mover in the plan to gather together the Prince of Wales' tour artists for the Prince's Trust. If anything, his life is fuller than it has ever been. And at its heart is his passionate desire to celebrate in paint the world he lives in, as well as his great good luck at being alive in that world.

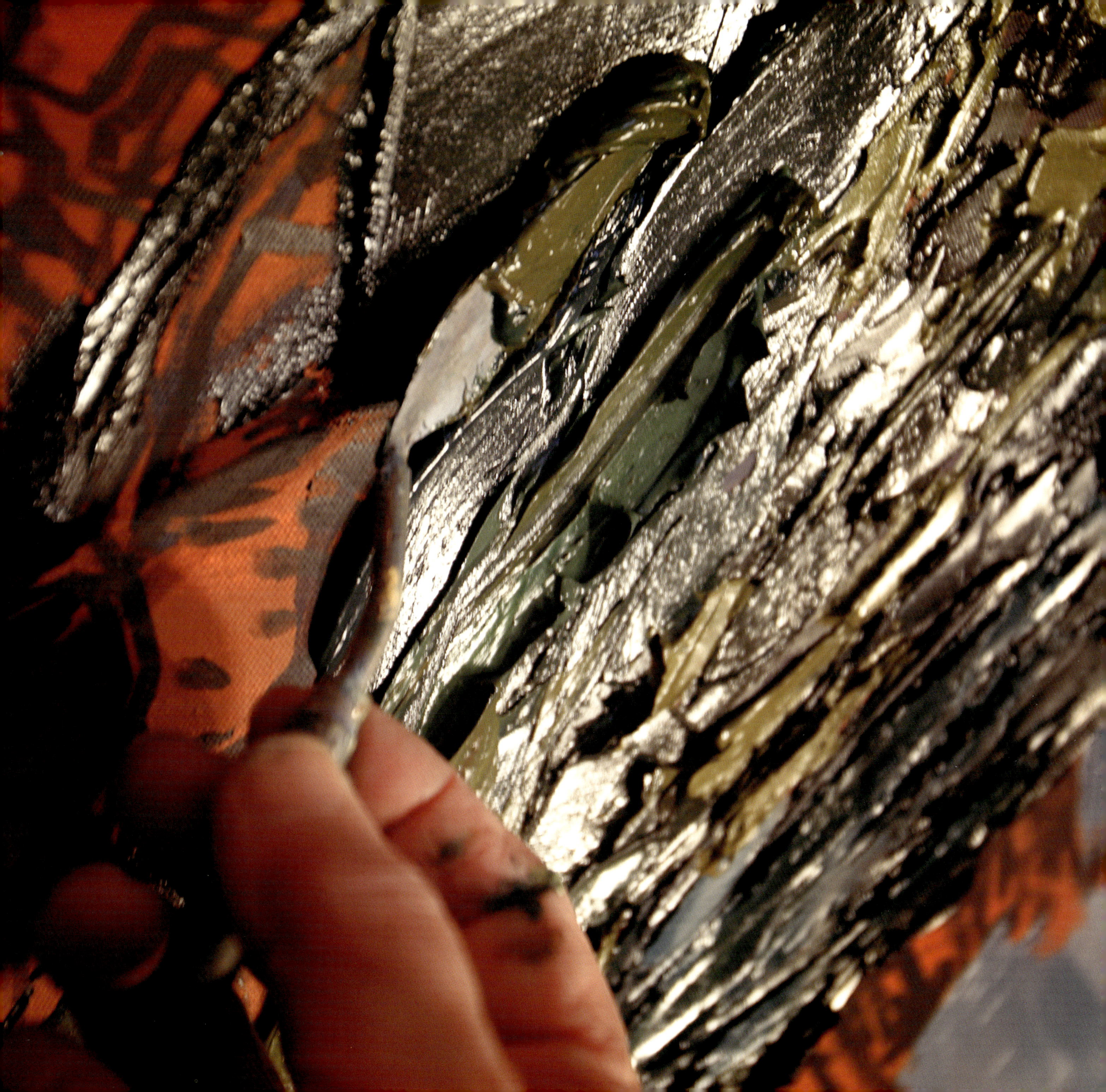

ALAN HAS PAINTED THE COAST from Hartland Quay, in North Devon, innumerable times but has never lost the thrill of seeing the waves constantly buffeting the rocky cliff edges. Part of the thrill lies in the danger of working close to the cliff edge, and once, accidentally dropping the lens of his camera over the edge, he saw it smash to pieces on the rocks below. The rocky strata of these cliffs lend themselves to knife painting, and Alan 'builds' the landscapes with broad slabs and sweeps of paint laid onto canvas with painting knives, the knife edges created in the thick paint catching the light in the same way as the rock edges. This square painting, in subtle tertiary colours, has the satisfying directness and strength that have become a hallmark of all Alan's painting.

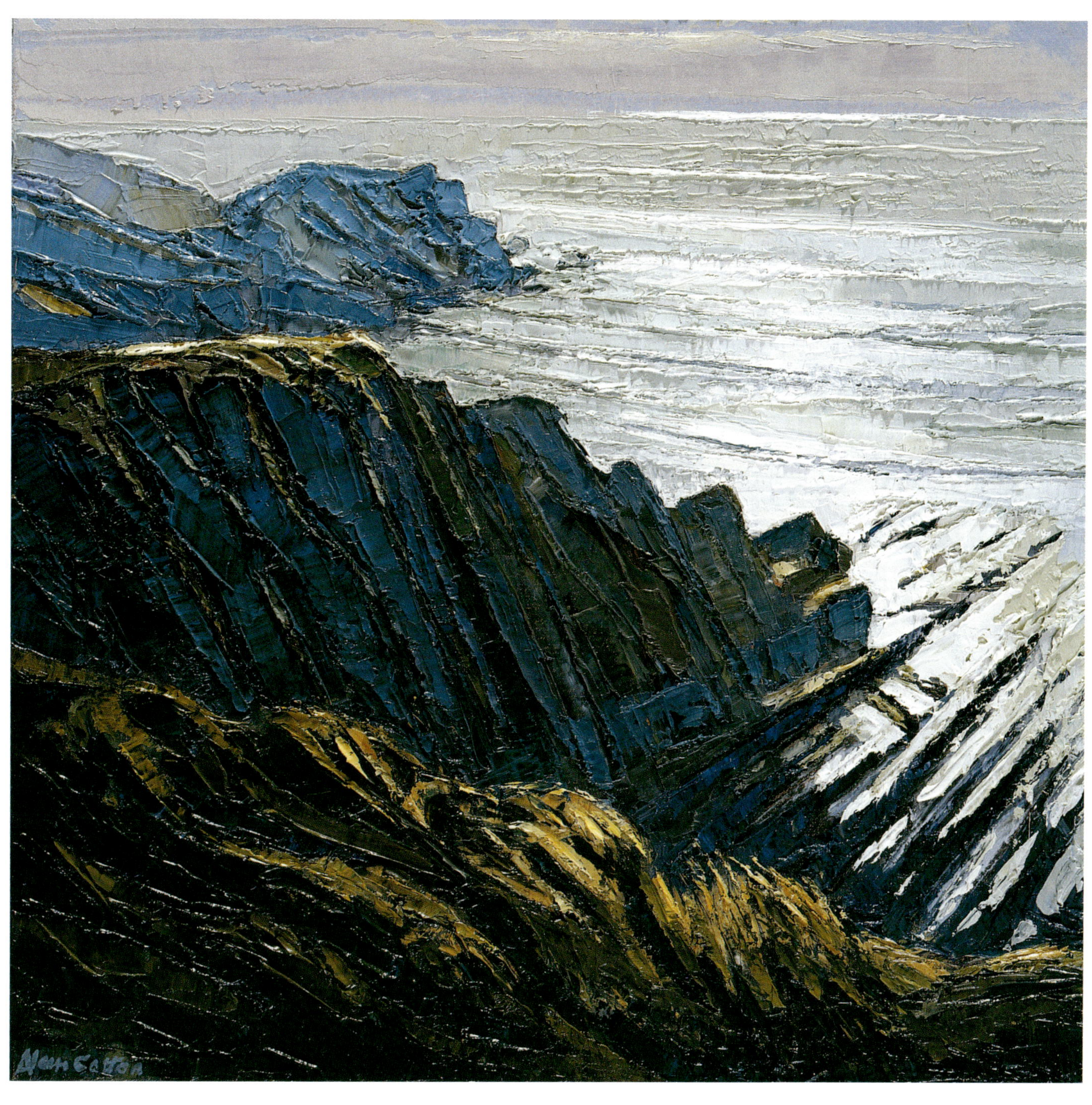

Devon – Sheer Cliffs at Hartland, 2008
oil on canvas 20 x 20 ins
Collection John Nettles

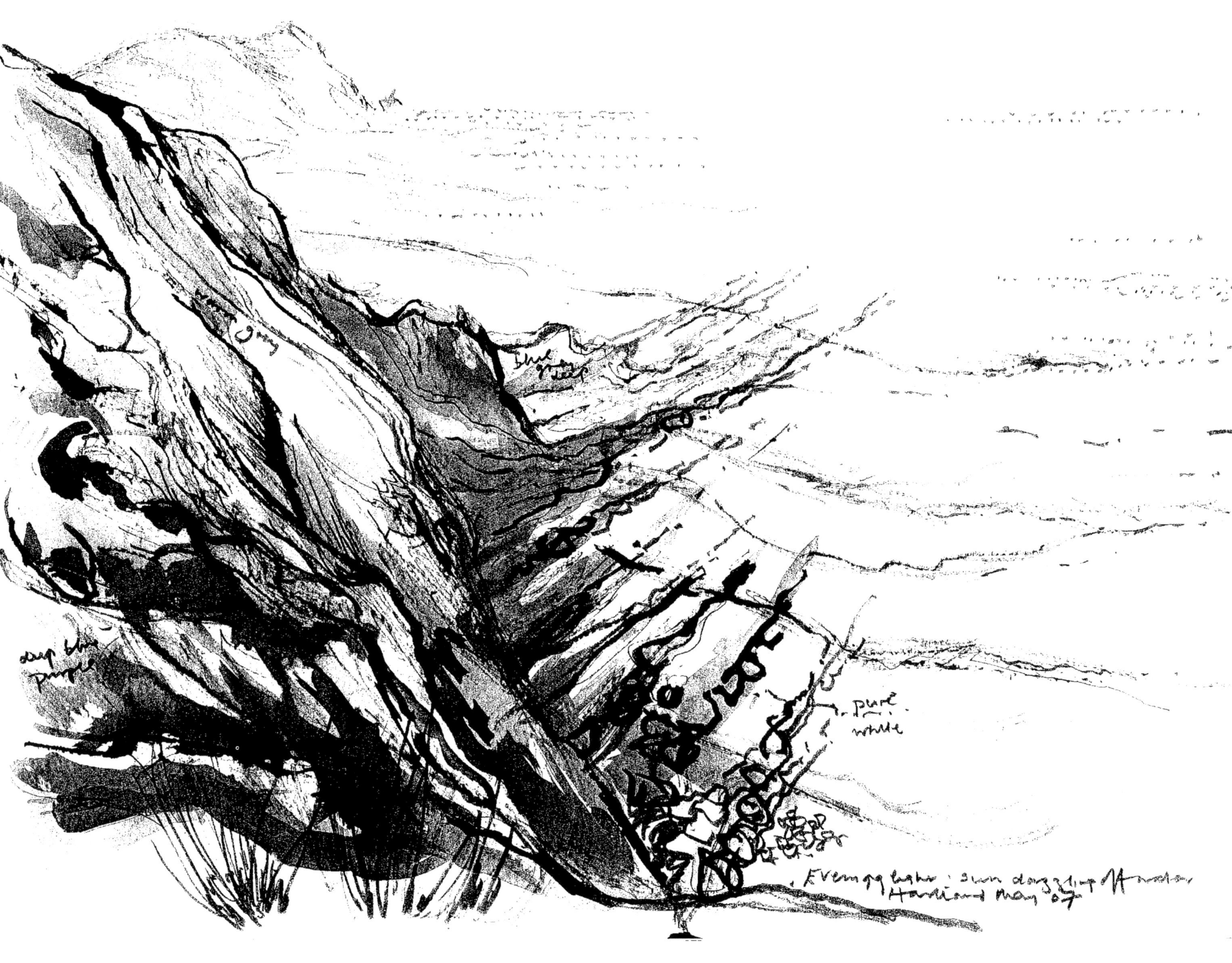
deep blue purple
pure white
Evening light: sun dazzling off rocks
Hartland May 07

Chapter Eight

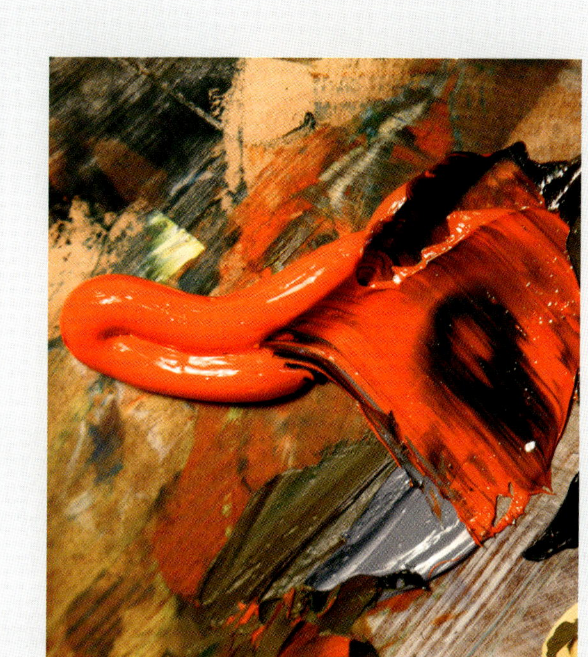

Here, There and Everywhere

In The Studio

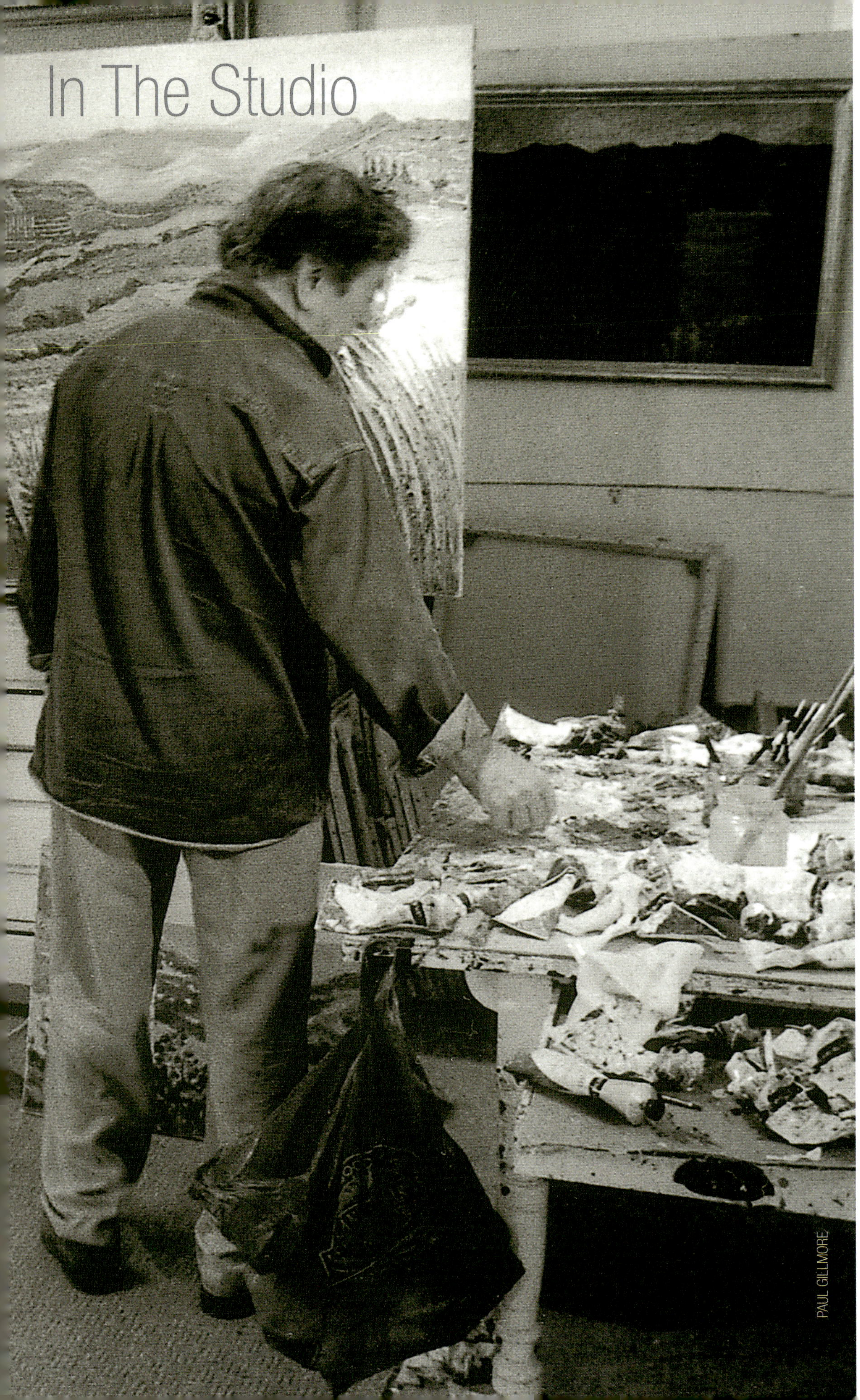

PAUL GILLMORE

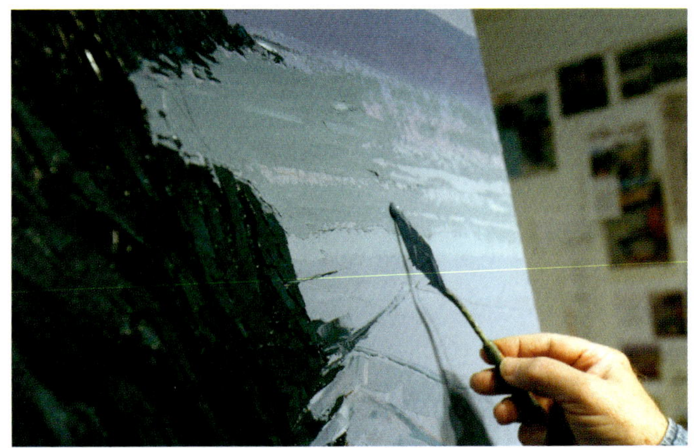

In the lead-up to an exhibition Alan's studio becomes the hub of intense activity. He starts work early in the morning, having prepared for action the day before. Pat is his éminence grise, *dealing with all the details of everyday life, and providing him with much-needed sustenance.*

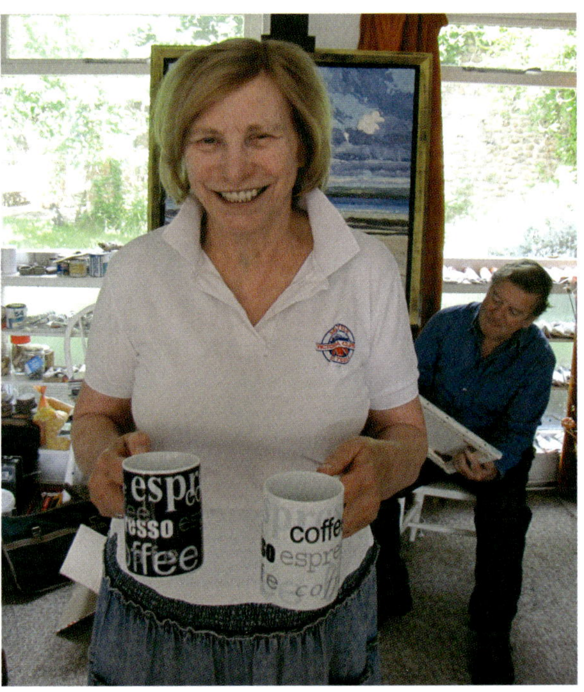

LIS McGILL

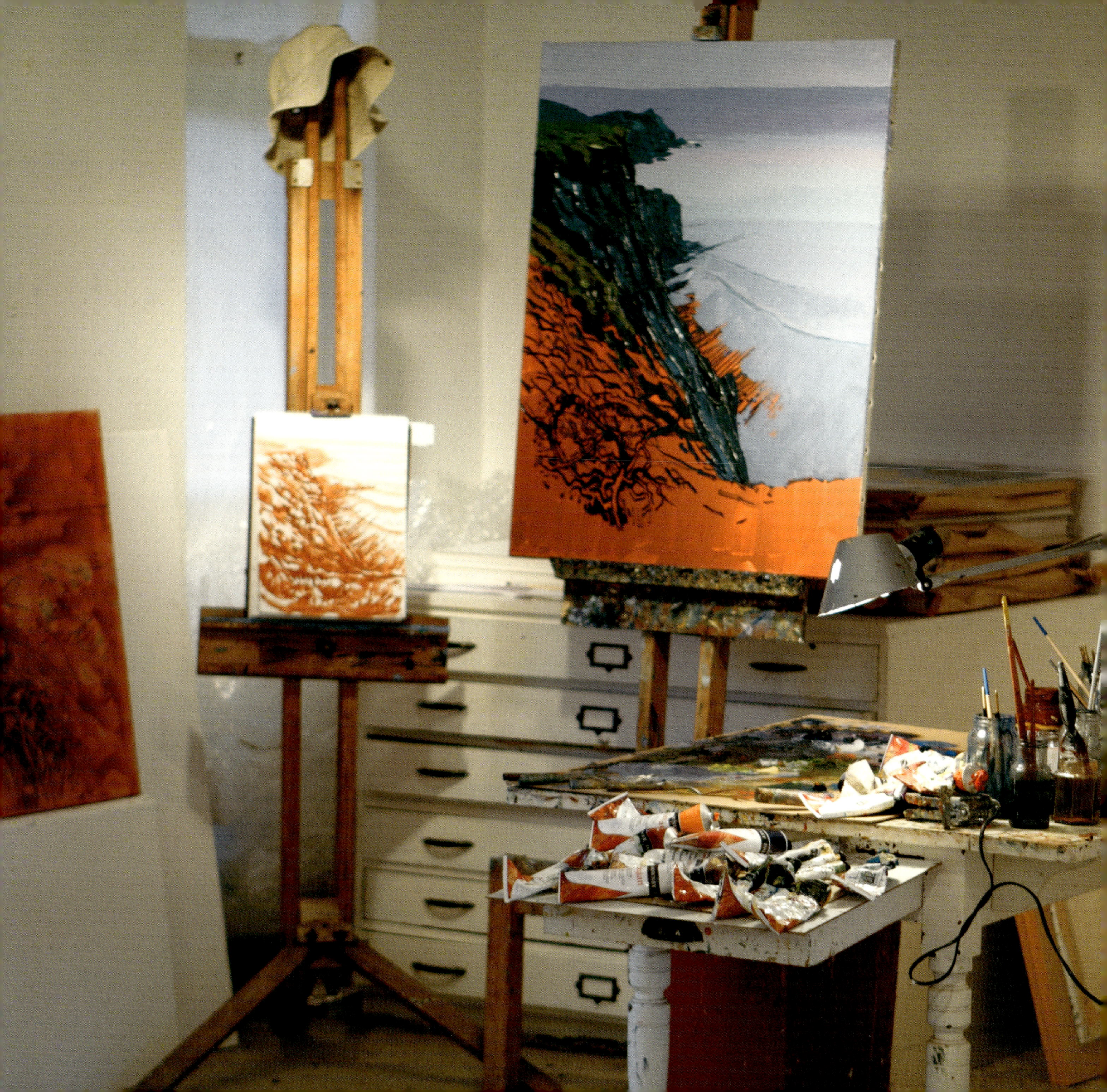

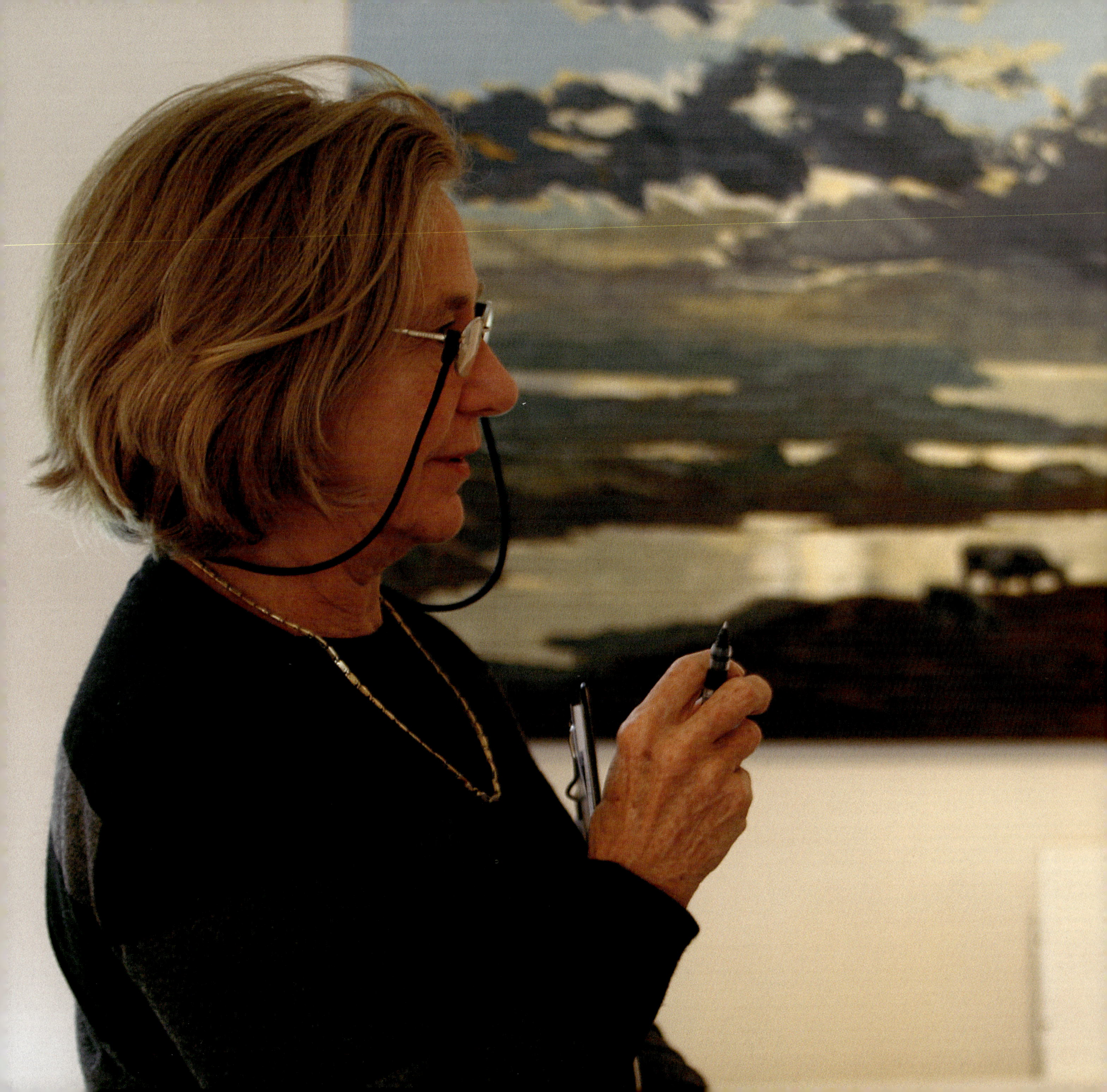

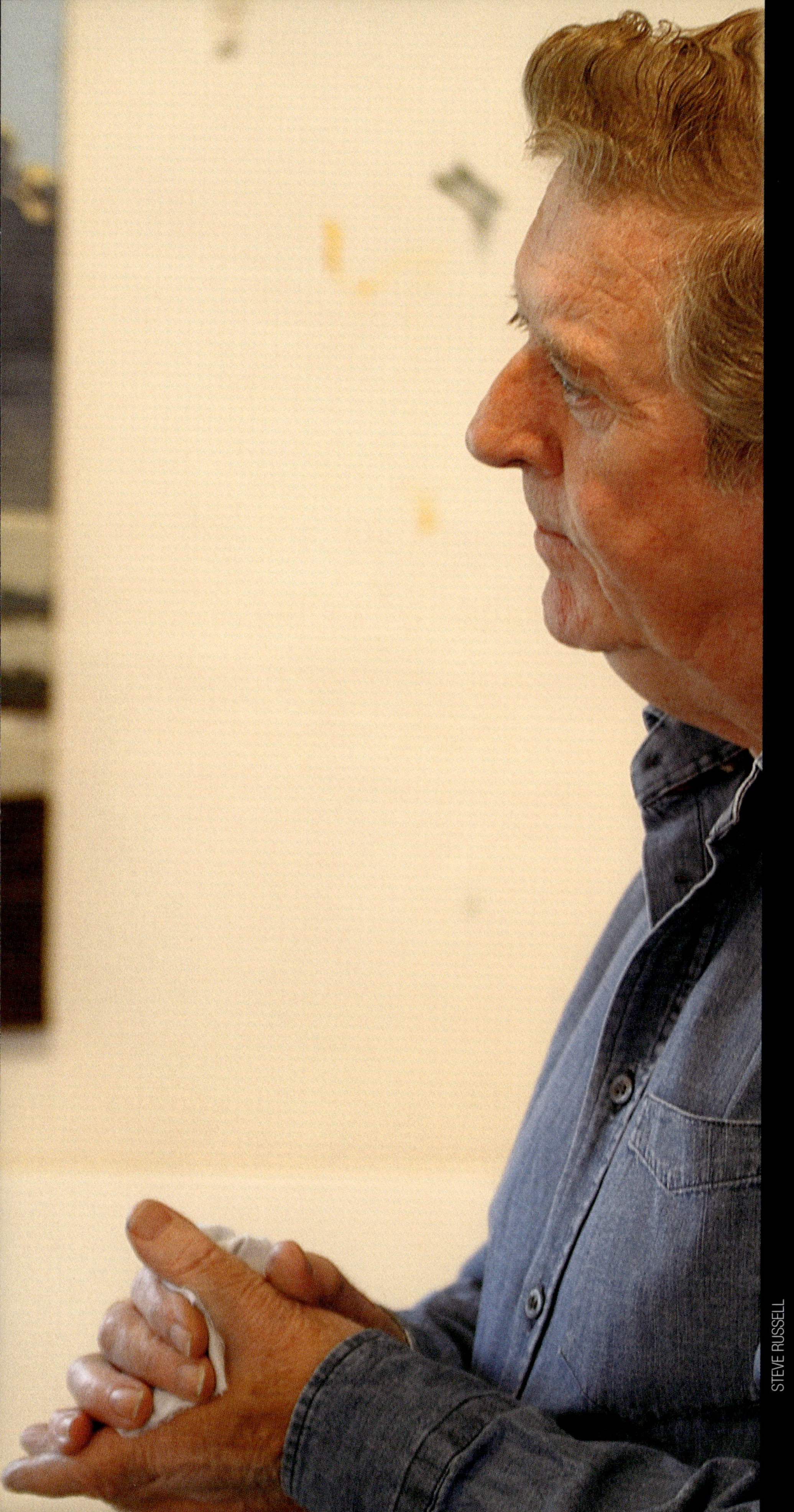
STEVE RUSSELL

After innumerable discussions about art and life, Alan Cotton and Jenny Pery have reached a rare degree of understanding. Here Alan seems quite resigned to his fate at the hands of the author!

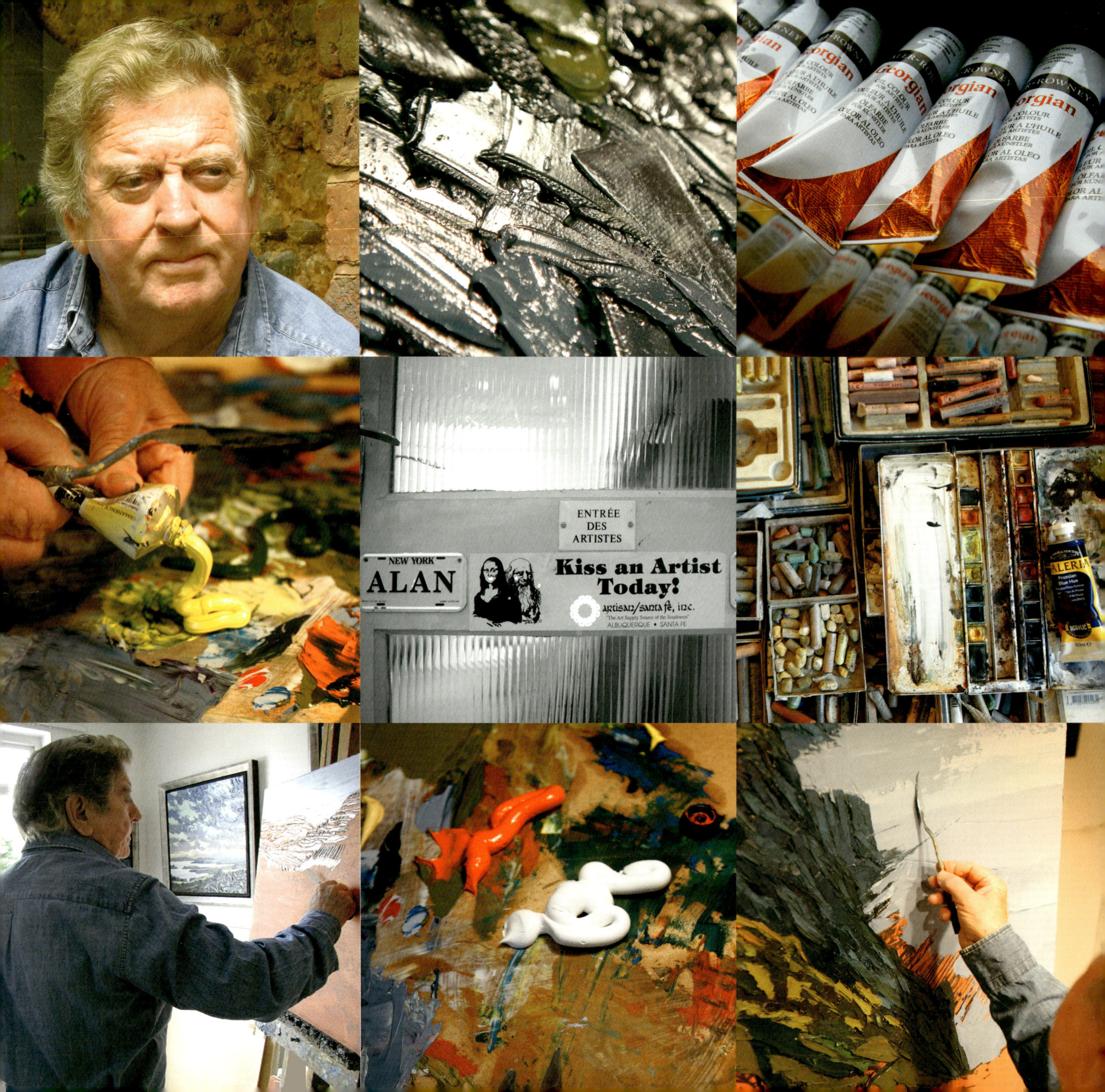
Georgian
ENTRÉE
DES
ARTISTES
NEW YORK
ALAN
Kiss an Artist
Today!
artisan/santa fe, inc.
"The Art Supply Source of the Southwest"
ALBUQUERQUE • SANTA FE

Alan often lays paint onto a reddish ground, which offsets the deep grey-greens of rock and grass particularly well. He glories in the paint, squeezing out large quantities and experimenting with different colour mixes on the table top that he uses as a palette. He remarks that many of his colours are found by mixing on the palette.

STEVE RUSSELL

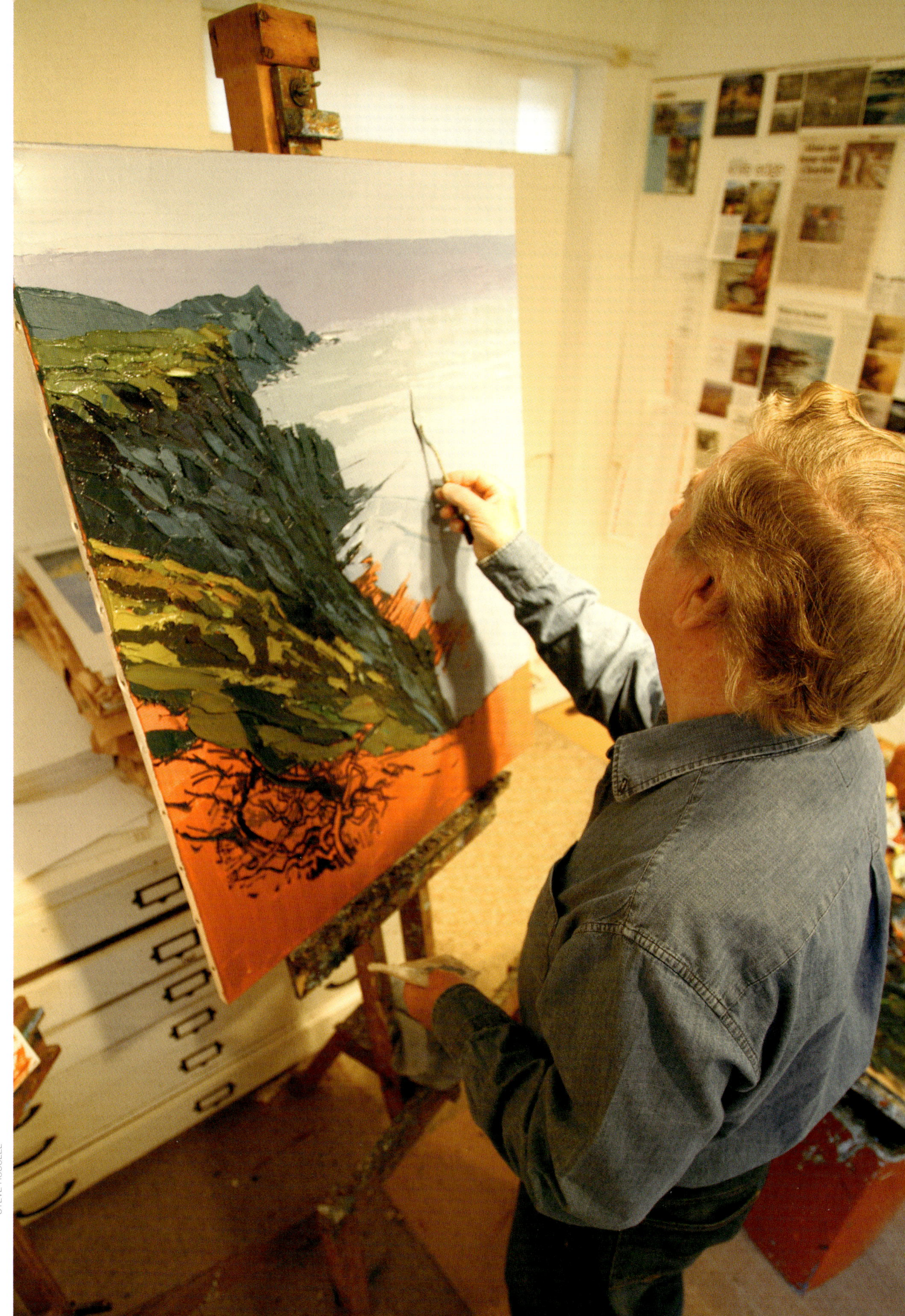

On Location

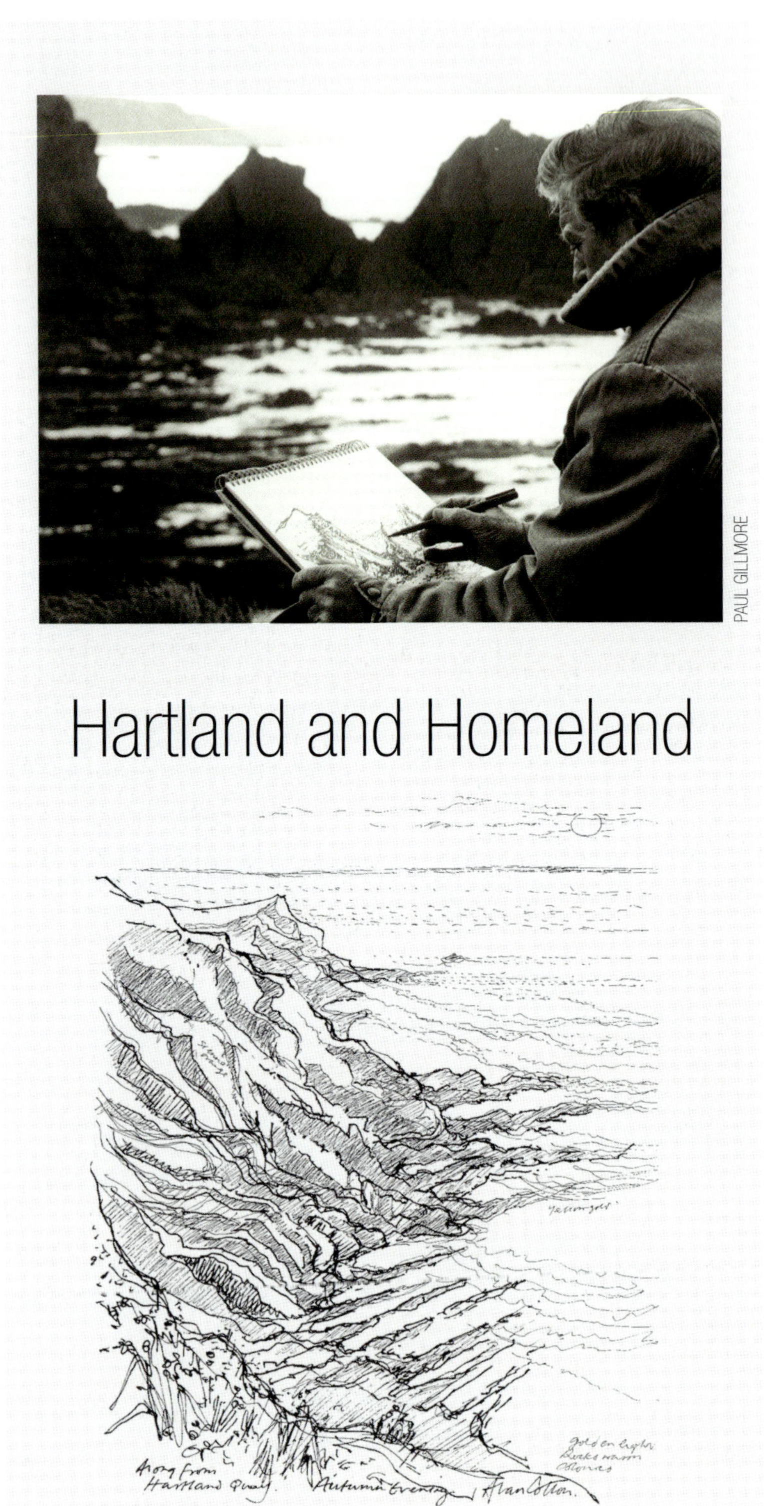

PAUL GILLMORE

Hartland and Homeland

The drama of the North Devon coast at Hartland has had Alan in thrall for many years. The dark cliffs set in opposition to the luminous sea demand the use of a full range of tones, from pure white to deepest blue-black. Into the light tones of water and sky Alan filters opalescent pinks and lilacs, and heightens the dark tones of land and rock with sombre ochres.

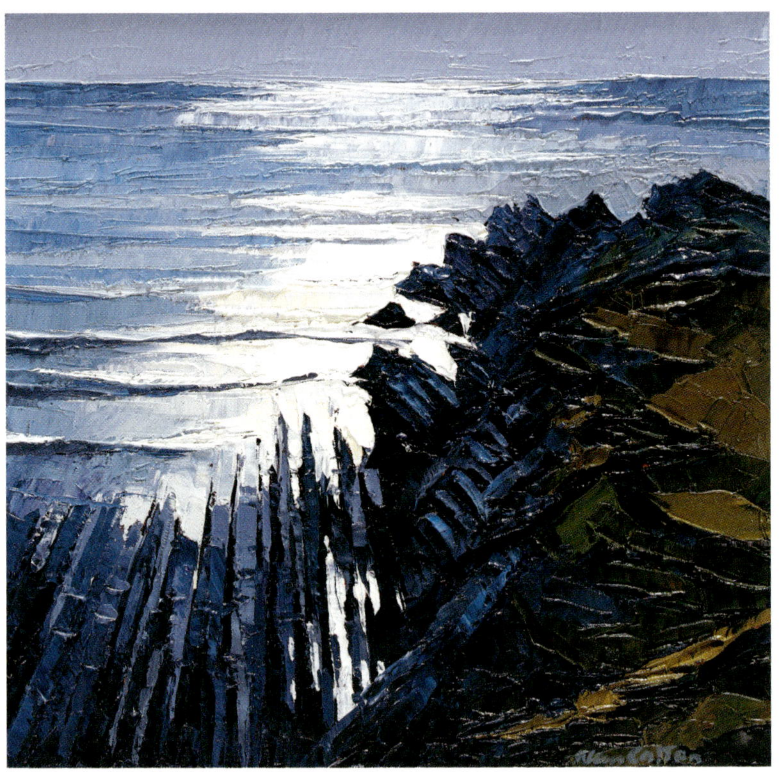

Devon – Dazzling Evening Light at Hartland
oil on canvas 14 x 14 ins

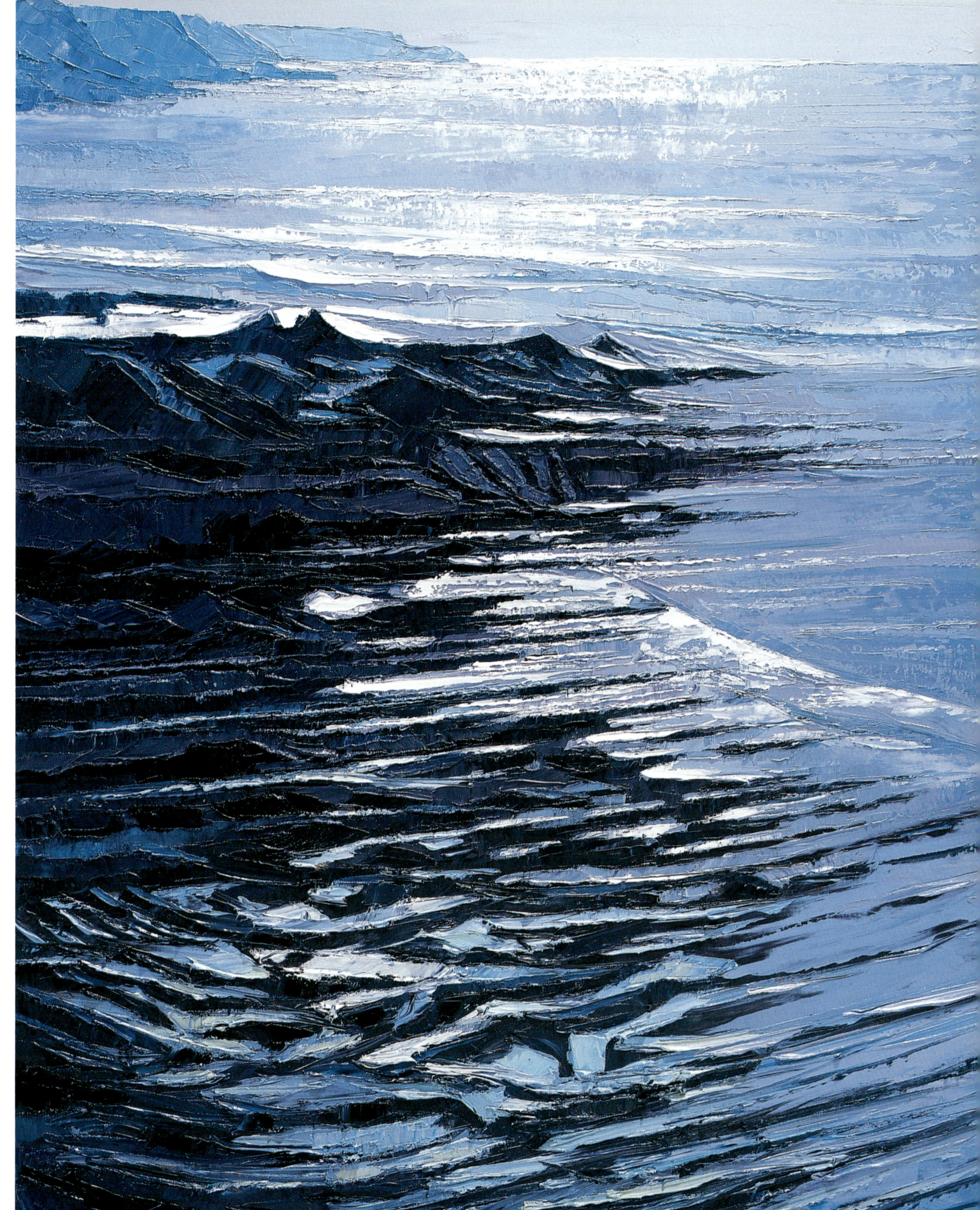

Devon – Calm Seas at Hartland
oil on canvas 46 x 36 ins

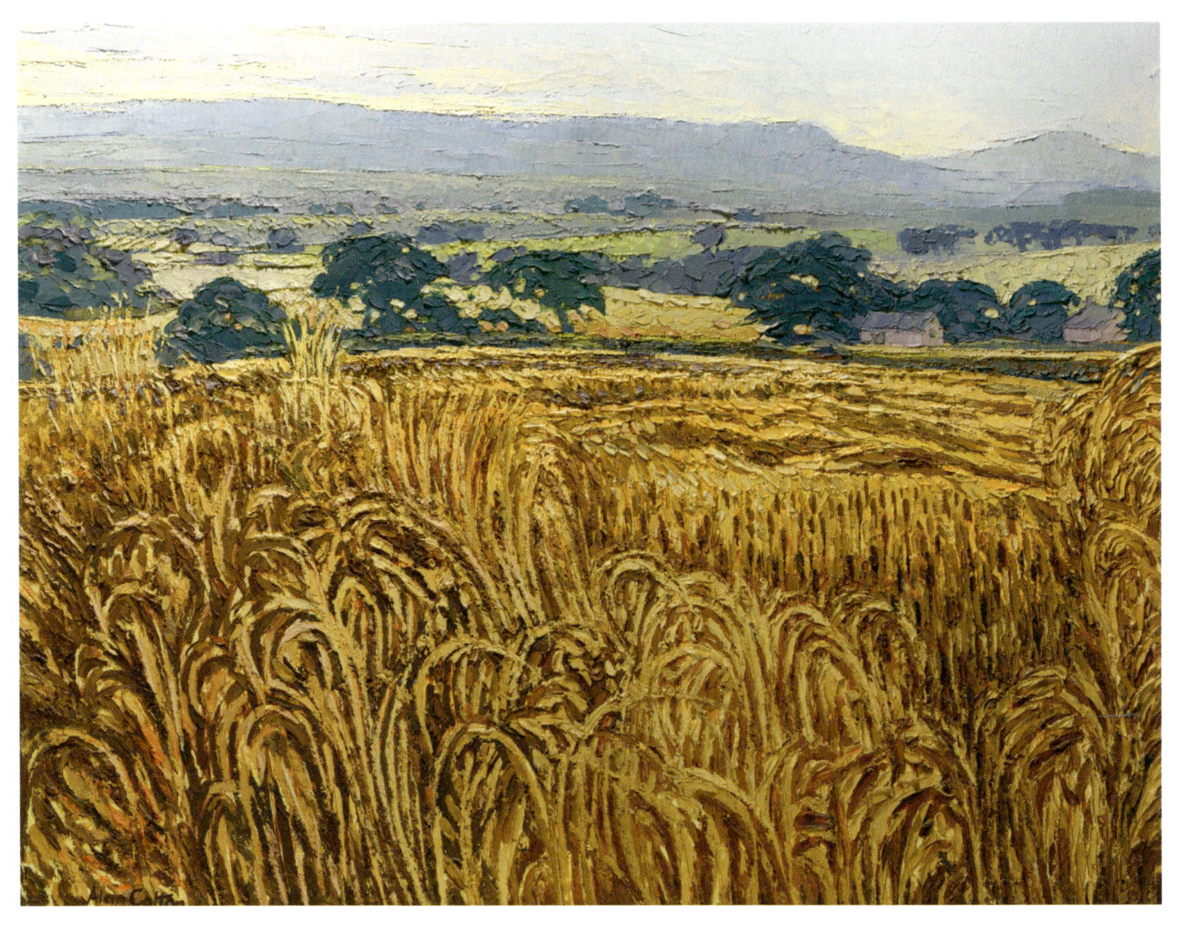

Devon – Otter Valley Harvest
oil on canvas 24 x 30 ins

Devon – Hartland Quay, Sunset
oil on canvas 30 x 24 ins

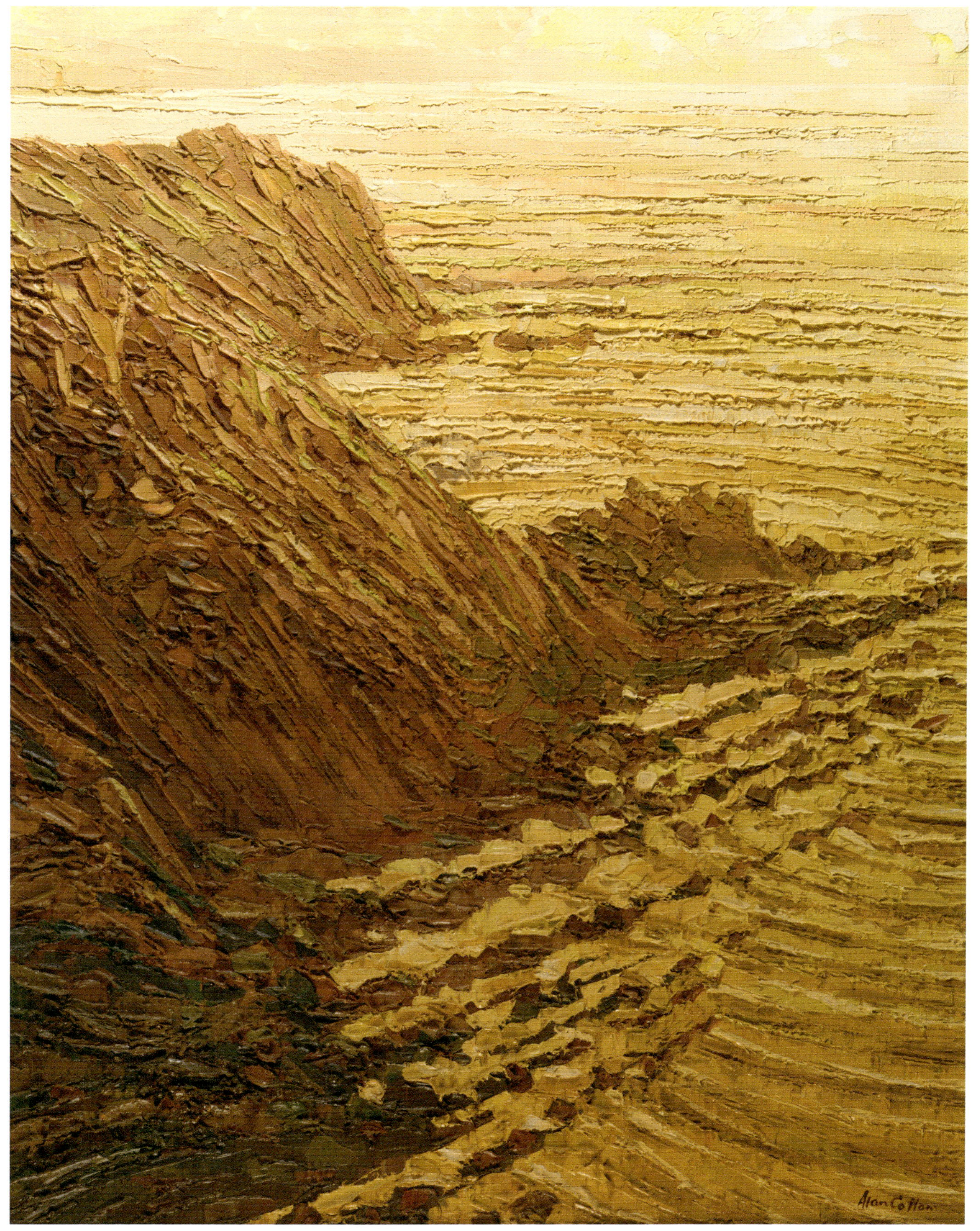

On Location

Donegal – Ebbing Tide Along the Estuary (opposite)
oil on canvas 36 x 36 ins

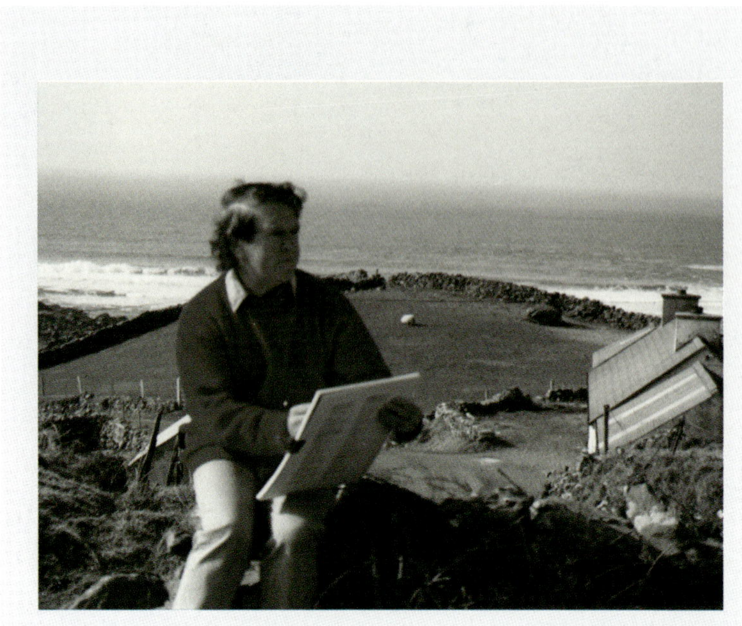

Ireland

Where the sea is the main protagonist at Hartland, in Ireland it is the sky that dominates. Alan depicts the weight of the rain-laden clouds in broad sweeps of indigo, puce and violet. The land is subdued under the wind-borne activity of the clouds, and the horizon line is lowered accordingly.

THE BOLDNESS of the painting opposite, with the canvas bisected horizontally by a series of vivid indigo stripes, and the blue shapes of the clouds contrasting with the greyish-ochre swirls of the land, make this one of Alan's most striking paintings. The broad sweeps of paint applied with knives hold their sheen in much the same way that recently wetted sand gleams. In his paintings of Ireland, where the light is never constant, Alan is able to explore the widest possible range of colour combinations.

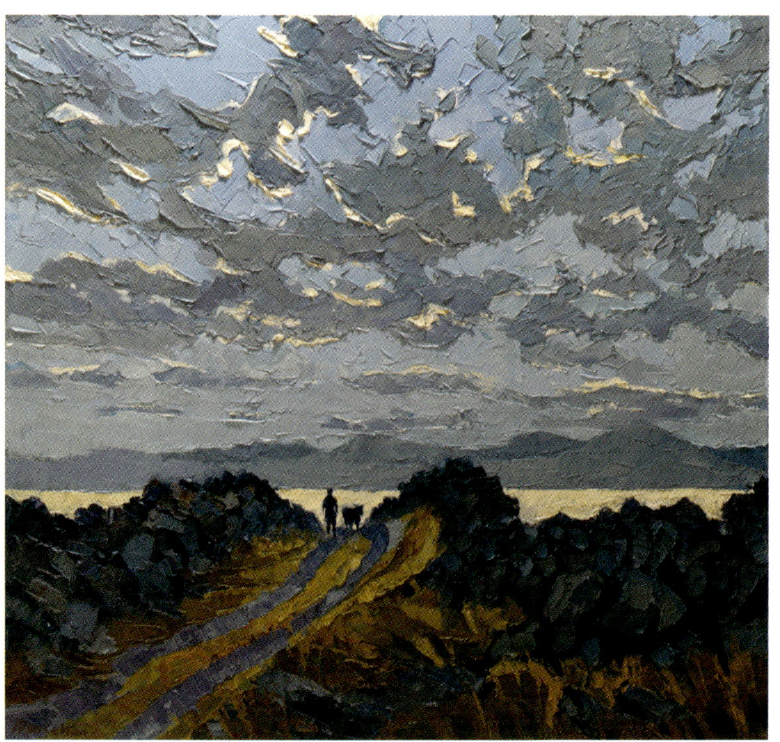

Connemara – Lonely Lane to Estuary
oil on canvas 24 x 24 ins

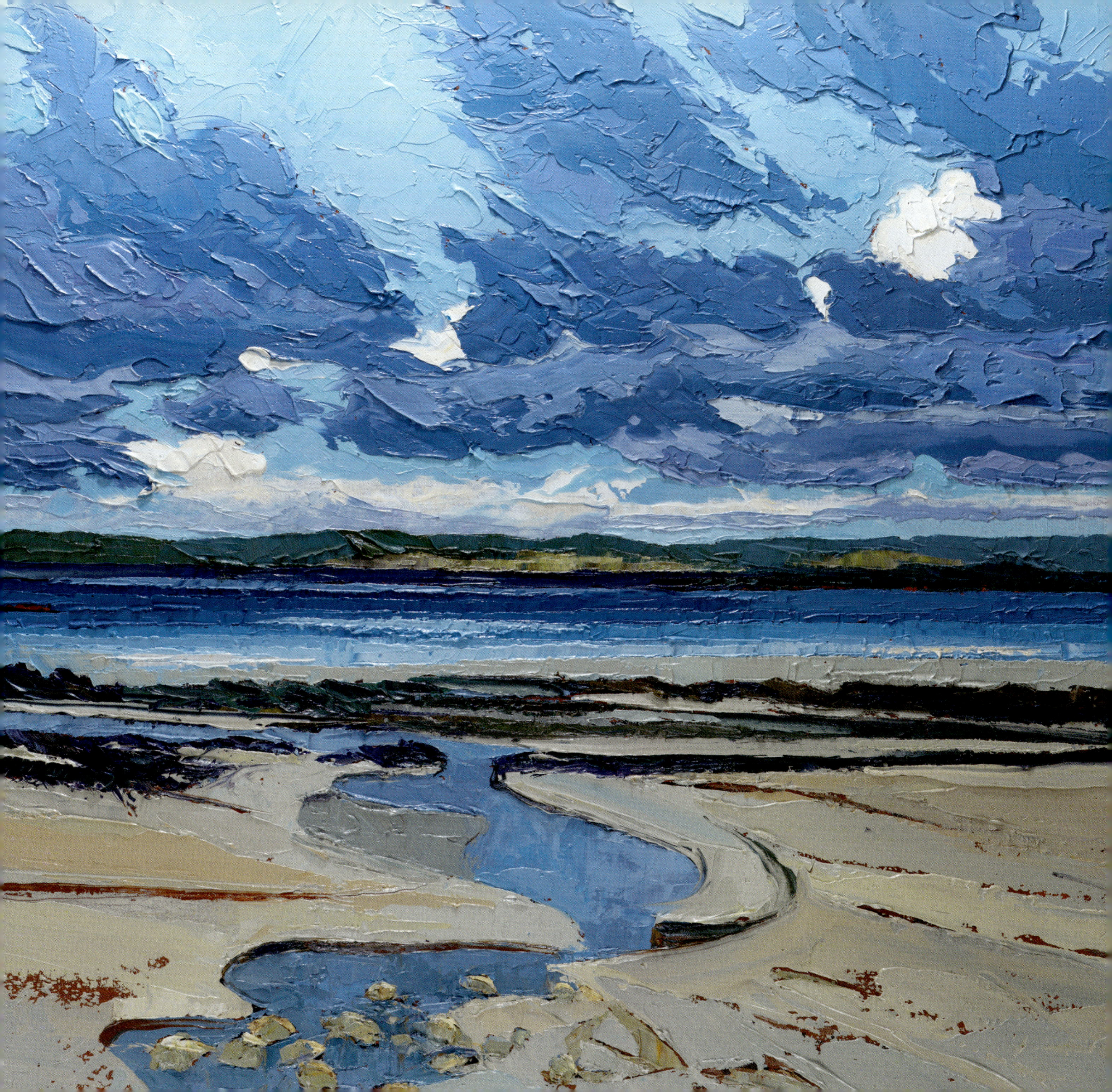

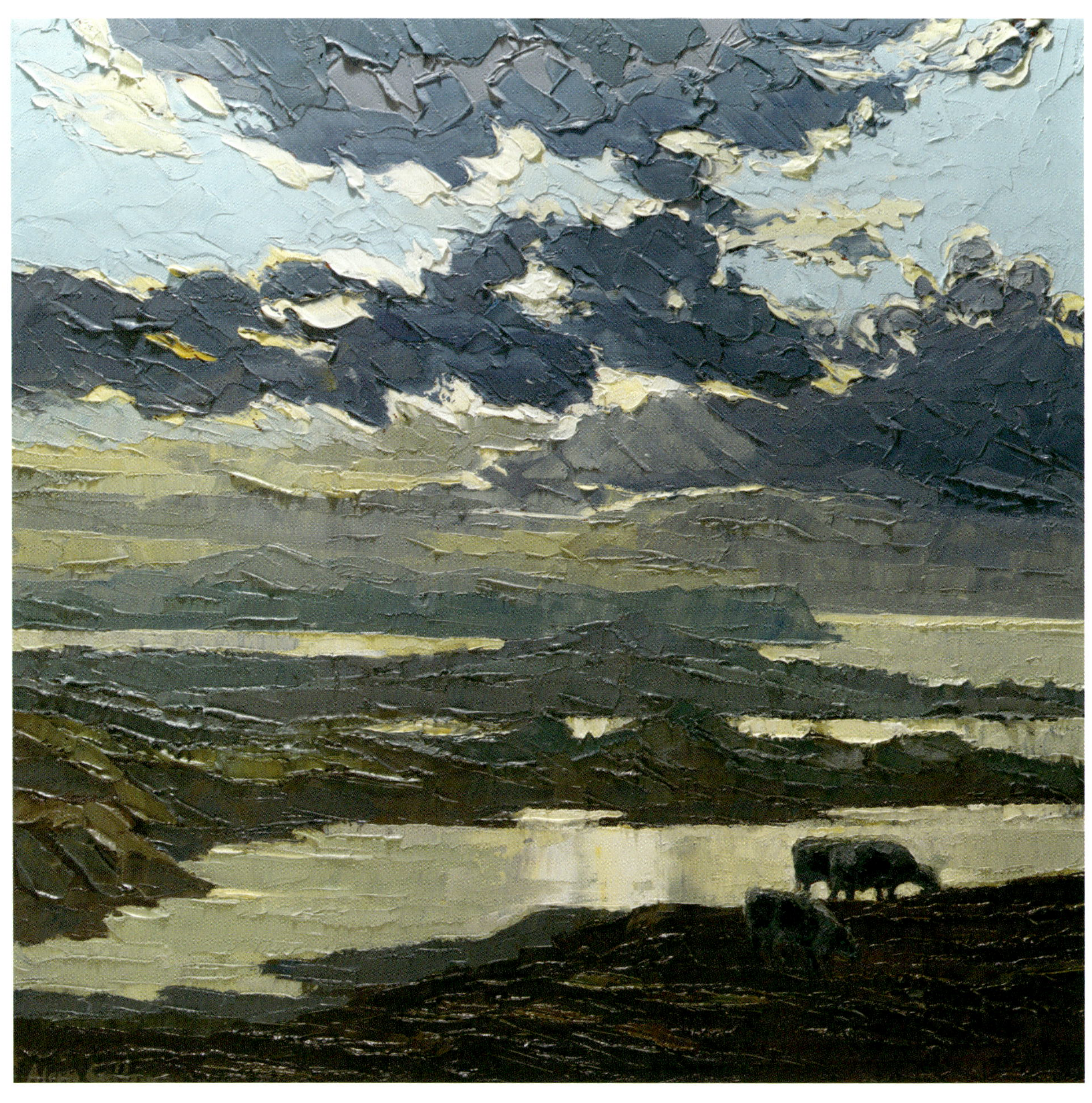

Donegal – Cruit Island Towards Evening
oil on canvas 24 x 24 ins

Donegal – Curving Stream into the Estuary (opposite)
oil on canvas 14 x 14 ins

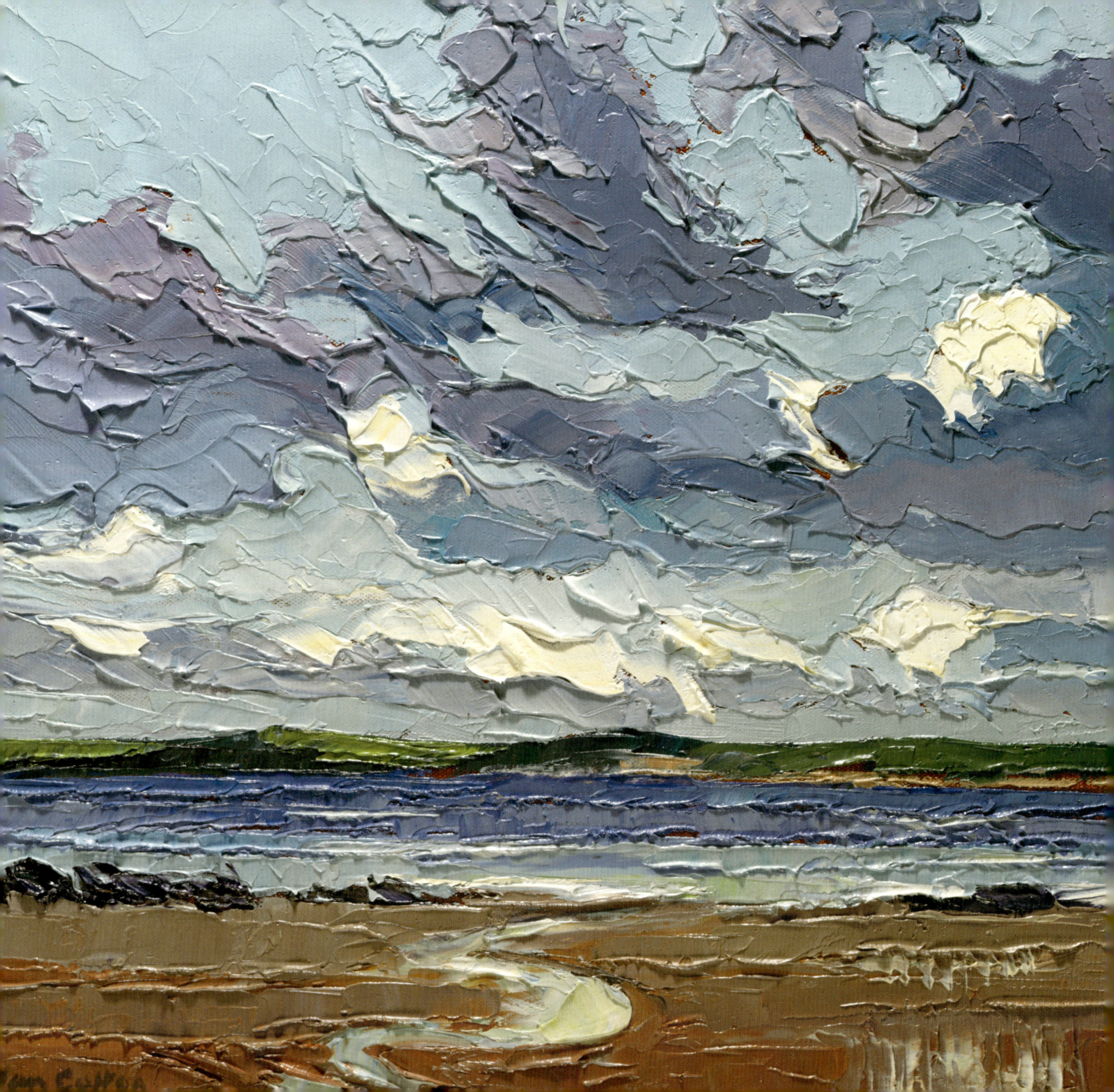

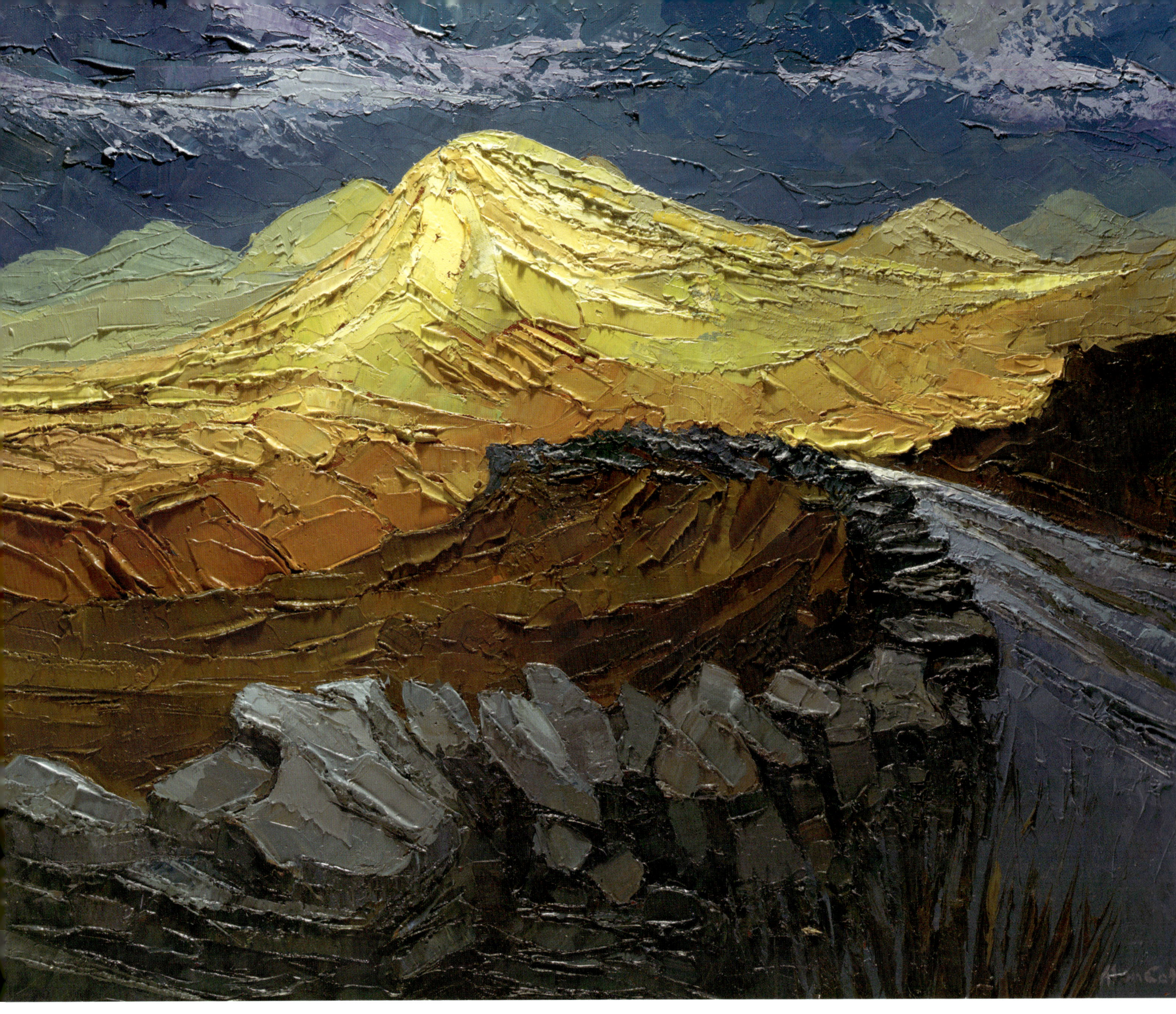

Connemara – The Twelve Pins – Golden Light after the Storm
oil on canvas 20 x 24 ins

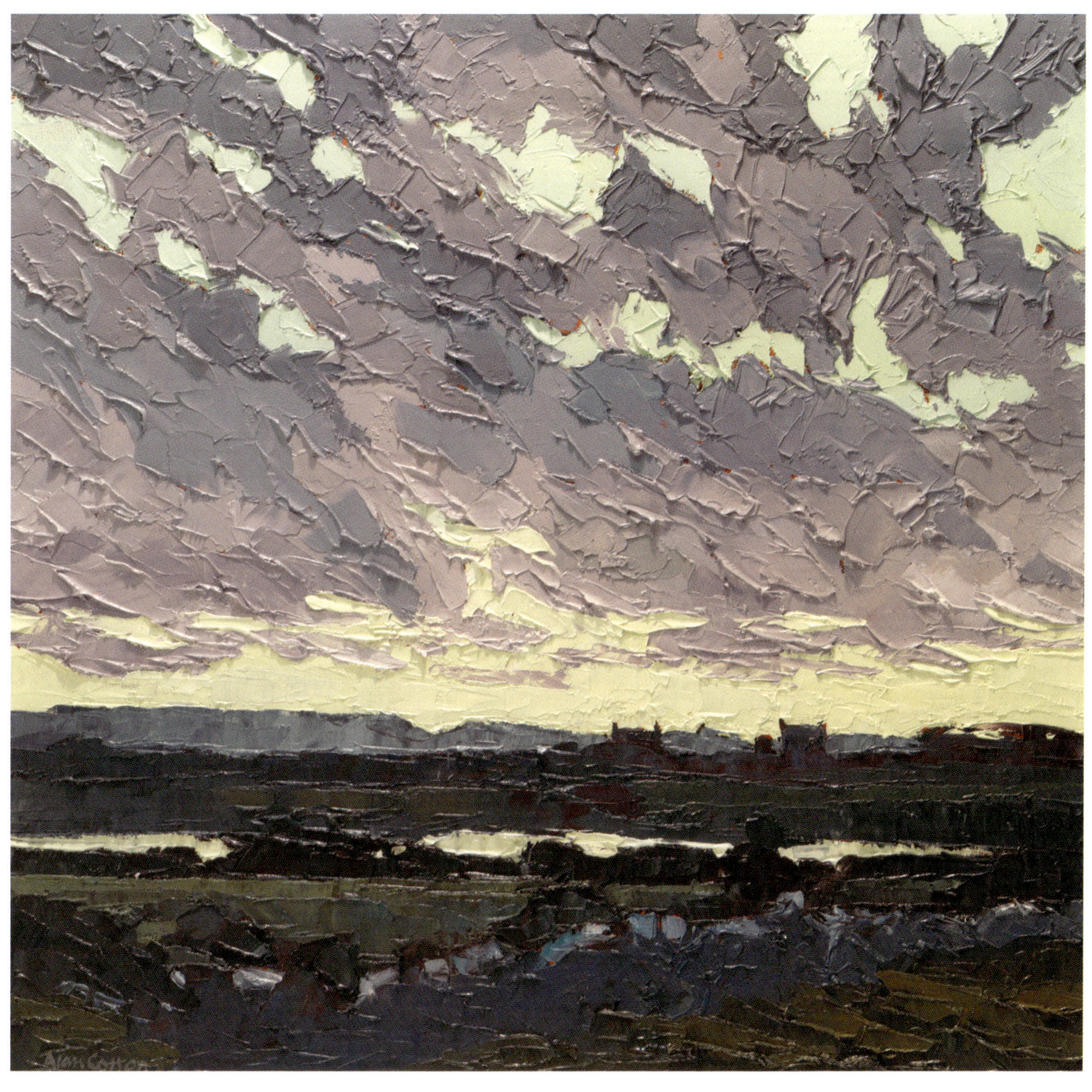

Donegal – Clearing Skies at Day's End
oil on canvas 24 x 24 ins

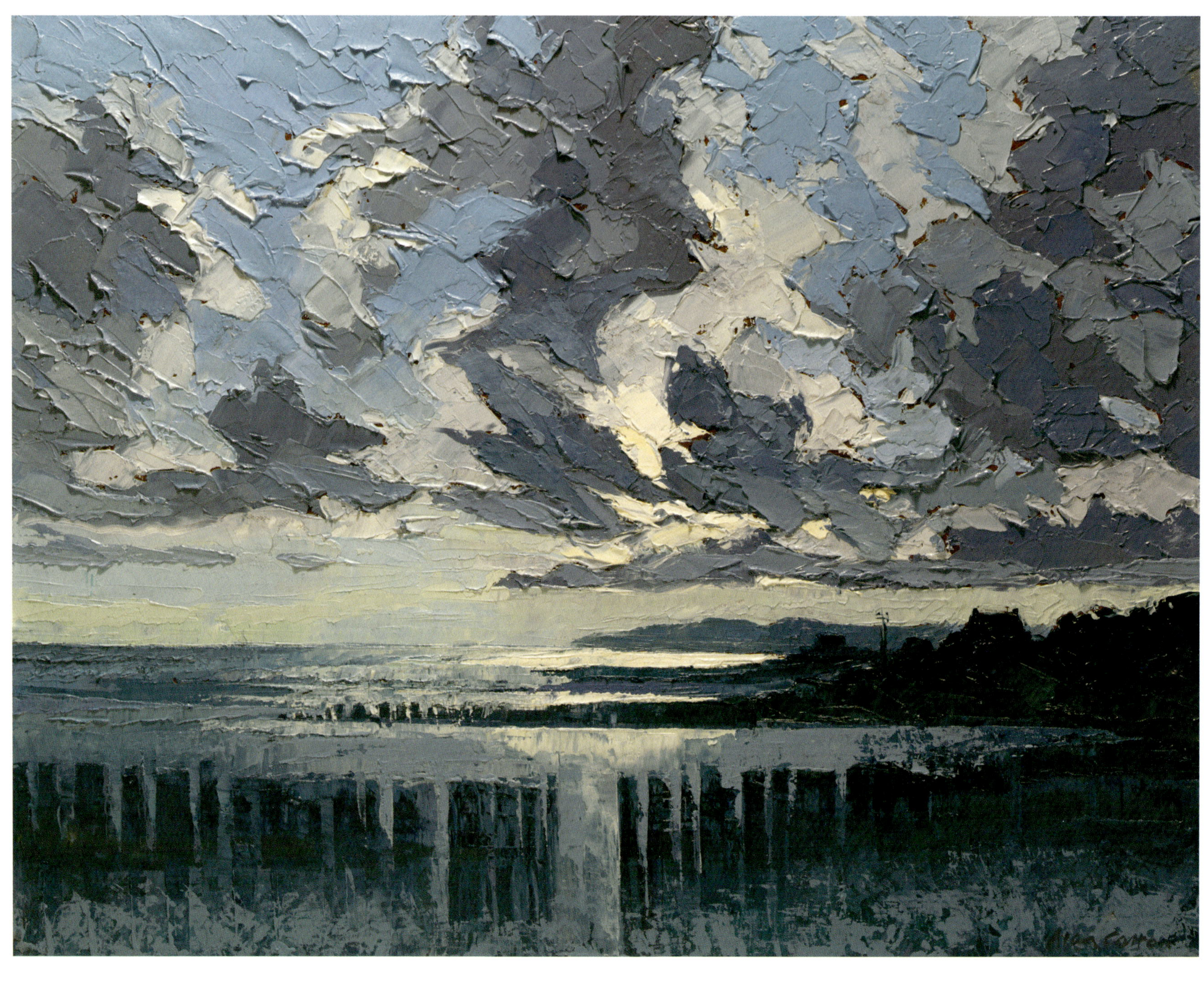

Donegal – Receding Tide Beyond the Wind Breaks
oil on canvas 16 x 20 ins

Donegal – Evening Light After the Storm (opposite)
oil on canvas 24 x 24 ins
Collection James Kidner

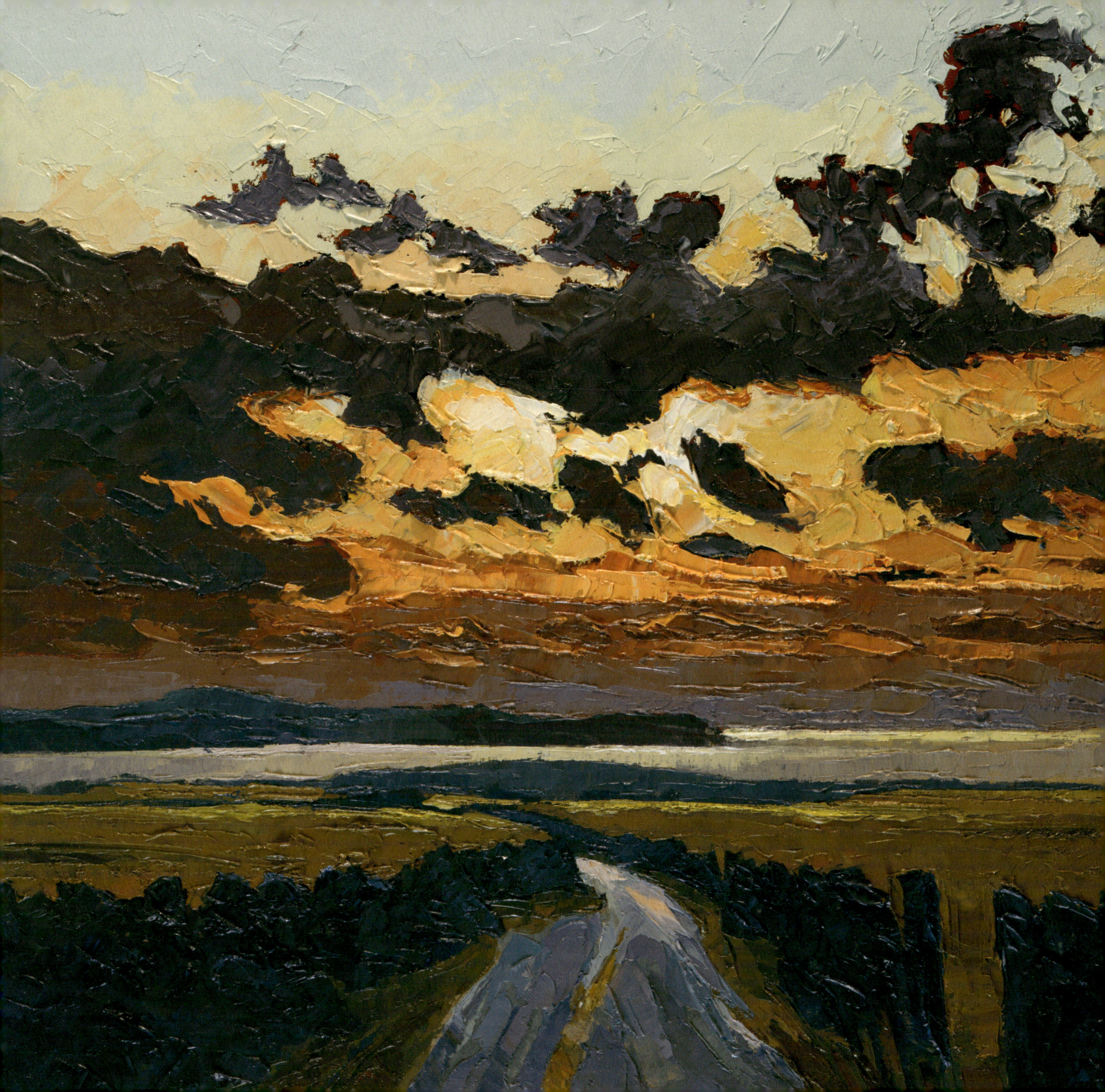

On Location

Morocco – Berber Dellings on the Telouet Road (opposite)
oil on canvas 24 x 24 ins

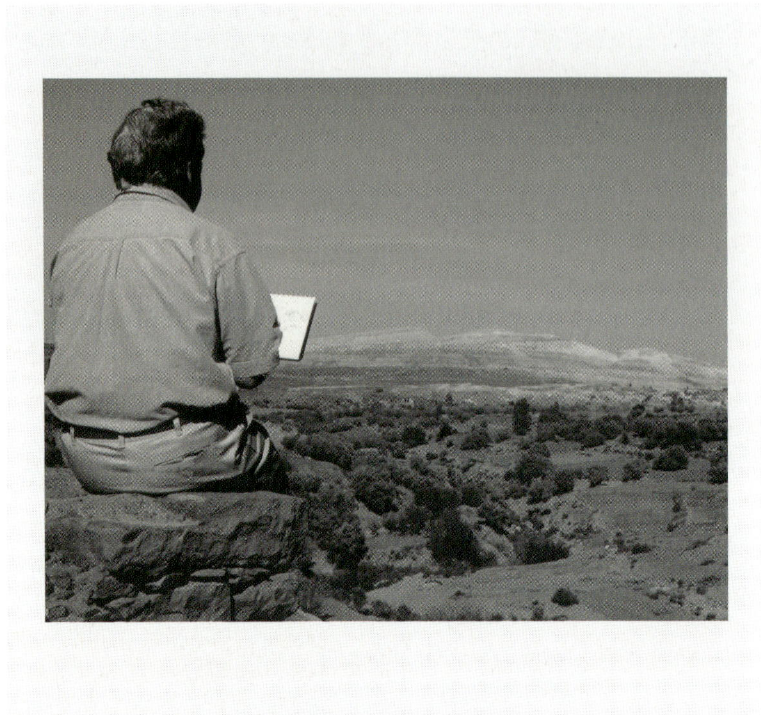

In Morocco Alan found colour combinations he had never seen before, as well as a harsher light than that he was used to in Europe. He experimented with new ways of laying on paint, dragging and scumbling one colour over another to achieve the richness of hue and luminosity he required.

Morocco

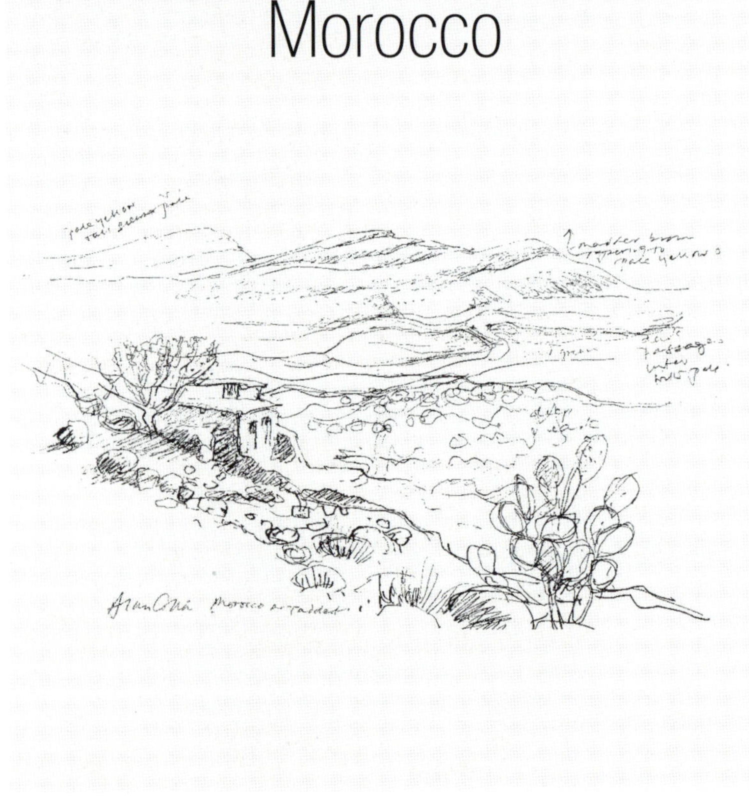

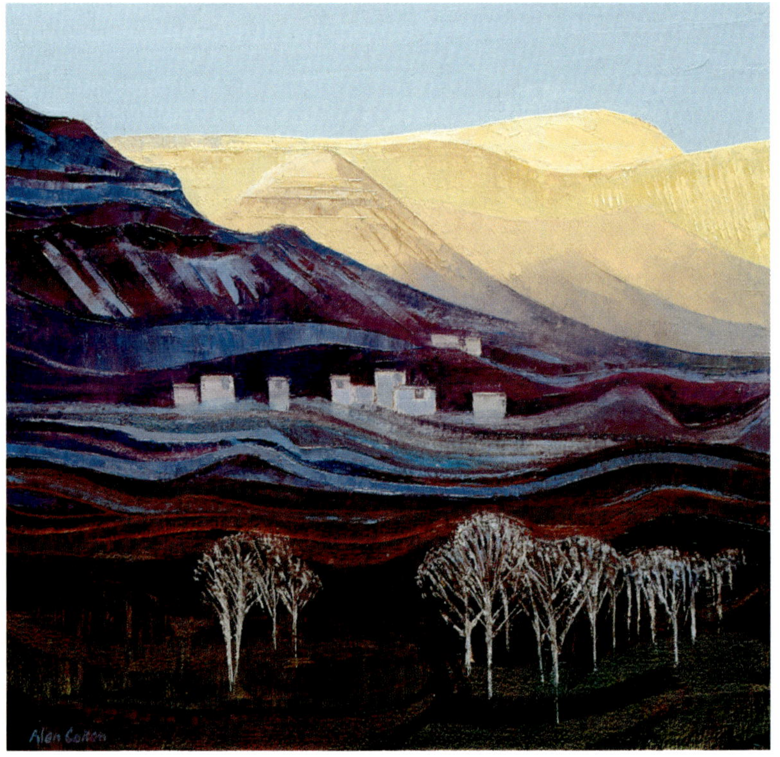

Morocco – Evening in the Asif Imini Valley
oil on canvas 20 x 20 ins

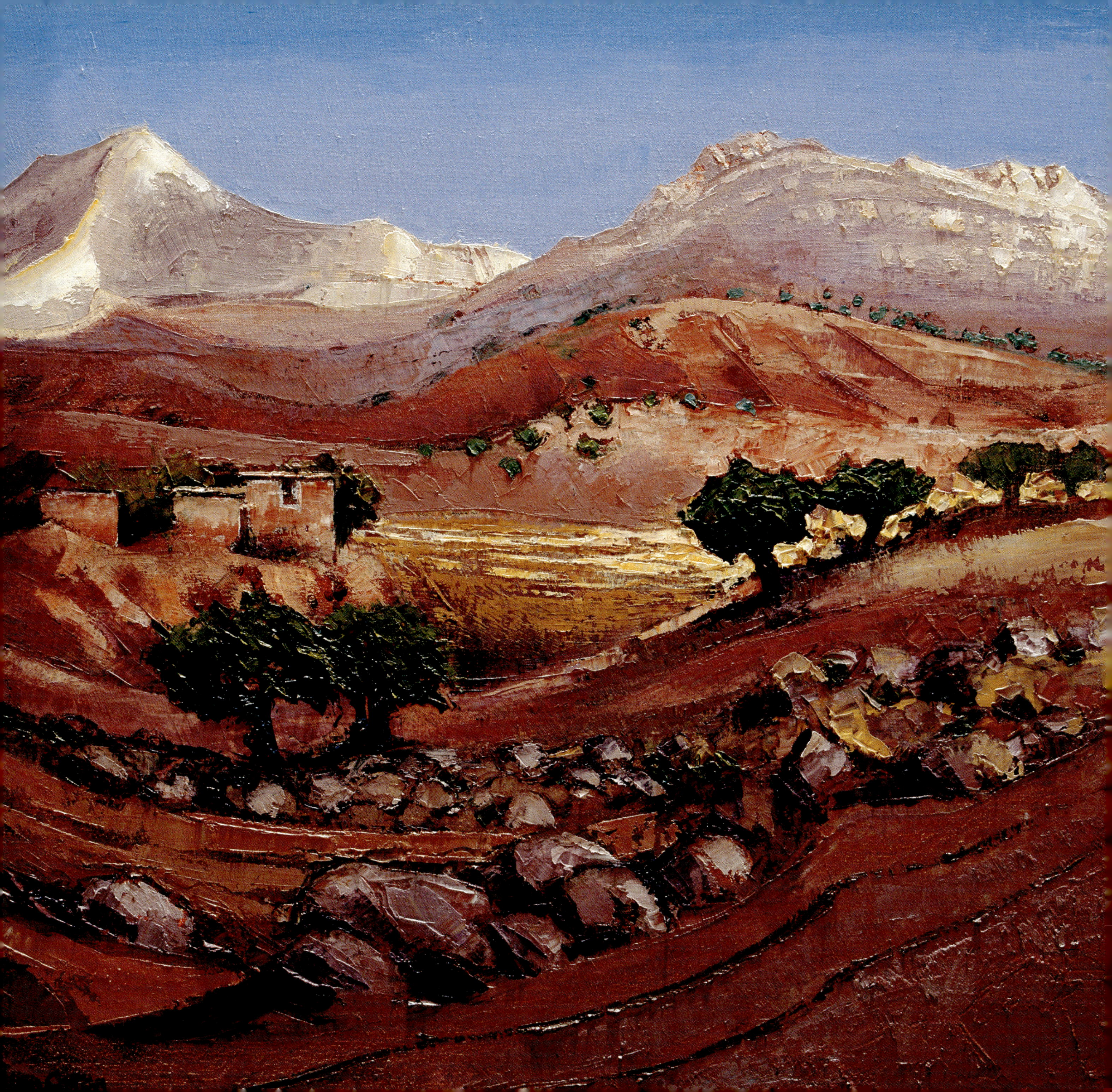

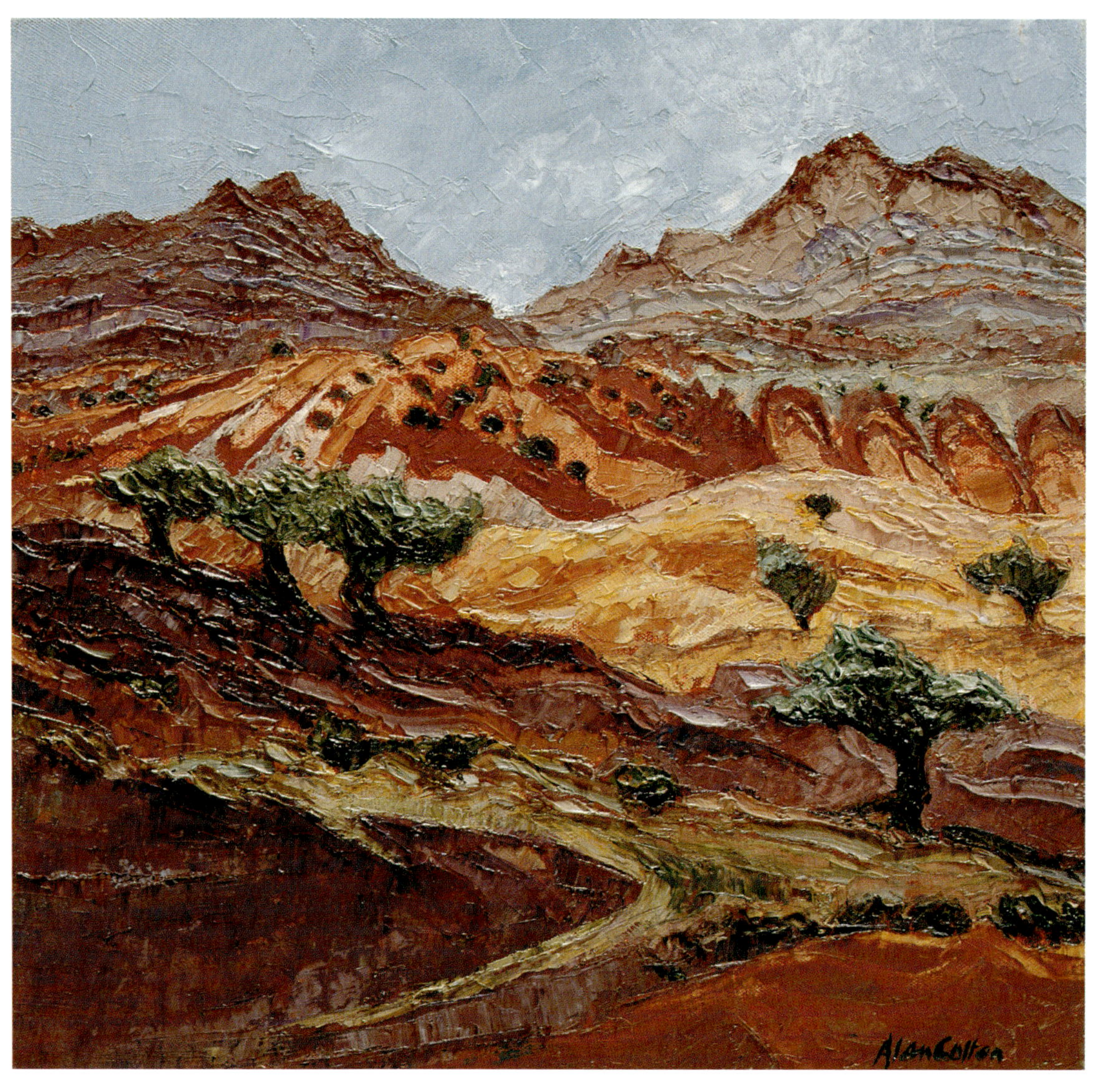

Morocco – Landscape near the Kasbah at Telouet
oil on canvas 14 x 14 ins

Morocco – Deepening Shadows in the Tizi-n-Tichka Pass (opposite)
oil on canvas 36 x 36 ins

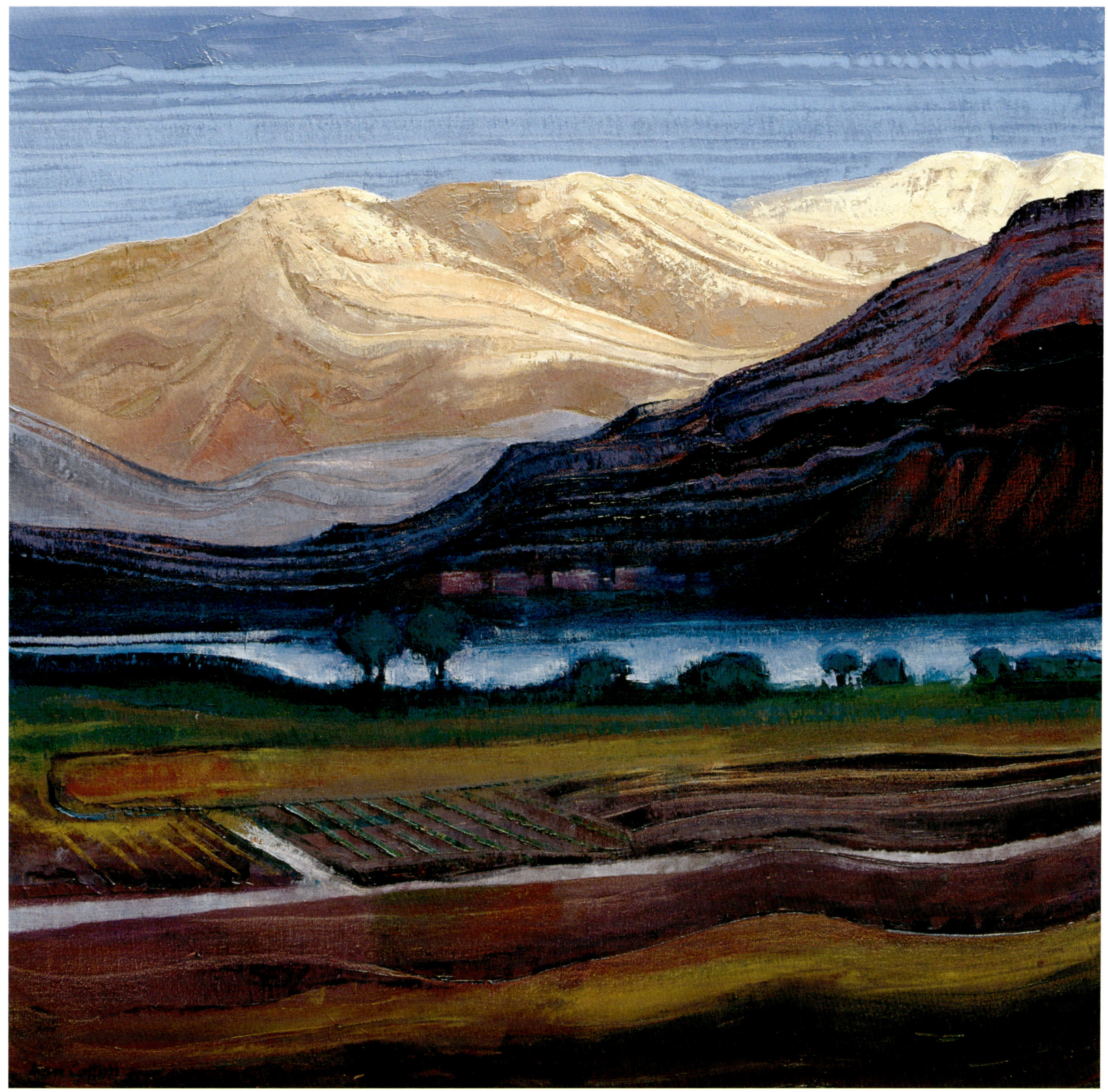

On Location

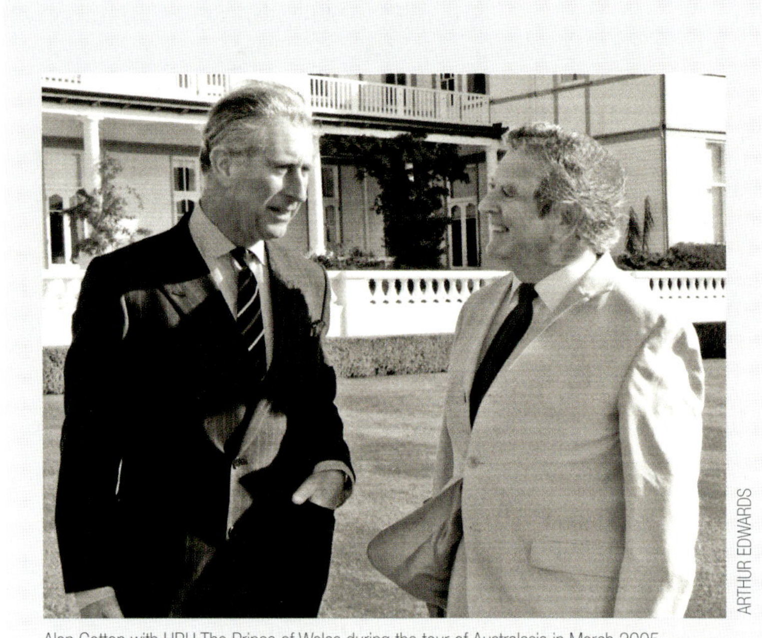

Alan Cotton with HRH The Prince of Wales during the tour of Australasia in March 2005.

Alan's impressive series of New Zealand paintings were the product of one intensive day's drawing at Taiaora Head, near Dunedin, on the South Island. Here the wind is the main protagonist, lifting the albatrosses on thermals and smashing the waves against the rocks.

New Zealand

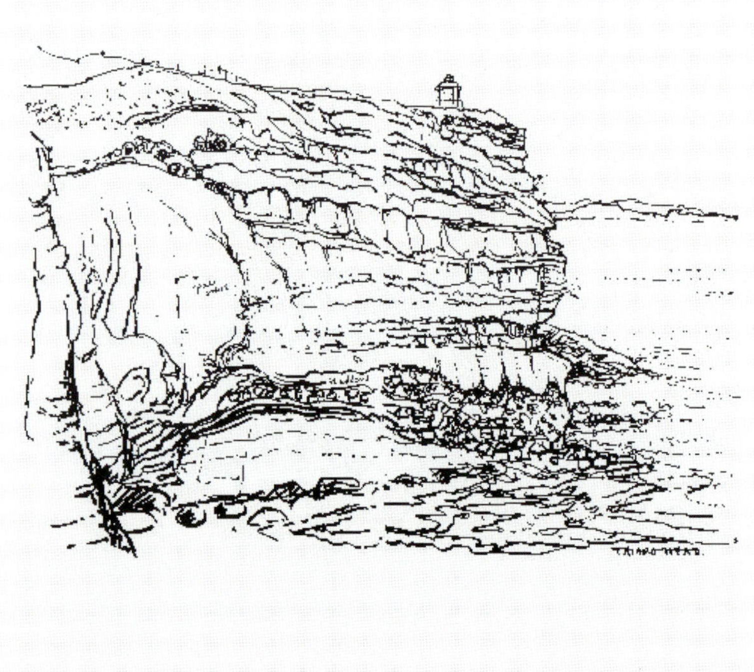

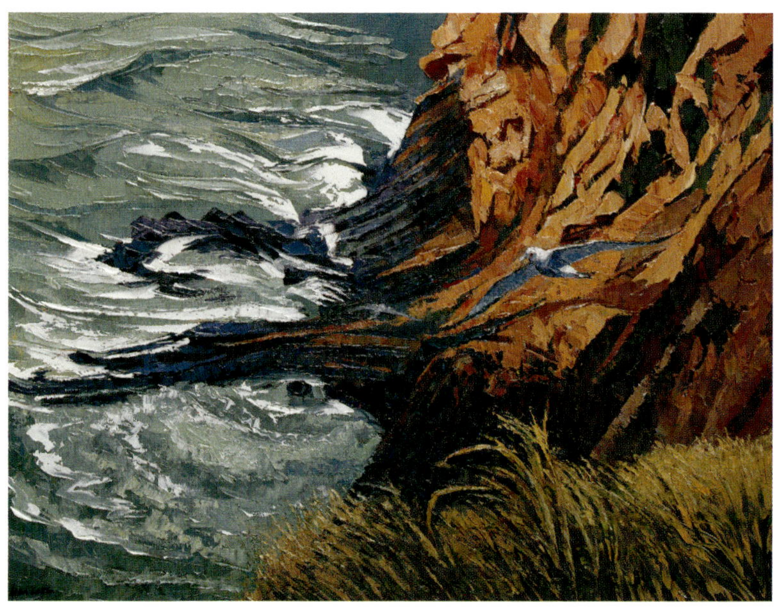

New Zealand – Riding the Thermals at Taiaroa Head
oil on canvas 28 x 36 ins

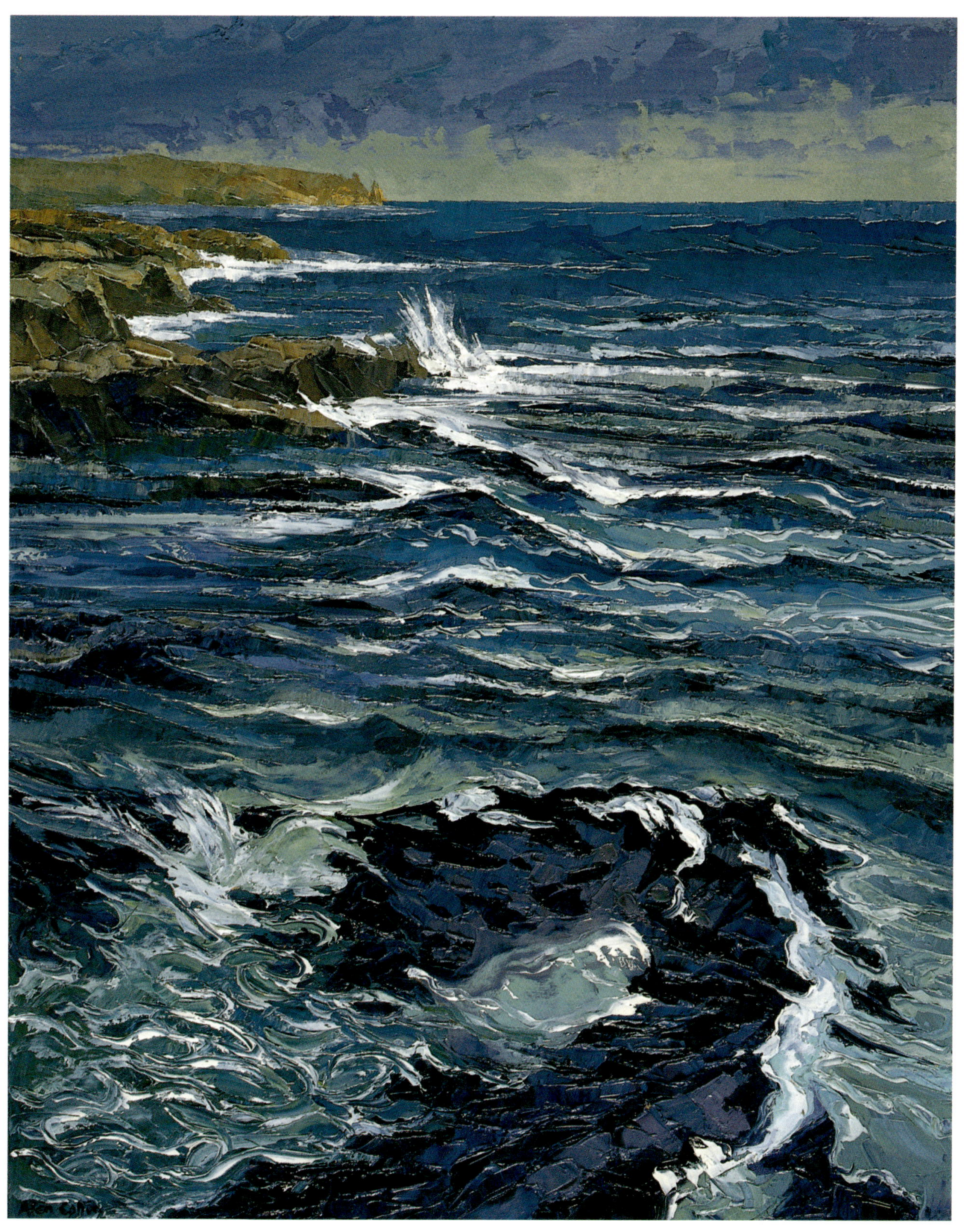

New Zealand – Surging Waves at Taiaroa Head
oil on canvas 36 x 28 ins

On Location

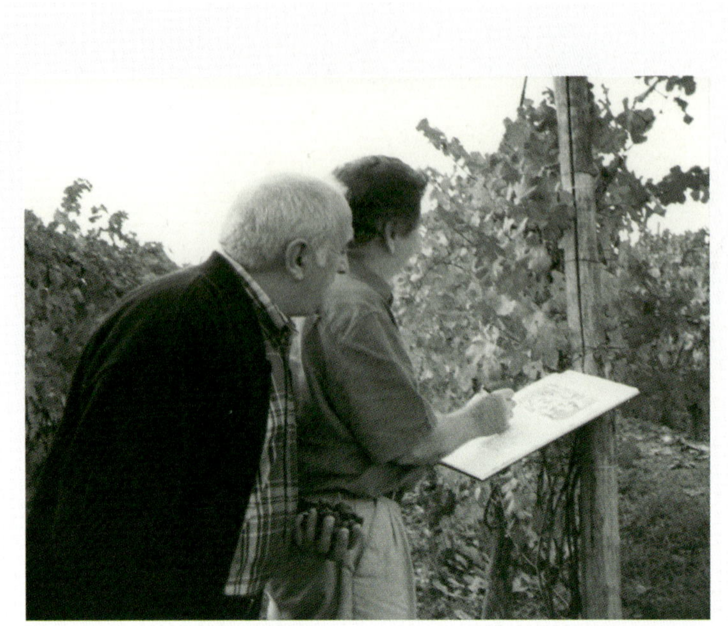

Amongst the vines with Mario

The criss-crossed, latticed hillsides of Piemonte, worked by man over many centuries, have continued to fascinate Alan, and he has returned to draw there many times. The opposition of soft light and luminous shadow present him with endless compositional possibilities.

Piemonte

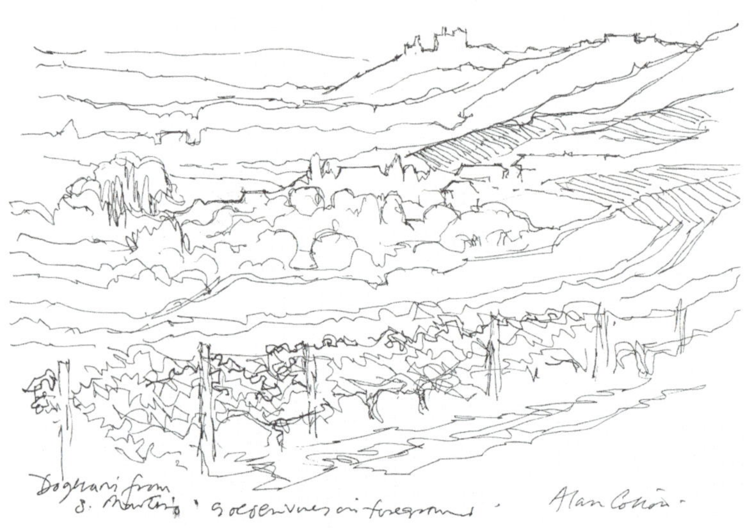

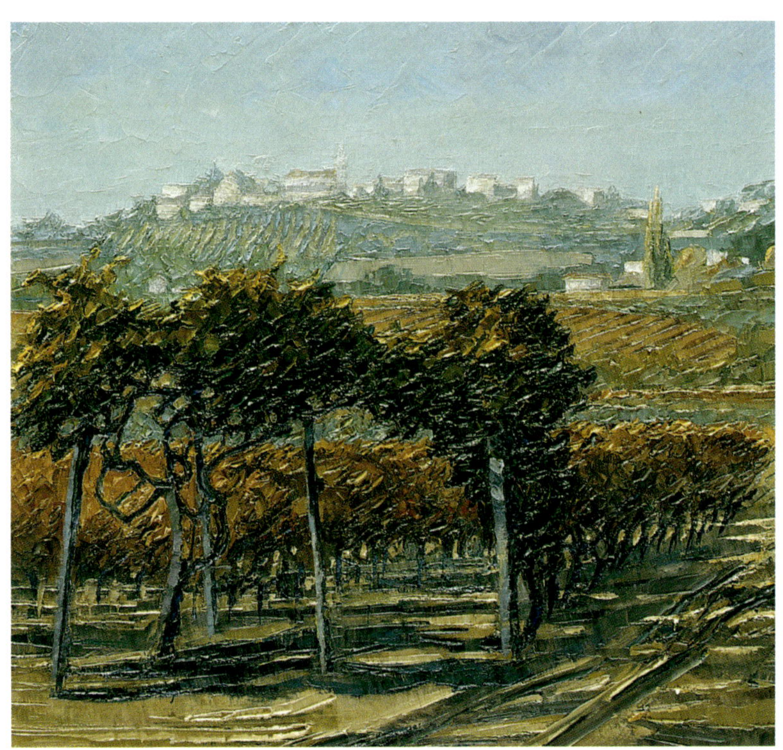

Piemonte – Pergolata in Olivero's Vineyard at Diano d'Alba
oil on canvas 24 x 24 ins

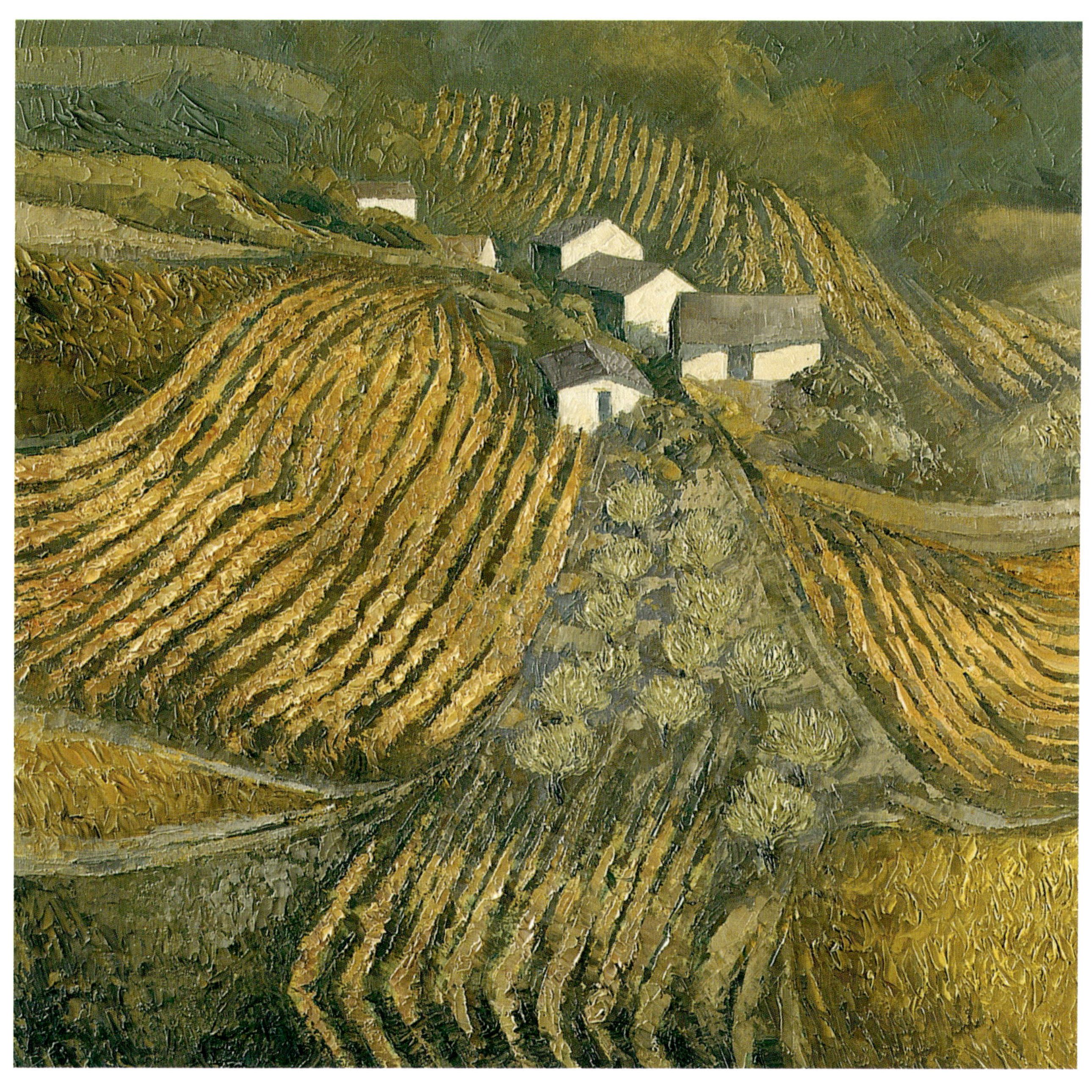

Piemonte – Rhythms of the Vines
oil on canvas 36 x 36 ins

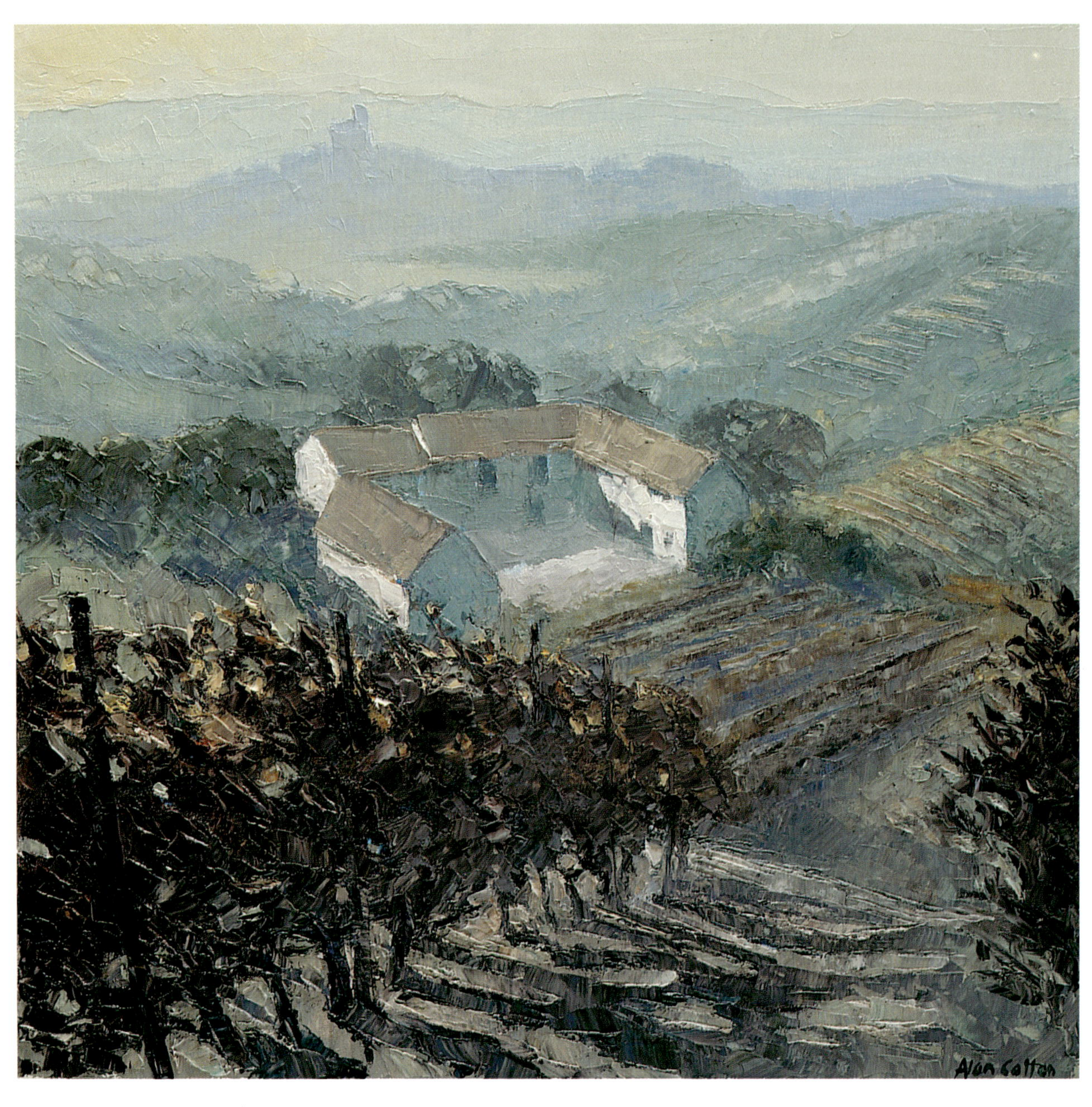

Piemonte – Farm Buildings from Caterina's Vineyard
oil on canvas 24 x 24 ins

Piemonte – Evening Vines (opposite)
oil on canvas 20 x 20 ins

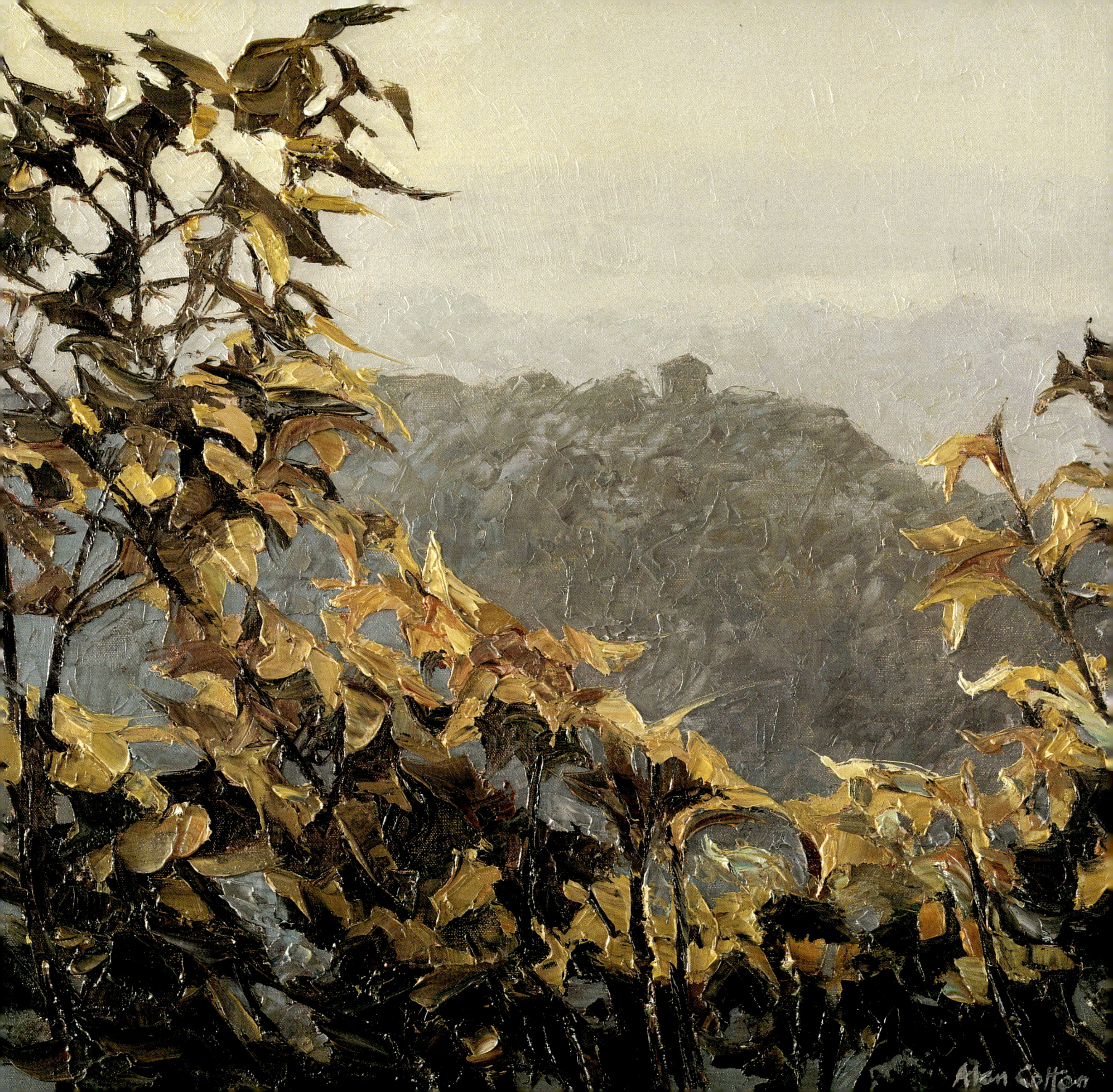
Alan Cotton

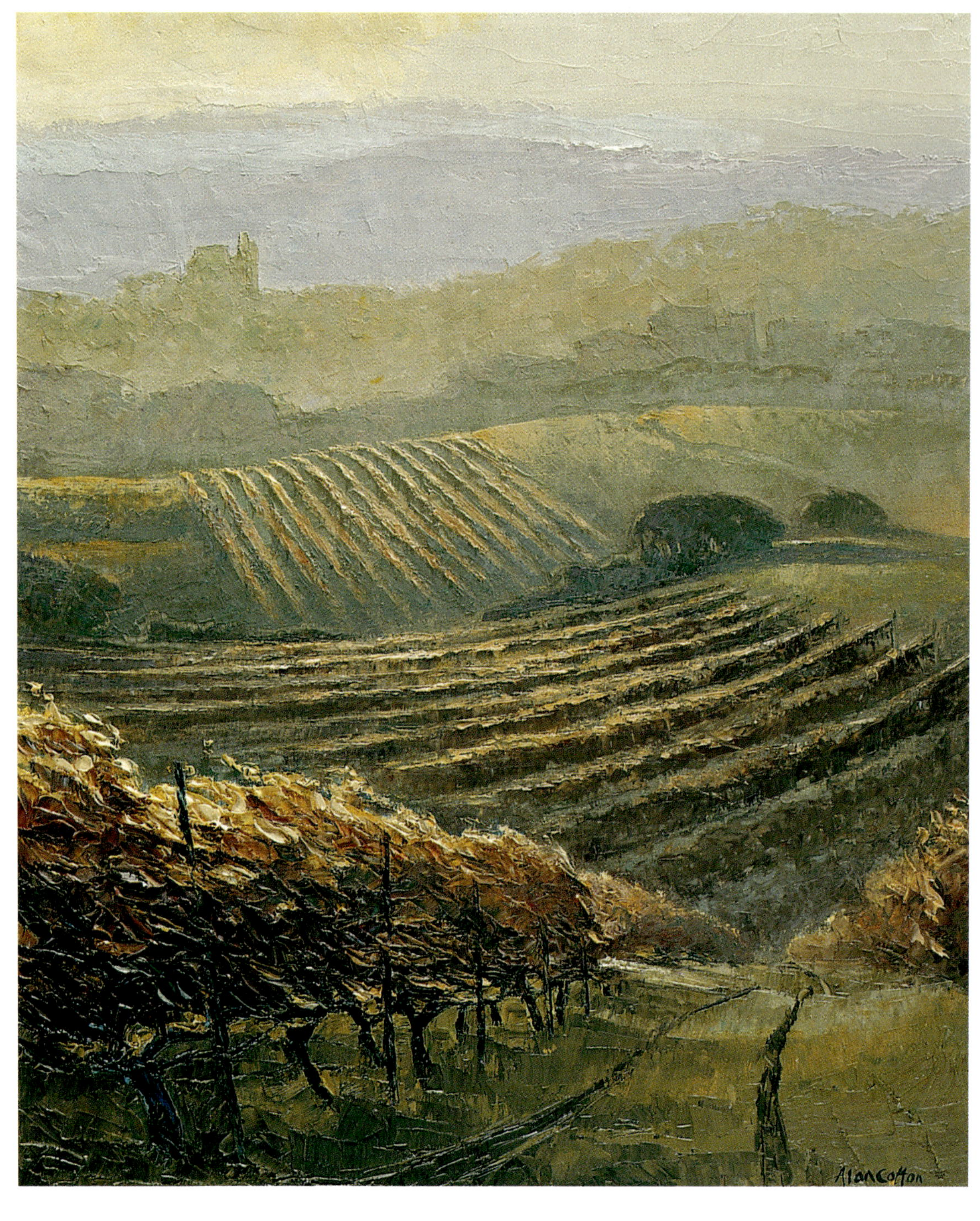

Piemonte – Autumn Vines in Hazy Sunlight
oil on canvas 30 x 24 ins

Rows of Vines at Montelupo Albese (opposite)
oil on canvas 36 x 36 ins

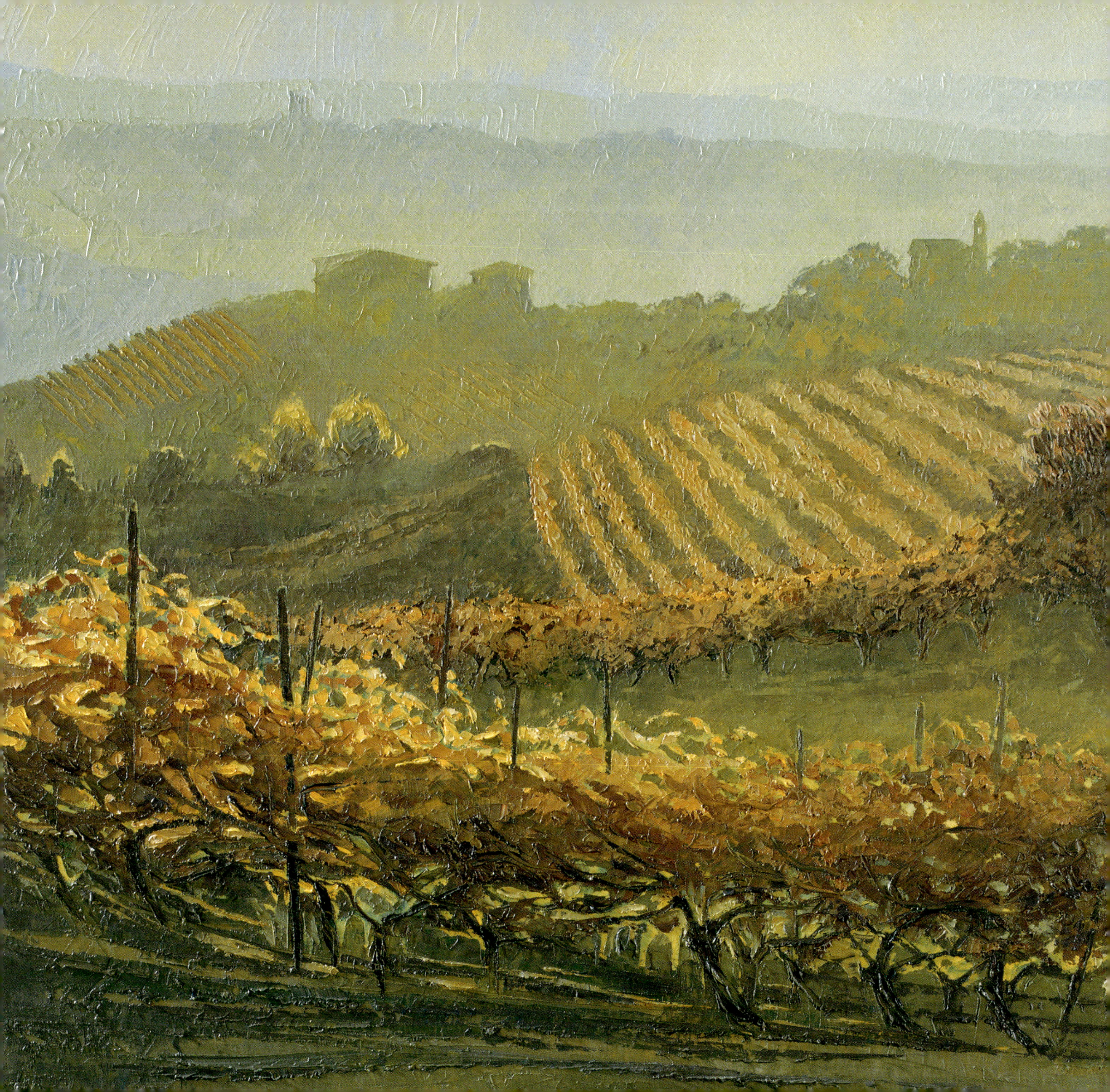

On Location

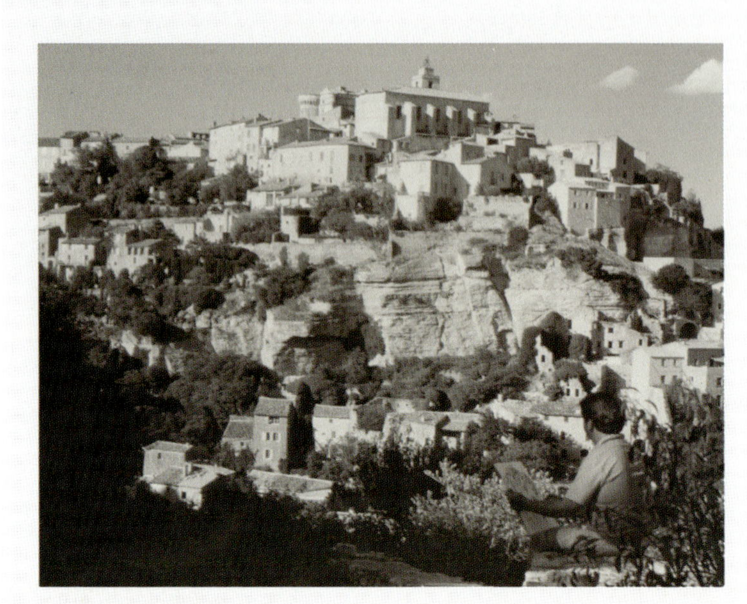

Provence was Alan's first great artistic love. Following in the footsteps of Cézanne, he went there as a student, and returned many times to search for subjects that he could make specifically his own. He found his subject matter in the Luberon plains with their orchards and lavender fields, and in the hill towns of Gordes and Bonnieux.

Provence

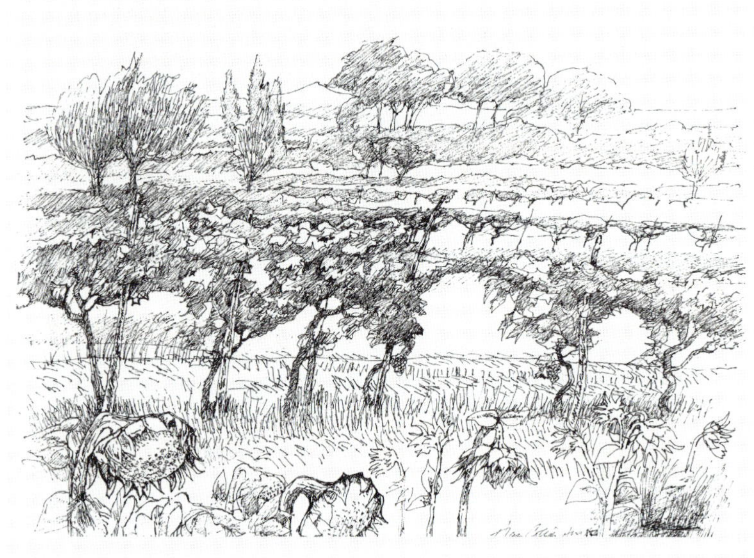

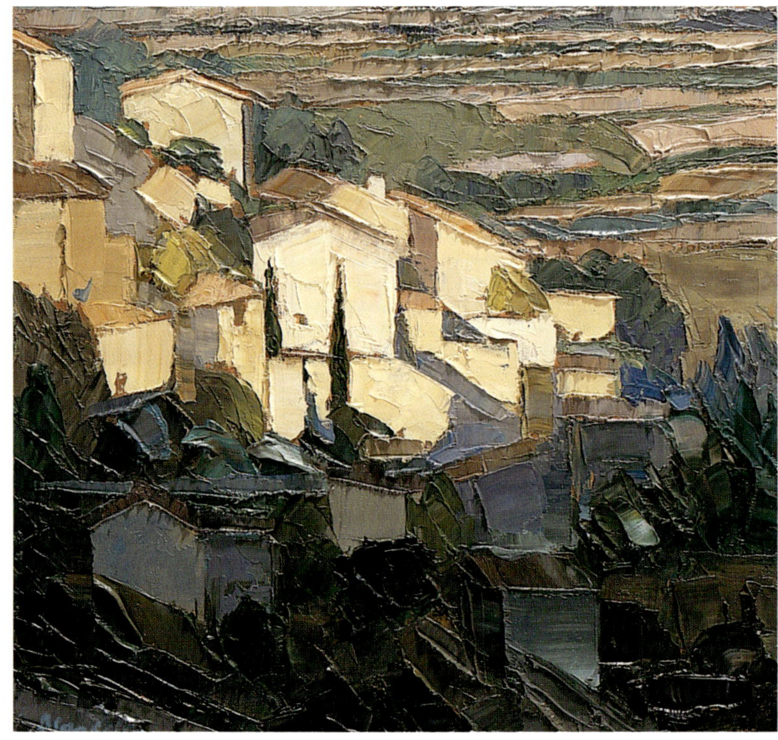

Provence – Gordes Façades in Evening Light
oil on canvas 14 x 14 ins

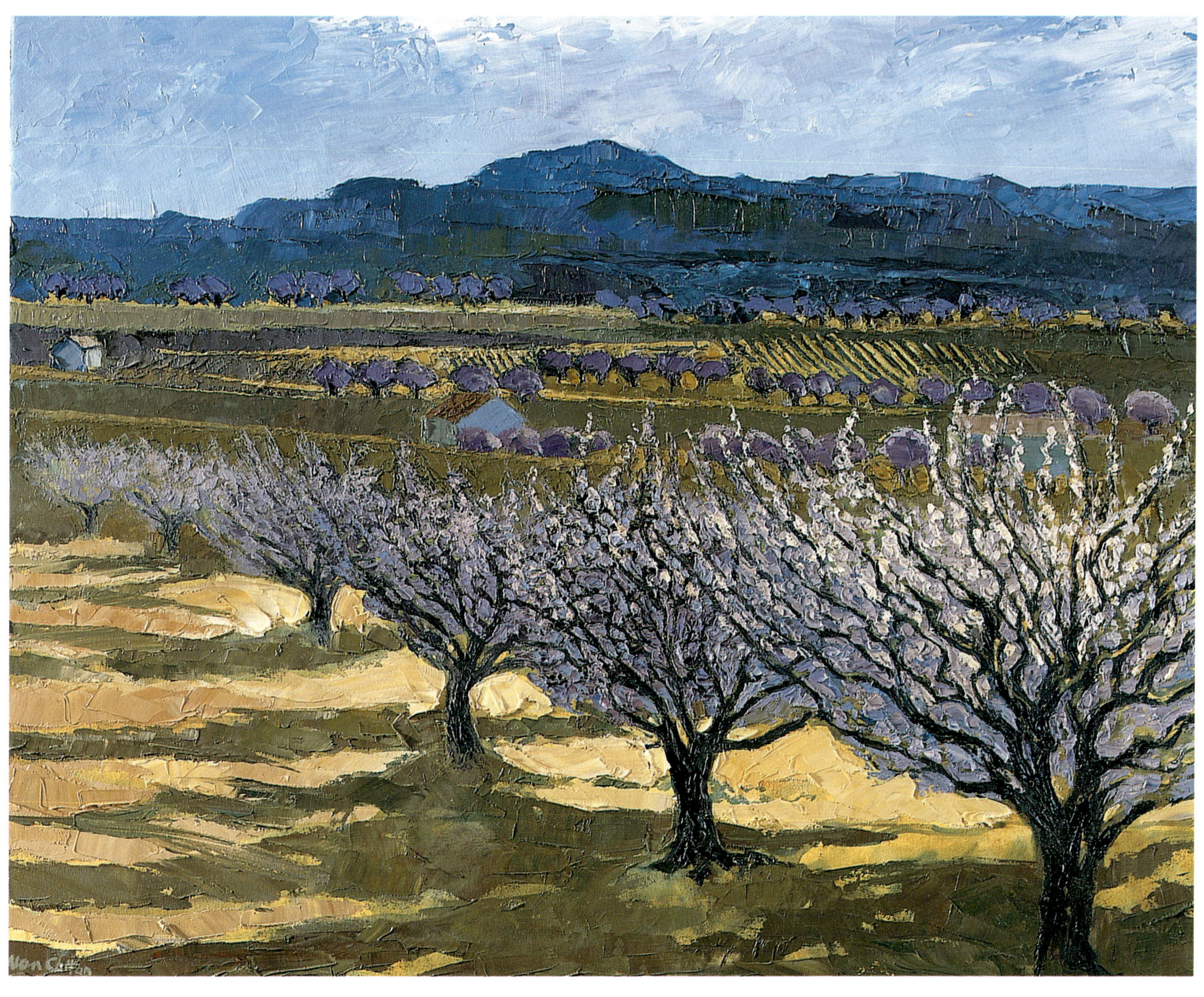

Provence – Cherry Orchard in the Luberon
oil on canvas 30 x 36 ins

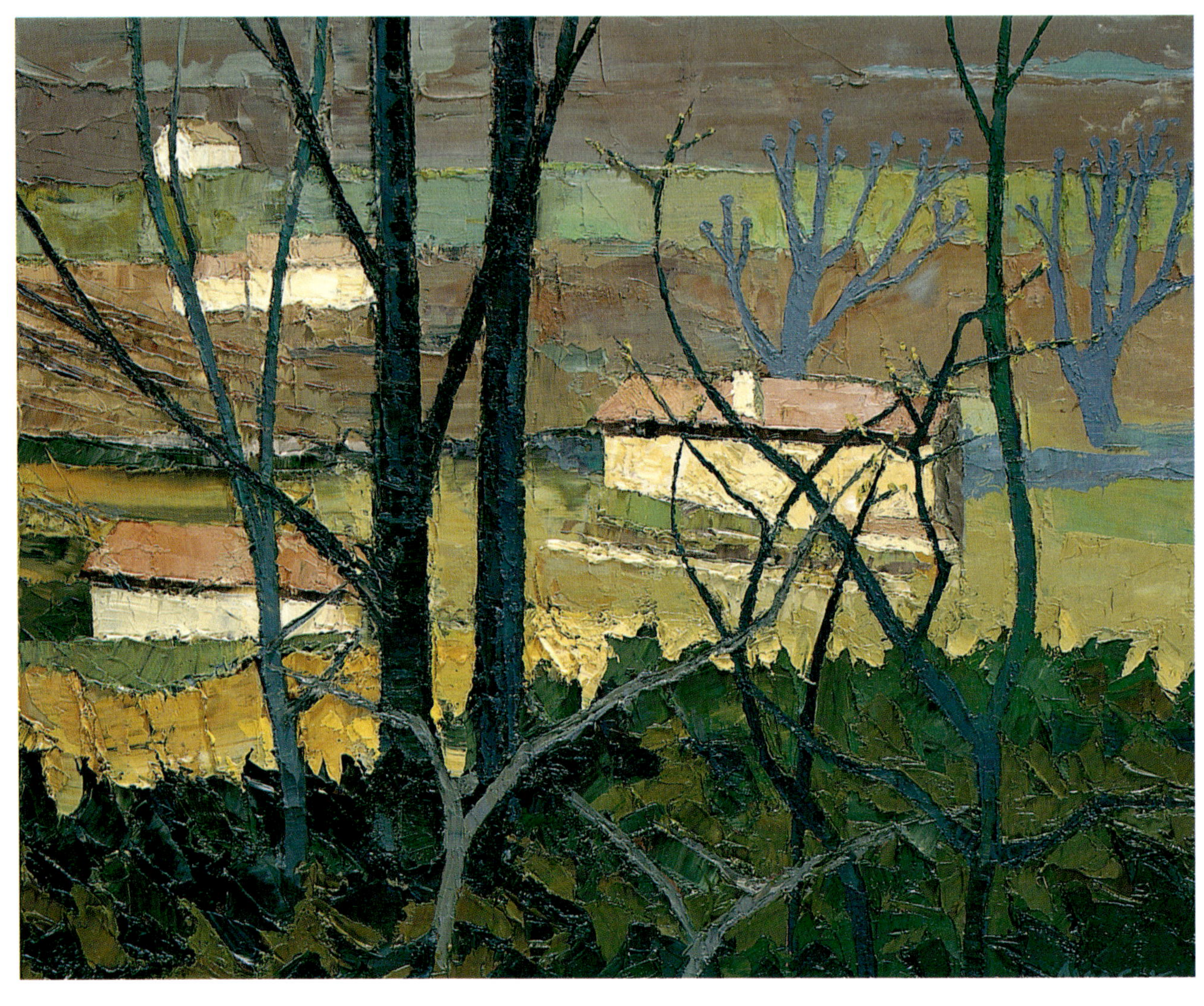

Provence – Spring in the Luberon with Plane Trees
oil on canvas 20 x 24 ins

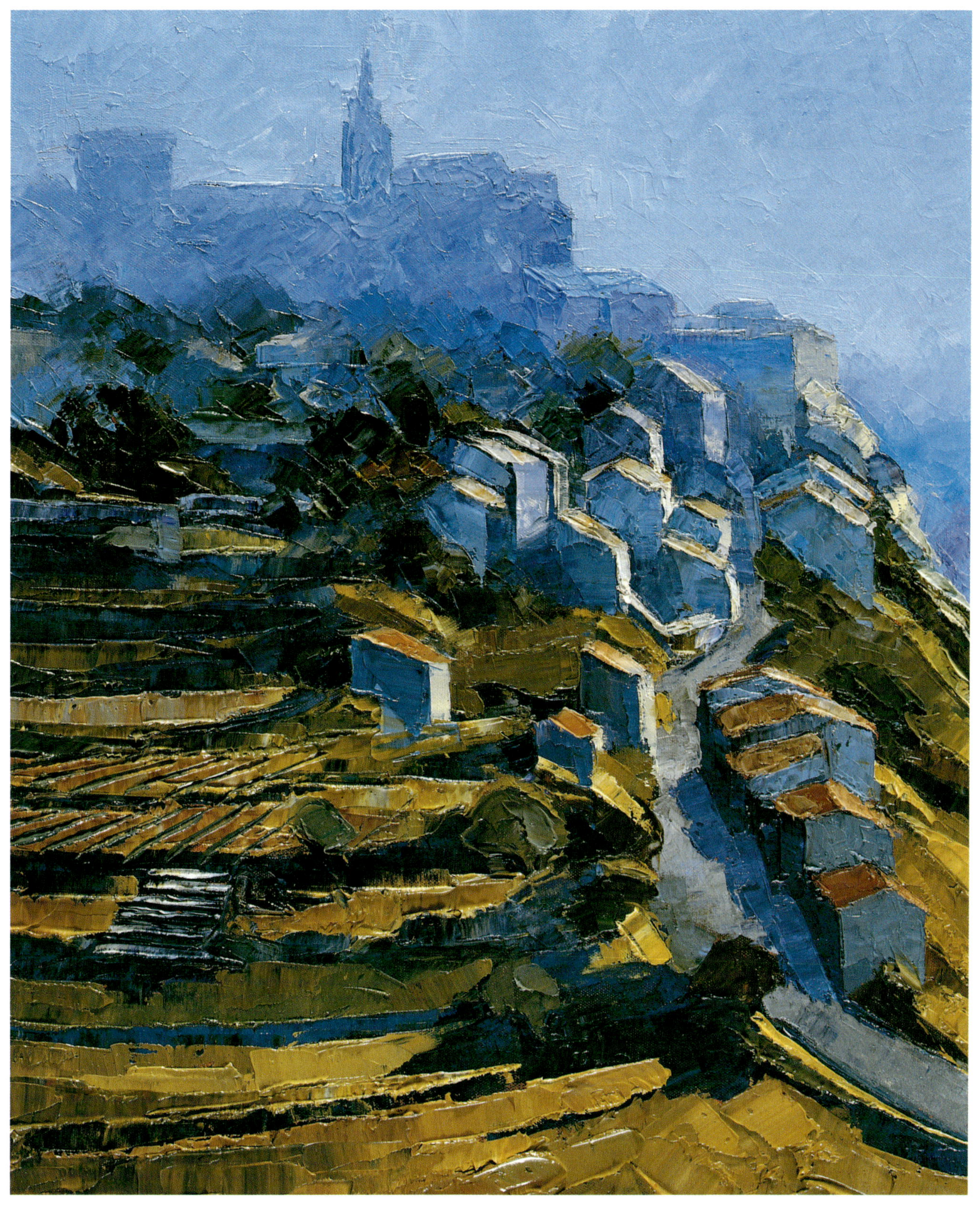

Provence – Gordes in Misty Light
oil on canvas 24 x 20 ins

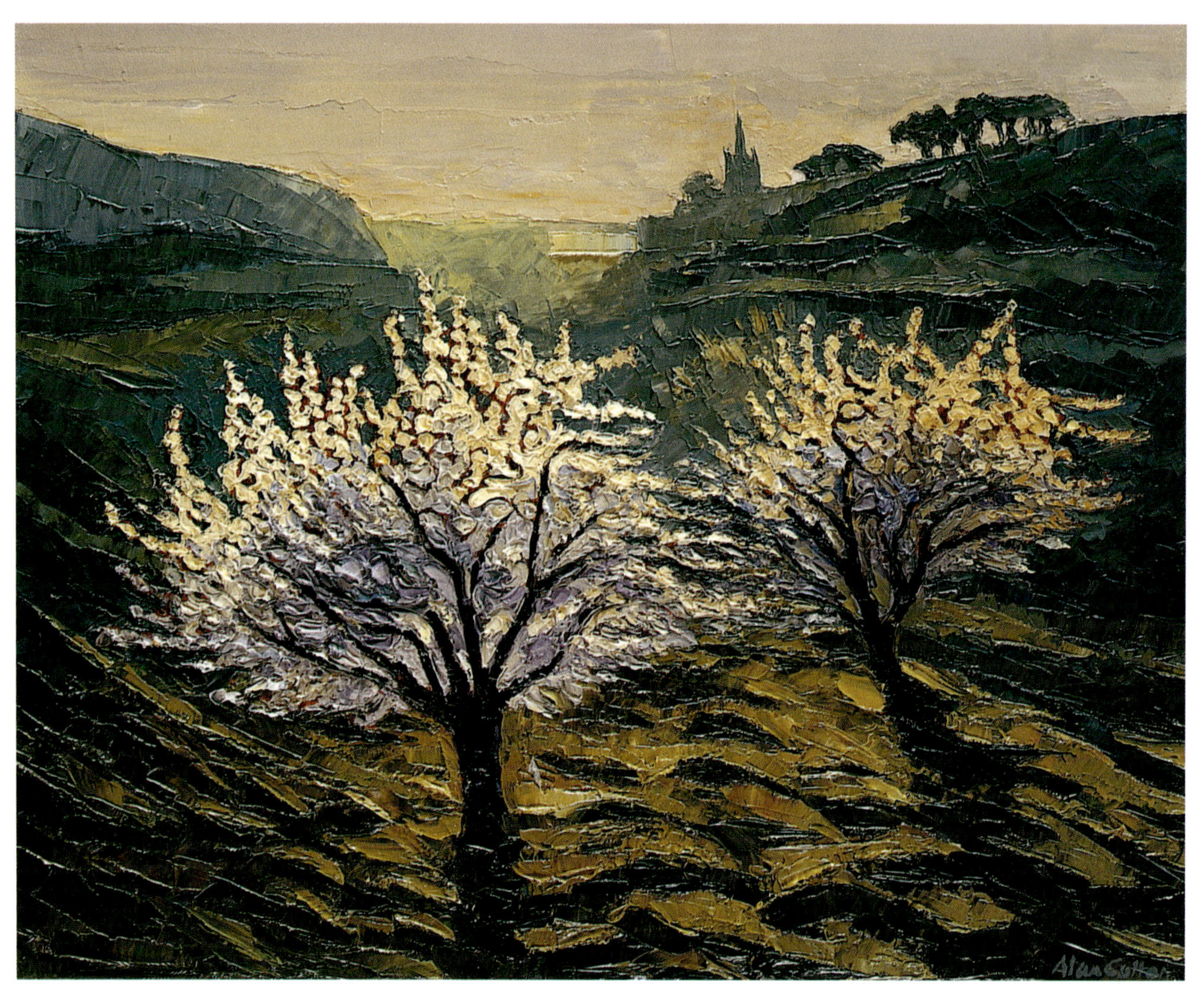

Provence – Cherry Trees below Bonnieux
oil on canvas 20 x 24 ins

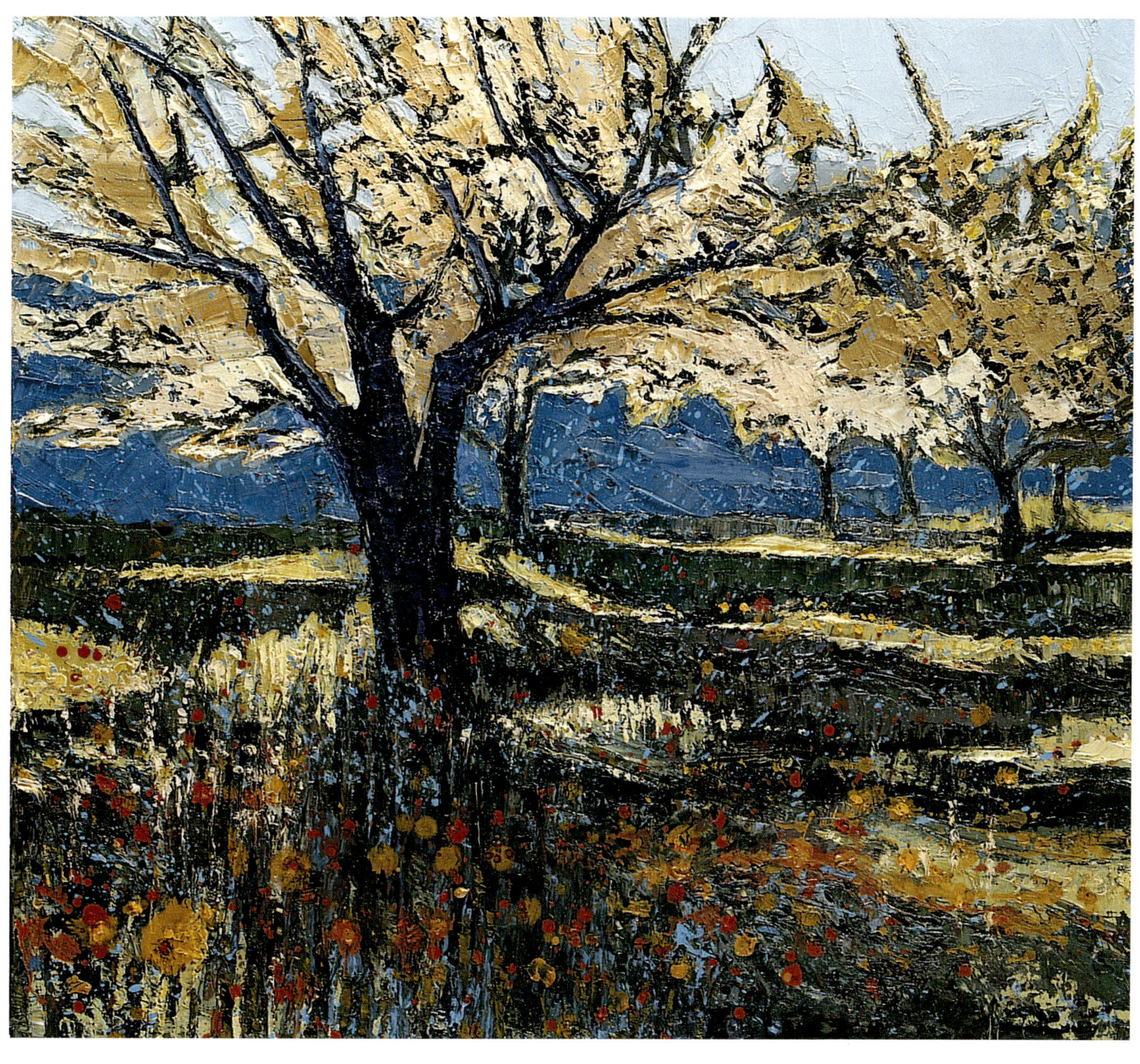

Provence – Spring Cherry Orchard
oil on canvas 24 x 24 ins

On Location

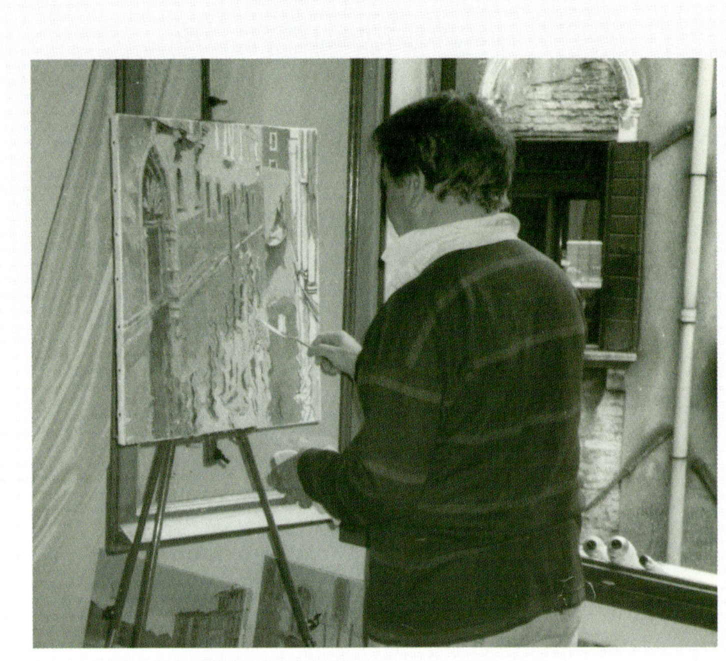

Venice is so picturesque that the challenge was to find a subject that had not been exploited by artists over many generations. Alan found his inspiration in the water. The reflections of boats and buildings in still or disturbed water offered endless semi-abstract possibilities..

Venice

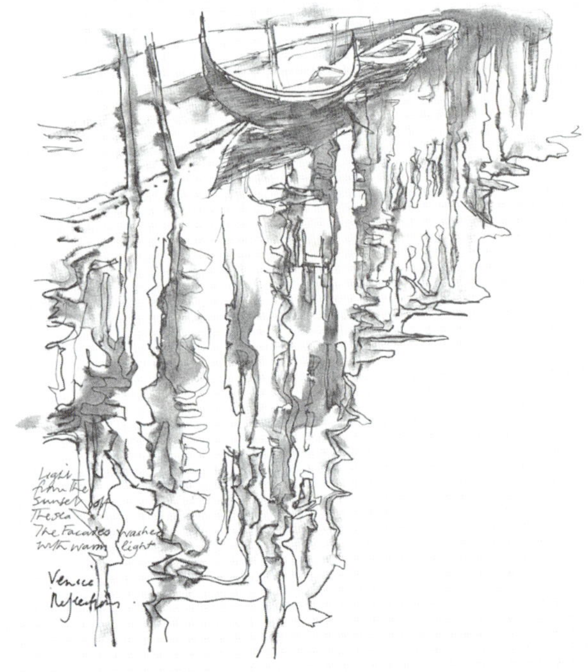

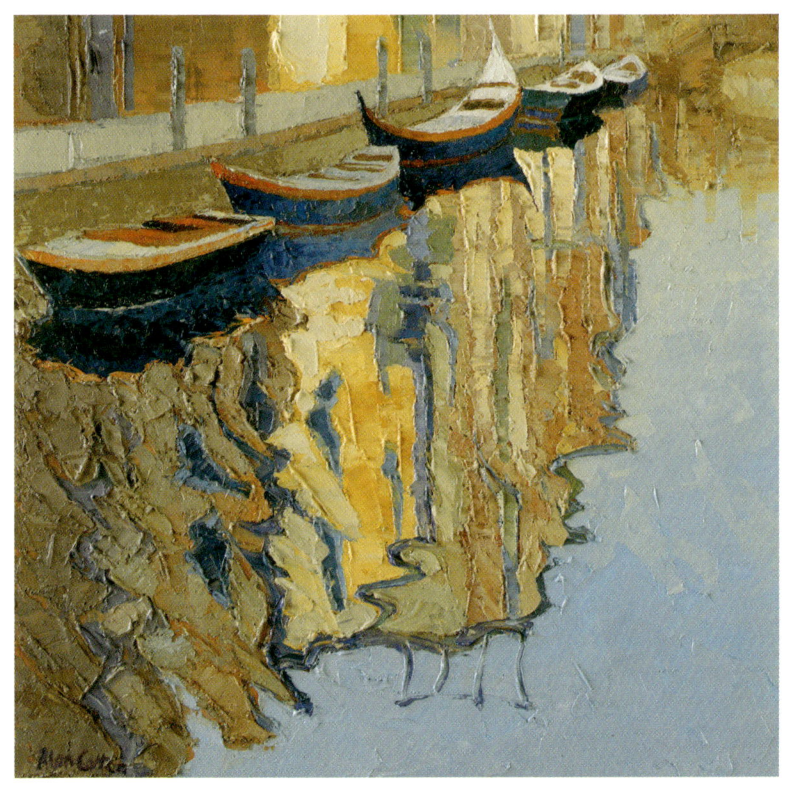

Venice – Reflections along the Fondamenta dei Mori
oil on canvas 20 x 20 ins

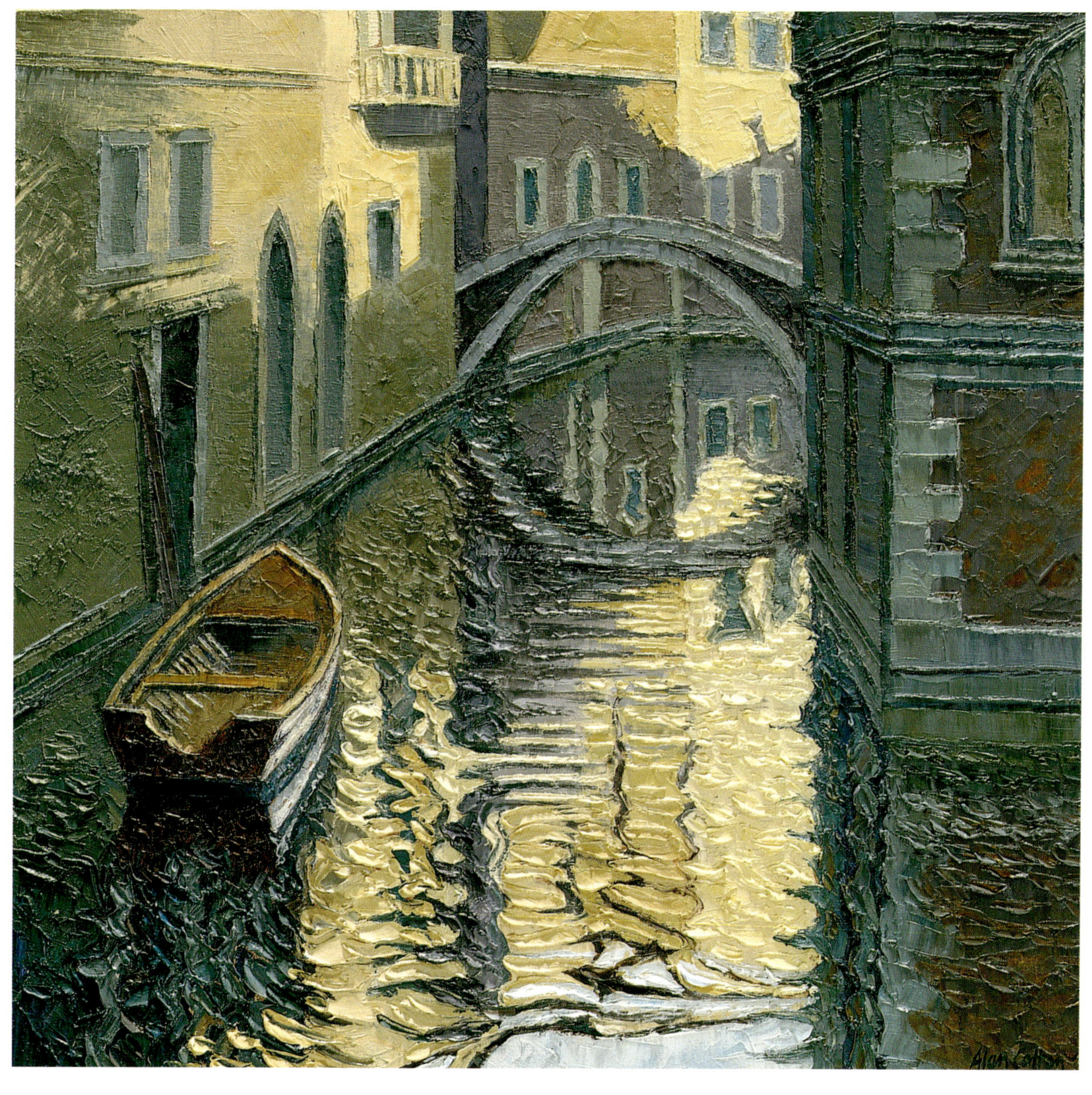

Venice – Rippled Reflections in Early Morning
oil on canvas 24 x 24 ins

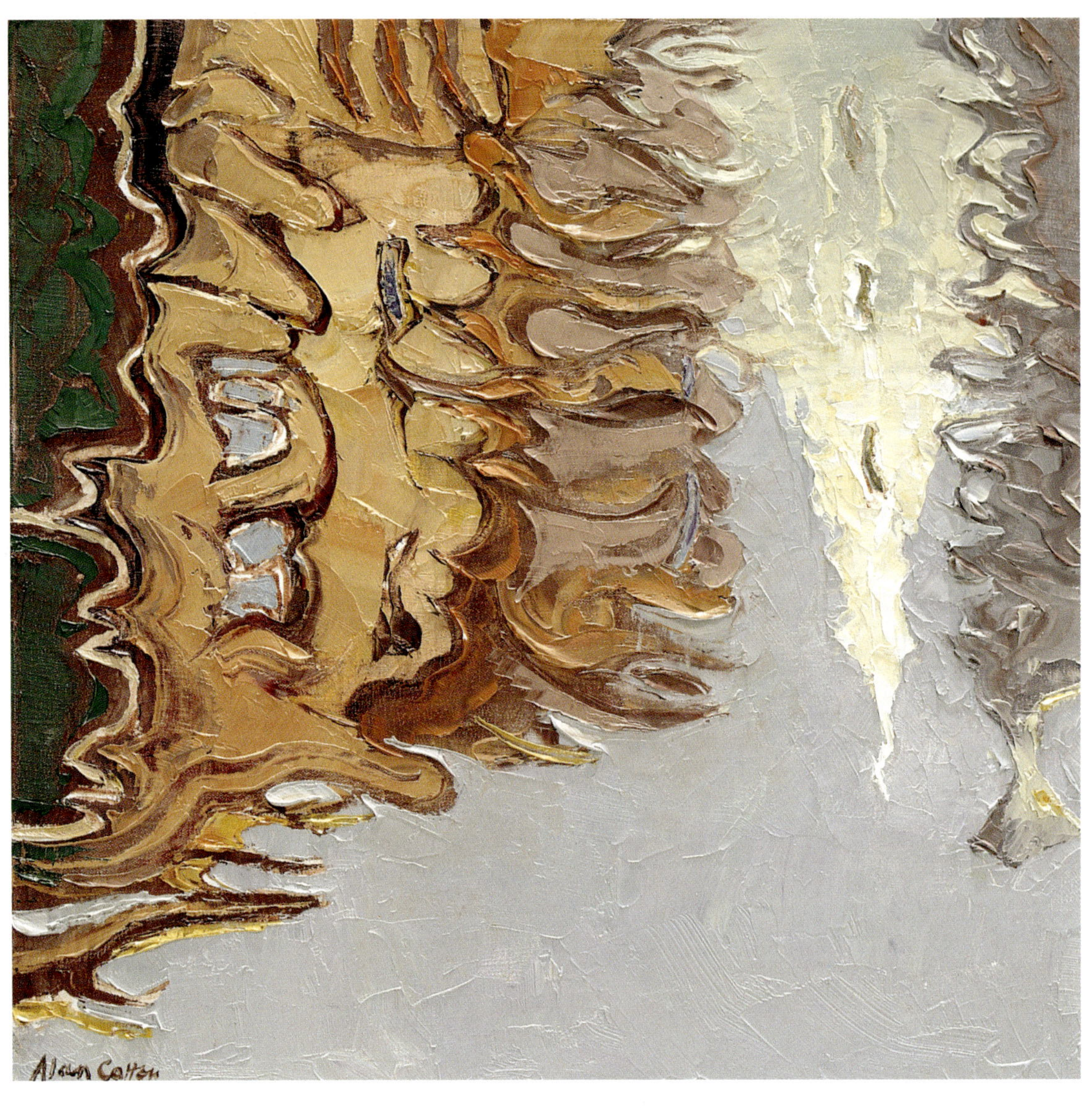

Venice – Burano Façades
oil on canvas 20 x 20 ins

Venice – Sunlight through the Narrow Canal (opposite)
oil on canvas 24 x 24 ins

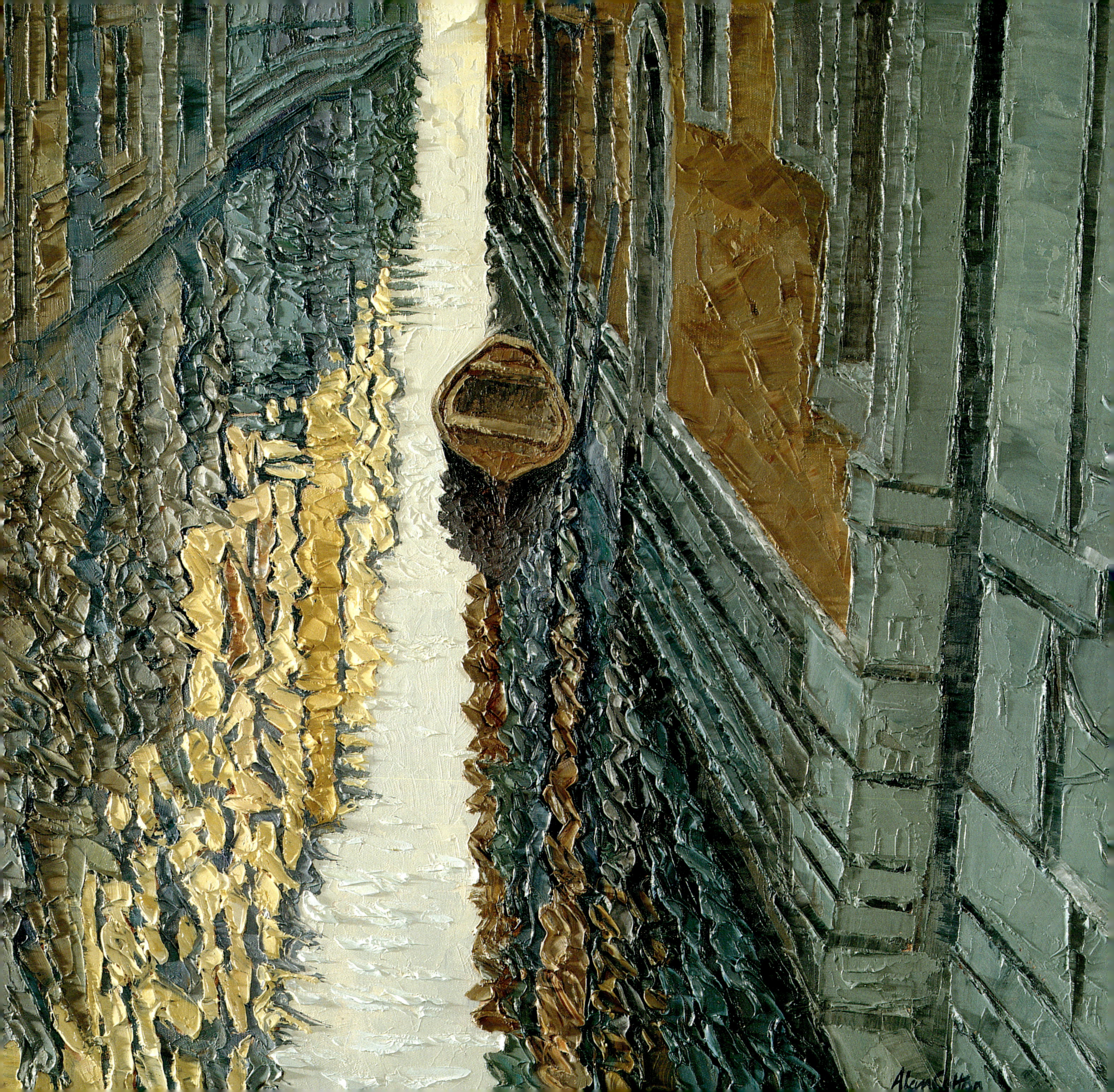

Acknowledgements

Over the years Alan and I have had many discussions about art, especially about the interrelationship of drawing and painting. For Alan, who composes his paintings in the studio from drawings made outside in the landscape, this is a pertinent matter. His drawings must contain the necessary spark for him to re-enter the mood of the place where they were made, and to recapture the magic of that place in paintings. We had already thought of writing about the role of drawing in Alan's work, so when David Messum suggested another book (as a sequel to *Alan Cotton: On a Knife Edge*, published Halsgrove 2003) to bring the painter's story up to date and explore his working methods in greater detail, I was naturally eager to be involved. Once again it has been a pleasure to work with Alan and Pat Cotton on this project, and my thanks go to them for their unstinting help and hospitality over many enjoyable working lunches. My thanks go as well to David Messum and Carol Tee, who have been the prime movers in planning the style and content of the book, and also for their generous hospitality, particularly for Messums' memorable Artists' Party in Cork Street! I am most grateful to Martin Bralsford, Gina Cox, Mary Engel Frank, Michael Morgan and Judi Spiers, admirers and collectors of Alan Cotton's work, for having spared the time and made the effort to meet me in order to talk about Alan and his art. I hope that this book may offer a deeper understanding of the personality and working methods of a painter who is truly in love with the world he inhabits.

Jenny Pery

Alan Cotton is represented internationally by David Messum Fine Art Ltd.

www.messums.com

www.alancotton.co.uk

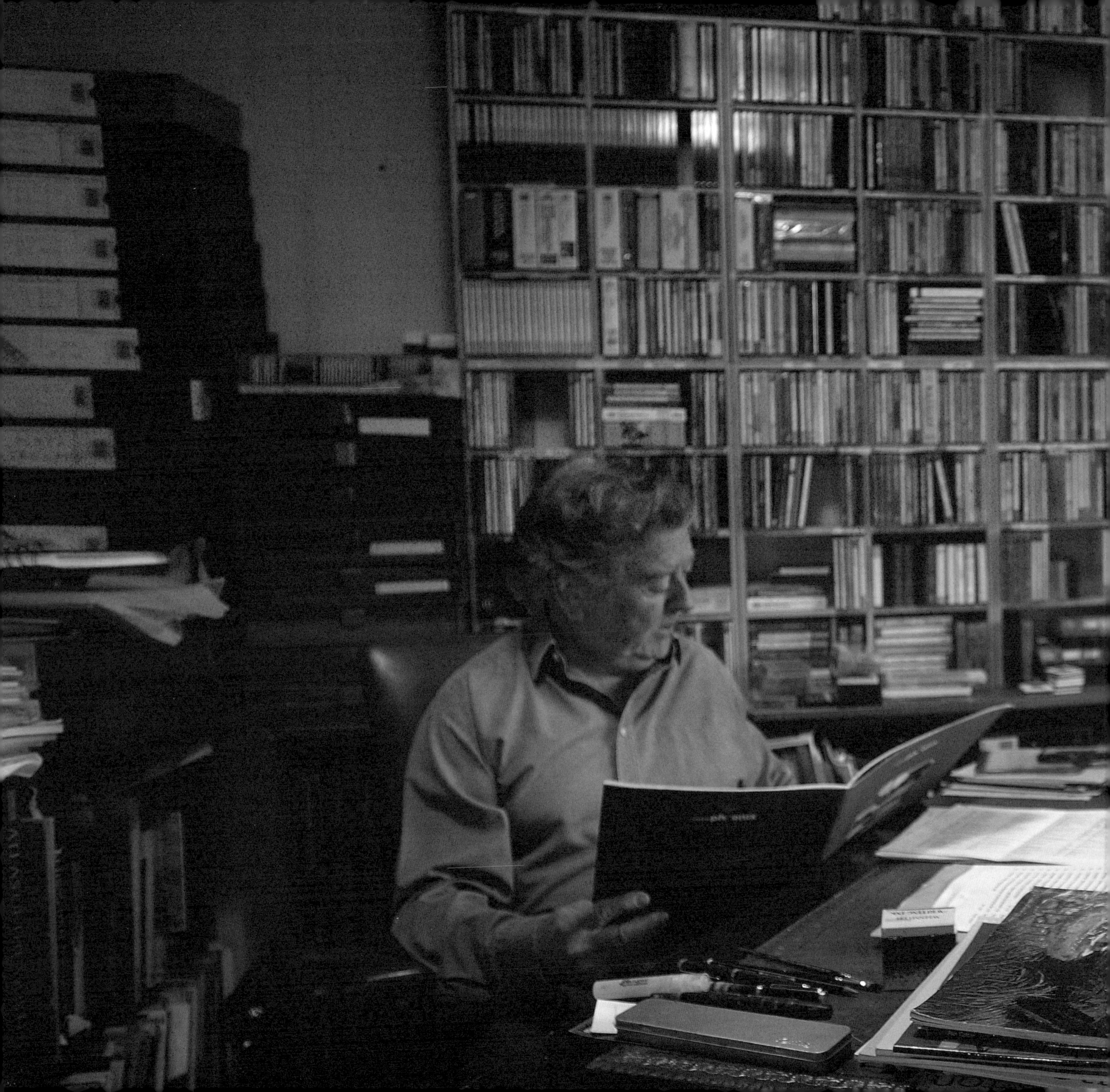